STUDENTS' BOOK
with digital resources and mobile app

Amanda Maris

Contents

FAST-TRACK ROUTE

MAIN LESSON	GRAMMAR/FUNCTION	VOCABULARY	PRONUNCIATION	SPEAKING GOAL
UNIT 1 page 6				
1A Hello page 6	be: *I* and *you*	countries	short forms of *be*	introduce yourself to other students
1B Jobs page 8	be: *he/she/it*	jobs	short forms of *be*	ask and answer about jobs
1C Nationalities page 10	be: *you/we/they*	nationalities	short forms of *be*	talk about different nationalities
1D English in action page 12	ask for and give contact information			ask for and give contact information
Check and reflect page 13 Go online for the Roadmap video.				
UNIT 2 page 14				
2A Families page 14	possessive *'s*, *I/my*, *you/your*, etc.	family	words that sound the same	talk about your family
2B Everyday things page 16	*this, that, these* and *those*	everyday objects (1)	*this* and *these*	talk about everyday objects
2C Numbers page 18	question words with *be*	numbers 1-100	forms of *be* with question words	ask questions about other people
2D English in action page 20	pay for things in a shop			pay for things in a shop
Check and reflect page 21 Go online for the Roadmap video.				
UNIT 3 page 22				
3A My town page 22	*There is/There are*; singular and plural nouns	places in town	short forms of *there is* and *there are*	say what's in a town
3B Is there wifi? page 24	*Is there a/an ...?/Are there any ...?*	rooms and things in a home	intonation in questions and answers	talk about a flat
3C It's expensive! page 26	position of adjectives	describing places	sentences stress	describe a town or a city
3D English in action page 28	ask for and give directions			ask for and give directions
Check and reflect page 29 Go online for the Roadmap video.				
UNIT 4 page 30				
4A You've got a friend page 30	*have/has got*	describing people	short forms of *have/has got*	describe people
4B Have you got it? page 32	*have/has got*: questions	everyday objects (2)	strong and weak forms of *have* and *has*	prepare for a trip
4C Dos and don'ts page 34	imperatives	common verbs	sentence stress	give advice
4D English in action page 36	tell the time			tell the time
Check and reflect page 37 Go online for the Roadmap video.				
UNIT 5 page 38				
5A My week page 38	present simple: *I/you/we/they*	days of the week, everyday activities	sentence stress	describe part of your week
5B A long journey page 40	present simple questions: *I/we/you/they*	travel and transport	strong and weak forms of *do*	talk about how you travel to work/university
5C Food and drink page 42	present simple with frequency adverbs	food and drink	word stress in frequency adverbs	take part in a survey about being healthy
5D English in action page 44	order food and drink			order food and drink
Check and reflect page 45 Go online for the Roadmap video.				

EXTENDED ROUTE

DEVELOP YOUR SKILLS LESSON	GOAL	FOCUS
1A Develop your reading page 86	understand a simple online profile	understanding capital letters
1B Develop your listening page 87	understand short conversations about personal details	understanding answers to questions
1C Develop your writing page 88	write a short personal profile	using capital letters and full stops

2A Develop your reading page 89	read a description of a photo	understanding subject pronouns and possessive adjectives
2B Develop your writing page 90	complete a form	completing forms
2C Develop your listening page 91	understand a description of classmates	understanding numbers

3A Develop your reading page 92	read a description of a place	understanding *and* and *but*
3B Develop your listening page 93	understand a description of a house	noticing intonation in lists
3C Develop your writing page 94	write about your town	using *and* and *but*

4A Develop your reading page 95	understand a short text	understanding punctuation: apostrophes
4B Develop your listening page 96	understand a short, informal conversation	understanding questions
4C Develop your writing page 97	write a message to a friend	using basic punctuation

5A Develop your reading page 98	understand a blog	understanding sequence adverbs
5B Develop your listening page 99	understand short, factual conversations	using pictures to help you listen
5C Develop your writing page 100	write an informal message	using correct word order

Contents

FAST-TRACK ROUTE

MAIN LESSON	GRAMMAR/FUNCTION	VOCABULARY	PRONUNCIATION	SPEAKING GOAL
UNIT 6 page 46				
6A Good and bad habits page 46	present simple: he/she/it	time expressions	verb endings: /s/, /z/ and /ɪz/	talk about another person's habits
6B Jobs around the house page 48	present simple questions: he/she/it	jobs around the house	strong and weak forms of does	ask and answer about things people often do
6C Skills page 50	can/can't for ability	skills	strong and weak forms of can	ask and answer about things you can and can't do
6D English in action page 52	make requests			make requests
Check and reflect page 53 — Go online for the Roadmap video.				
UNIT 7 page 54				
7A Questions page 54	wh- questions	places	intonation in questions	ask and answer about a place
7B A good day page 56	was/were, there was/were	months, dates	short forms of was not and were not	talk about good days
7C How was it? page 58	was/were (questions), there was/were (questions)	adjectives	strong and weak forms of was and were	ask and answer about past events
7D English in action page 60	buy travel tickets			buy travel tickets
Check and reflect page 61 — Go online for the Roadmap video.				
UNIT 8 page 62				
8A When I was young page 62	past simple (regular verbs)	verb phrases	verb endings: /t/, /d/ and /ɪd/	give a talk about when you were young
8B You had a bad day page 64	past simple (irregular verbs)	irregular verbs	silent letter in didn't	talk about a bad day
8C Good places page 66	past simple (questions)	holiday activities	linking sounds	talk about a holiday
8D English in action page 68	greet people			greet people
Check and reflect page 69 — Go online for the Roadmap video.				
UNIT 9 page 70				
9A Family photos page 70	object pronouns (me, him, her, etc.)	prepositions of place	weak form of object pronouns	talk about the people in a photo
9B Hobbies page 72	like/enjoy/love/hate + -ing	hobbies	weak form of -ing	ask and answer about things you and I like doing
9C Study habits page 74	why and because	learning a language	because	ask and answer about study habits
9D English in action page 76	make and respond to suggestions			make and respond to suggestions
Check and reflect page 77 — Go online for the Roadmap video.				
UNIT 10 page 78				
10A Goals page 78	would like/love to	collocations	short form of would	ask and answer about dreams and wishes
10B Party time page 80	be going to	party vocabulary	going to	talk about plans for a class party
10C My plans page 82	be going to: questions	seasons, time expressions	linking words	ask and answer about plans for the year
10D English in action page 84	make and respond to invitations			make and respond to invitations
Check and reflect page 85 — Go online for the Roadmap video.				

Grammar bank page 116   Vocabulary bank page 136   Communication review 146

EXTENDED ROUTE

DEVELOP YOUR SKILLS LESSON	GOAL	FOCUS
6A Develop your writing page 101	write about a daily routine	using time expressions
6B Develop your listening page 102	understand short conversations	linking between words
6C Develop your reading page 103	understand a short text	understanding titles

7A Develop your writing page 104	write directions	using sequence adverbs
7B Develop your listening page 105	understand a short conversation about events	understanding present and past
7C Develop your reading page 106	understand short texts	finding dates, times and place names

8A Develop your reading page 107	understand a short story	understanding *a/an* and *the*
8B Develop your writing page 108	write a description of your last birthday	planning your writing
8C Develop your listening page 109	understand directions	listening for sequence adverbs

9A Develop your reading page 110	understand short messages	understanding subject and object pronouns
9B Develop your listening page 111	understand people's feelings	listening for how people feel
9C Develop your writing page 112	write a short text	using *because*

10A Develop your reading page 113	understand a short article	understanding paragraphs
10B Develop your listening page 114	understand a conversation about plans	checking information and showing understanding
10C Develop your writing page 115	write a short message for an online discussion	using subject and object pronouns

Communication bank page 151   Irregular verbs page 160

1A Hello

A John Miller, the UK
B Maria Fernandez, Spain
C Ela Atan, Turkey

> **Goal:** introduce yourself to other students
> **Grammar:** *be*: *I* and *you*
> **Vocabulary:** countries

Vocabulary

1 a Match flags 1–12 with the countries in the box.

Argentina	Brazil	~~Canada~~	Italy	Japan
Mexico	Poland	Spain	Thailand	the UK
the US	Turkey			

1 Canada

b 🔊 1.1 Listen and check your answers. Then listen again and repeat.

2 a 🔊 1.2 Listen and complete the table.

| Argentina | Brazil | Canada | Italy | ~~Japan~~ |
| Mexico | ~~Poland~~ | Spain | Thailand | Turkey |

o	Oo	oO	Ooo	ooOo
___	Poland	Japan	___	___
___	___	___	___	___
___	___	___	___	___

b Listen again and repeat.

c How do you say your country in English? Underline the stressed syllable.

Bra<u>zil</u>, <u>It</u>aly

3 Work in pairs. Look at photos A–F and roleplay conversations.

A: Hello, I'm Maria.
B: Hi, Maria. I'm John.
A: Where are you from?
B: I'm from the UK. Where are you from?

📱 Go to your app for more practice.

Reading and listening

4 a 🔊 1.3 Listen to two conversations at a language conference. Complete them with the correct countries.

Conversation 1
A: Hello, I'm Juan. Nice to meet you.
B: Nice to meet you, too. I'm Akiko.
A: Hi. Are you here for the conference?
B: Yes, I am. Are you a teacher?
A: No, I'm not. I'm the manager of a language school.
B: Where are you from?
A: I'm from ¹_____ . How about you?
B: I'm from ²_____ . I'm a university teacher.

Conversation 2
A: Hi, are you Lucy?
B: Yes, I am. Barbara?
A: Yes, I'm Barbara. Nice to meet you. Sorry, am I late?
B: No, you aren't.
A: Great. So where are you from, Lucy?
B: I'm from ³_____ . Are you from Spain?
A: No, I'm not. I'm from ⁴_____ .

b Listen again and repeat.

c Work in pairs. Practise the conversations.

Amy Desmond, the US D   Santos Flores, Mexico E   Masayuki Ogawa, Japan F

Grammar

5 Read and complete the grammar box.

be: I and you

+	I'm Juan.		
	I'm a university teacher.		
	You're on time.		
?	Am I late?	+	Yes, you are.
		–	No, you aren't.
?	Are you a teacher?	+	Yes, I am.
	Are you from Spain?	–	No, I'm not.

with *where*
Where are you from?   I'm from Mexico.

Short forms
¹_____ = I am
²_____ = you are
³_____ = are not

6 a 🔊 1.4 Listen to the sentences. Notice the pronunciation of the short forms in blue.
1 I'm from Mexico.
2 I'm not a teacher.
3 You're on time.
4 You aren't late.

b Listen again and repeat.

7 a Complete the conversation with the correct form of *be*.
A: Hello. ¹_____ you here for the conference?
B: Yes, I ²_____ . I ³_____ Laura.
A: I ⁴_____ Elif.
B: Nice to meet you.
A: Nice to meet you, too. ⁵_____ you from the US?
B: No, I ⁶_____ not. I'm from Toronto in Canada. Where ⁷_____ you from?
A: I ⁸_____ from Ankara in Turkey.

b 🔊 1.5 Listen and check your answers.

8 Work in pairs. Roleplay conversations with the information below. Use Exercise 7a to help you.

📱 Go to page 116 or your app for more information and practice.

Speaking

PREPARE

9 Complete the conference card with your information.

10th International Language Conference
Name:
City:
Country:
☐ student ☐ school teacher ☐ university teacher
☐ language school teacher ☐ manager

SPEAK

10 Work in groups. You are at the language conference. Introduce yourself to the other students.
A: Hi. I'm Mehmet Osman.
B: Hello. I'm Lana Cruz. Nice to meet you.
A: Nice to meet you, too. Where are you from?

Develop your reading
page 86

1B Jobs

> **Goal:** ask and answer about jobs
> **Grammar:** *be: he/she/it*
> **Vocabulary:** jobs

Name: Josh King
Job: ¹_____
City: Chicago
Country: the US

Name: Amy Gardner
Job: ²_____
City: Norwich
Country: the UK

Name: Yolanda Alvarez
Job: ⁵_____
City: Guadalajara
Country: Mexico

Name: Santiago Castillo
Job: ⁶_____
City: Mendoza
Country: Argentina

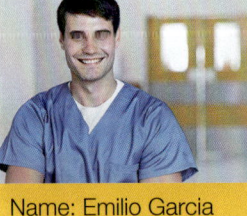

Name: Emilio Garcia
Job: ⁷_____
City: Valencia
Country: Spain

Name: Mali Arak
Job: ⁸_____
City: Chiang Mai
Country: Thailand

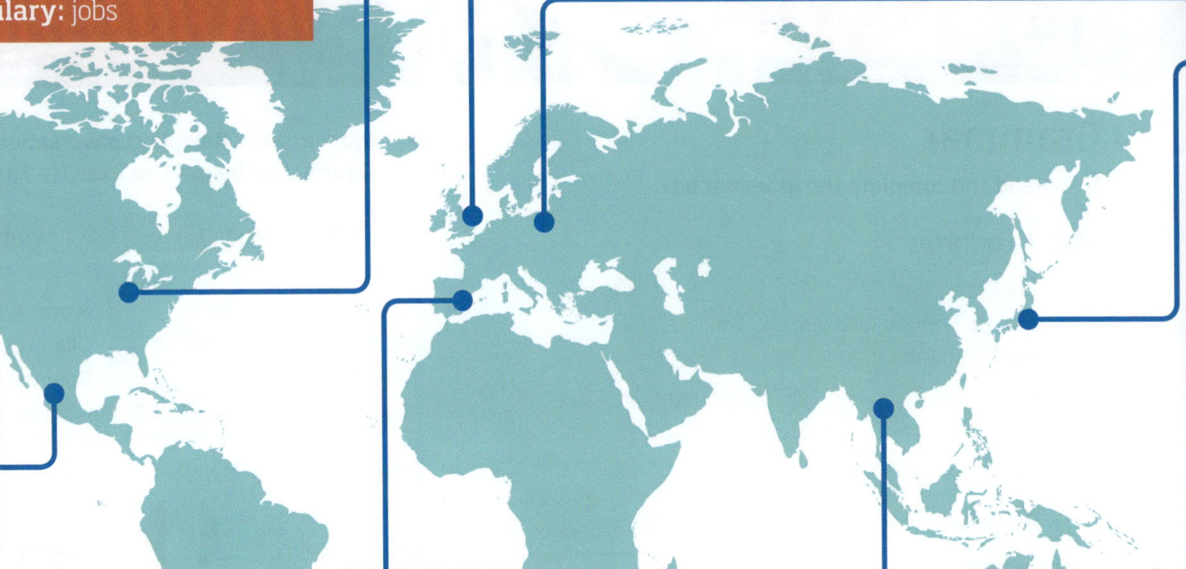

Vocabulary

1 a Look at the map and the profiles. Where are the people from?

b Complete 1–8 in the profiles with jobs a–h.

- **a** football player
- **b** doctor
- **c** school teacher
- **d** pilot
- **e** farmer
- **f** nurse
- **g** taxi driver
- **h** office worker

c 🔊 1.6 Listen and underline the stressed syllables in the jobs in Exercise 1b. Then listen again and repeat.

football player

2 Work in pairs. Choose a person from Exercise 1a. Then ask and answer questions about the person.

A: Are you from Poland?
B: No, I'm not.
A: Are you a football player?
B: Yes, I am. I'm Santiago.

📱 Go to page 136 or your app for more vocabulary and practice.

Reading

3 Read the web page. Match people 1–3 with jobs a–c.

1 Lucy a office worker
2 Paul b doctor
3 Mila c nurse

➕ Green Cross Hospital

About us

Green Cross Hospital is a small hospital. It's in Manchester in the UK.

Hospital staff

Lucy Brown
Lucy is from London. She's a doctor.

Paul Turner
Paul is from Manchester. He's a nurse.

Mila Kowalski
Mila is from Toronto. She's an office worker at the hospital.

Name: Lidia Nowak
Job: ³_____
City: Torun
Country: Poland

Name: Sakura Sato
Job: ⁴_____
City: Nagoya
Country: Japan

4 a Read the web page again. Choose the correct option, a or b, to answer the questions.

1 Is the hospital in London?
  a Yes, it is.
  b No, it isn't.
2 Is Paul from the UK?
  a Yes, he is.
  b No, he isn't.
3 Is Mila a doctor?
  a No, she isn't a doctor. She's a nurse.
  b No, she isn't a doctor. She's an office worker.

b Underline all the examples of *'s, is* and *isn't* in Exercises 3 and 4a.

Grammar

5 a Read and complete the grammar box with *'s* and *isn't*.

be: he/she/it

+	−
He's a nurse.	**He isn't** from the UK.
She ¹_____ a doctor.	**She isn't** from Canada.
It ²_____ a small hospital.	It ³_____ a big hospital.

?	+	−
Is he from the UK?	Yes, **he is**.	No, **he isn't**.
Is she a doctor?	Yes, **she is**.	No, **she isn't**.
Is it in London?	Yes, **it is**.	No, **it isn't**.

with where
Where's she from?   She ⁴_____ from Spain.

b 🔊 1.7 Listen to the sentences. Notice the pronunciation of the short forms in blue.

1 She's a doctor.
2 He's a nurse.
3 It's a small hospital.
4 Where's she from?
5 She isn't a doctor.
6 Mila's an office worker.

c Listen again and repeat.

6 🔊 1.8 Choose the correct alternatives. Then listen and check your answers.

A: So, Patrick are you a football player?
B: Yes, ¹*I'm / it is* a football player in the UK.
A: ²*It is / Is it* a good team?
B: Yes, ³*it is / it's*.
A: ⁴*Is the manager / The manager is* nice?
B: Yes, ⁵*he's / is he* OK.
A: ⁶*He's / Is he* from the UK?
B: No, he ⁷*isn't / not*.
A: Where ⁸*'s he / he* from?
B: ⁹*He's / Is* from Argentina.

7 a Look at the profiles in Exercise 1a again. Answer the questions.

1 Is Mali from Japan?
  No, she isn't. She's from Thailand.
2 Is Santiago a pilot?
3 Is Sakura a farmer?
4 Is Emilio a nurse?
5 Is Josh a school teacher?
6 Is Yolanda a doctor?

b Complete the profiles for two people. Work in pairs and tell your partner about them.

Name: _____
Job: _____
City: _____
Country: _____

Name: _____
Job: _____
City: _____
Country: _____

A: *This is Diego. He's a teacher. He's from Córdoba in …*

📱 Go to page 116 or your app for more information and practice.

Speaking

PREPARE

8 Work in pairs. Student A: Turn to page 151. Student B: Turn to page 152.

SPEAK

9 Ask and answer the questions and complete the profiles on pages 151/152.

A: *Is Julia a doctor?*
B: *No, she isn't. She's …*

Develop your listening
page 87

1c Nationalities

> **Goal:** talk about different nationalities
> **Grammar:** be: you/we/they
> **Vocabulary:** nationalities

Vocabulary

1 a Work in pairs. Look at photos 1–6 and name the countries.

b Match countries 1–12 with nationalities a–l.

1	Spain	a	Thai
2	Canada	b	British
3	Japan	c	Polish
4	the US	d	Spanish
5	Poland	e	Turkish
6	Argentina	f	Mexican
7	Thailand	g	Japanese
8	the UK	h	Italian
9	Turkey	i	American
10	Mexico	j	Canadian
11	Brazil	k	Brazilian
12	Italy	l	Argentinian

2 a  1.11 Listen and underline the stressed syllables in nationalities a–l in Exercise 1b.

b Listen again and repeat.

c  1.12 Read the sentences. Is the stress in the countries and nationalities on the same (S) syllable or on different (D) syllables? Listen and check.

1 She's from Argen<u>ti</u>na. She's Argen<u>ti</u>nian. *S*
2 She's from Canada. She's Canadian.
3 He's from Japan. He's Japanese.
4 She's from Mexico. She's Mexican.
5 He's from Poland. He's Polish.

3 Write sentences about the nationalities of some famous people.

Tom Cruise is American.

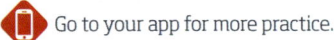 Go to your app for more practice.

Reading

4 a Read the blog. Match photos A–E with paragraphs 1–5.

Me and my friends

1 Hi! I'm Nina. I'm from London. I'm a university student and an office worker.
2 Tessa and Julia are my friends from university. Tessa is Turkish and Julia is Polish. They're student nurses.
3 This is my office. We aren't all British. We're from all over the world. Diego is from Spain, Carlos is from Argentina and the manager is from Thailand. We're a good team.
4 Tim, Annie and Dan are my friends from school. They aren't in the UK now. They're at an American university.
5 And this is my friend Marvin. He's from London, but he's in Vancouver in Canada now.

b Read the blog again. Are the sentences true (T) or false (F)? Correct the false sentences.

1 Nina is from the US.
   F – Nina is from the UK.
2 Tessa and Julia are from Turkey.
3 The office manager is Thai.
4 Tim, Annie and Dan are in the UK now.
5 Marvin is from Vancouver.

Grammar

5 a Read and complete the grammar box with *are* and *aren't*.

be: you/we/they

+	-
You're British.	You aren't American.
We're office workers.	We ¹_____ football players.
They're nurses.	They aren't doctors.

?	+	-
Are you British?	Yes, we ²_____.	No, we aren't.
Are we a good team?	Yes, you are.	No, you aren't.
³_____ they in the UK?	Yes, they are.	No, they ⁴_____.

with who

Who ⁵_____ they?   They're my friends.

b 🔊 1.13 Listen to the sentences. Notice the pronunciation of the short forms in blue.
1 They aren't in the UK now.
2 They're at an American university.
3 We aren't all British.
4 We're from all over the world.

c Listen again and repeat.

6 Complete the texts with the words in the box.

| 're | ~~are~~ | 're | aren't | 're |

Lidia and Wiktor ¹ *are* my friends. We ²_____ from Poland but Lidia and Wiktor ³_____ in Kraków at the moment. They ⁴_____ at university in the UK and they ⁵_____ very happy there.

| ~~are~~ | aren't | are | 're | are |

My office is in Chicago. My manager and I ⁶ *are* from Chicago, but some people ⁷_____ American. They ⁸_____ from different countries. Sally and Tim ⁹_____ British. Hana and Kaito ¹⁰_____ Japanese.

7 a Make questions using the prompts.
1 you and your friends / at university?
   Are you and your friends at university?
2 the teachers at your school / American?
3 your classmates / from different countries?
4 where / you and your classmates / now?
5 who / your teachers?
6 where / your teachers / from?

b Work in pairs. Ask and answer the questions in Exercise 7a.
   A: *Are you and your friends at university?*
   B: *Yes, we are. We're students at …*

📱 Go to page 116 or your app for more information and practice.

Speaking

PREPARE

8 a Work in pairs. Student A: Look at photo 1. Student B: Look at photo 2.

b Make notes about the people in your photo: names, nationalities, jobs.
   photo 2: Monika, the UK, student

SPEAK

9 Ask and answer questions about the people in the photographs.
   A: *Who are they?*
   B: *They're my friends.*
   A: *Who is she?*
   B: *She's Monika.*

Develop your writing
page 88

1D English in action

> **Goal:** ask for and give contact information

1. Look at the photo. Work in pairs. Where are the people?
   a at a conference
   b in a language school
   c in a hotel

2. 🔊 1.14 Listen to the conversation. Who is the student? Where is she from?

3. a Read the Useful phrases box. Listen to the conversation again and number the phrases in the order that you hear them.

   Useful phrases

   Asking for information
   What's your first name?
   What's your family name?
   What's your phone number?
   What's your email address?

   Checking information
   Sorry, can you say that again?
   How do you spell (your first name)?

   Giving information
   My first name is (Selin).
   My family name is (Atakan).
   My number is (020-555-7645).
   My email address is (selin2000@dmail.com).

   b Listen again and complete the form.

   NEW CONTACT
   1 _____: Selin
   2 _____: Atakan
   3 _____: 020-555-7645
   4 _____: selin2000@dmail.com

4. a Complete the conversation with the correct questions. Use the Useful phrases to help you.
   A: ¹_____?
   B: Dieter Neumann.
   A: ²_____ first name?
   B: D - I - E - T - E - R.
   A: And ³_____ again?
   B: Neumann. That's N - E - U - M - A - N - N.
   A: ⁴_____?
   B: It's 07700 900617.
   A: Sorry, ⁵_____?
   B: 07700 900617.
   A: And ⁶_____?
   B: It's dietern@intertalk.com.

   b 🔊 1.15 Listen, check and repeat.

5. Complete the form with your information.

   NEW CONTACT
   First name: _____
   Family name: _____
   Phone number: _____
   Email address: _____

6. Work in pairs. Ask and answer questions to complete the form with your partner's information.

   NEW CONTACT
   First name: _____
   Family name: _____
   Phone number: _____
   Email address: _____

Go online for the Roadmap video.

Check and reflect

1 Find the ten countries in the wordsearch.

Argentina	Brazil	Canada	Italy	Japan
Mexico	~~Poland~~	Spain	Thailand	Turkey

P	L	B	R	A	Z	I	L	L	M
O	T	U	X	O	P	R	N	N	E
L	U	R	I	T	A	L	Y	K	X
A	R	G	E	N	T	I	N	A	I
N	K	J	A	P	A	N	S	F	C
D	E	K	Z	Z	O	N	B	T	O
B	Y	U	S	P	A	I	N	K	C
T	H	A	I	L	A	N	D	R	S
U	K	V	S	J	J	K	P	K	N
C	A	N	A	D	A	I	B	B	E

2 a Put the words in the correct order to make sentences.

1 from / I / Brazil / am
  I am from Brazil.
2 am / London / from / not / I
3 you / class / my / in / Are ?
4 are / Where / from / you ?
5 my / you / are / No, / in / class / not

b Rewrite three of the sentences in Exercise 2a. Use short forms.

3 Complete the sentences with the correct form of *be*. Use short forms.

1 **A:** _____ you from Spain?
  B: No, I _____ from Mexico.
2 **A:** I _____ in Class 4. _____ you?
  B: No, I _____ . I _____ in Class 3.
3 **A:** Hi, I _____ Tomoko. I _____ from Japan.
  B: Nice to meet you. I _____ Burak from Turkey.
4 **A:** _____ I late?
  B: No, you _____ late.

4 Complete the names of the jobs.

1 f___b___ p*layer*
2 s_____ t_____r
3 f____r
4 o_____ w____r
5 p__o_
6 d__t__
7 t___ d____r
8 n____

5 Correct the sentences. Add *is* or *isn't*.

1 Lionel Messi a football player.
2 Marina from Italy?
3 Yes, Yoko in Class 5.
4 The White House in New York.
5 Pete a doctor?
6 No, he.

6 Correct the sentences. Use the information in brackets.

1 Jennifer Lopez is English. (American)
  Jennifer Lopez isn't English. She's American.
2 Cristiano Ronaldo is a doctor. (football player)
3 The students are at a British university. (American)
4 Celine Dion is from Spain. (Canada)
5 We are from Spain. (all over the world)

7 a Complete the sentences with the correct nationalities.

1 Gemma's from the UK. Gemma's *British*.
2 Murat's from Turkey. Murat's _____ .
3 Sonoko's from Japan. Sonoko's _____ .
4 Jake's from Canada. Jake's _____ .
5 Felipe's from Brazil. Felipe's _____ .
6 Manolo's from Spain. Manolo's _____ .
7 Maria's from Argentina. Maria's _____ .
8 Sergio's from Mexico. Sergio's _____ .
9 Agnieszka's from Poland. Agnieszka's _____ .
10 Anurak's from Thailand. Anurak's _____ .

b Write the names, nationalities and jobs of three people you know.

c Work in pairs. Tell your partner about the people in Exercise 7b.

Gino's my friend. He's Italian and he's a doctor.

8 Choose the correct alternatives.

1 Ana and Lydia are friends. *We're / They're* from Mexico.
2 Hey Luca, *we are / are we* in Classroom 2 today?
3 Mike and Sally are teachers. *Are they / They are* British.
4 **A:** Hello Yuki, hello Yumi. *Are we / Are you* from Tokyo?
  B: *We aren't / They aren't* from Tokyo. *You're / We're* from Osaka.
5 Hi Jaime, hi Abdul. Don't worry! *You aren't / They aren't* late.

9 Complete the text with *'re, are* and *aren't*.

Nick and Kelly _____ my friends in London. I'm from the UK, but Nick and Kelly _____ British. They _____ from Canada.

Reflect

How confident do you feel about the statements below? Write 1–5 (1 = not very confident, 5 = very confident).

- I can introduce myself to other students.
- I can ask and answer about jobs.
- I can talk about different nationalities.
- I can ask for and give contact information.

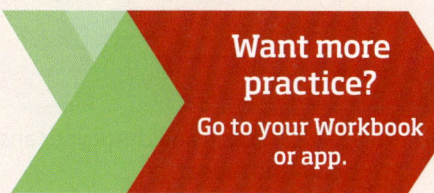

Want more practice?
Go to your Workbook or app.

2A Families

Luisa

Maria

Alonzo

José

> **Goal:** talk about your family
> **Grammar:** possessive 's, I/my, you/your, etc.
> **Vocabulary:** family

Vocabulary

1 Look at the photos and complete the family tree with the correct names.

2 a Look at the family tree again and complete the table below.

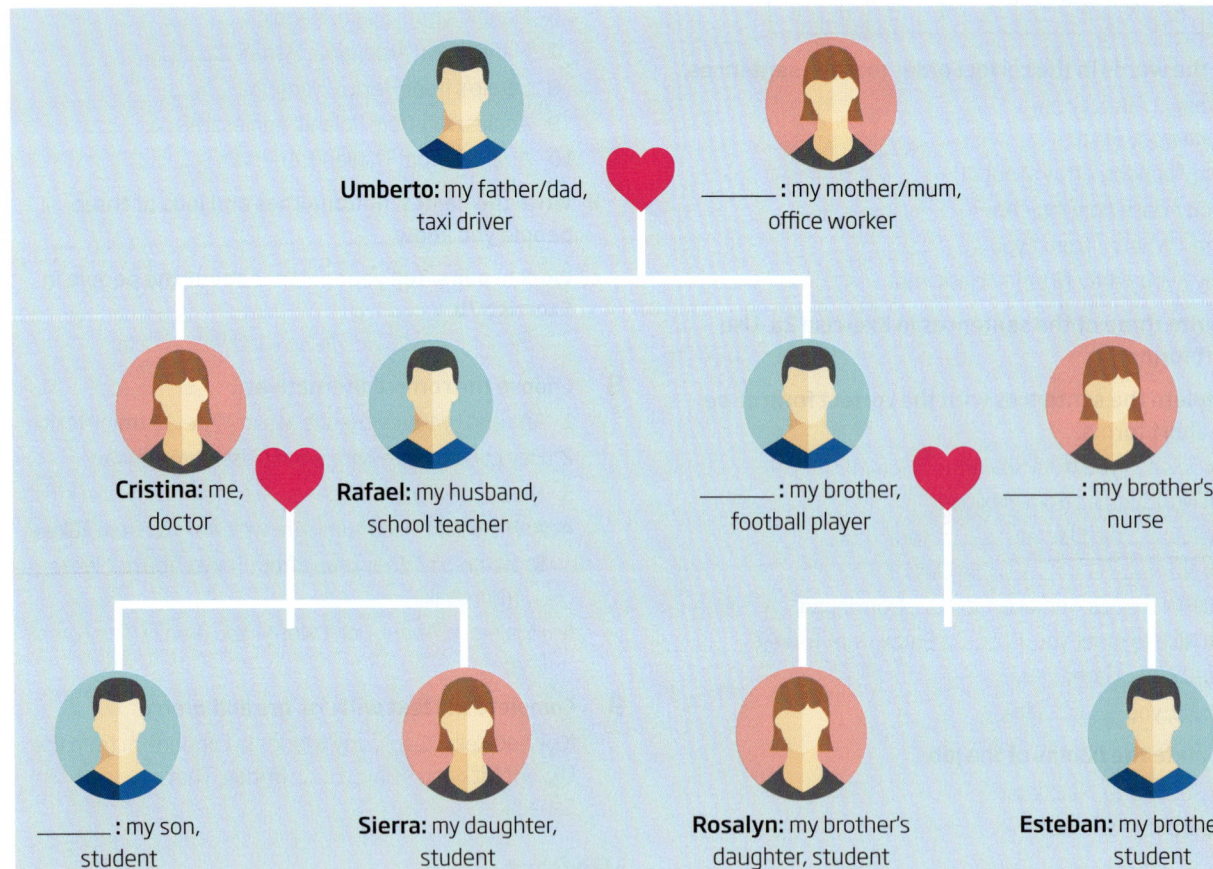

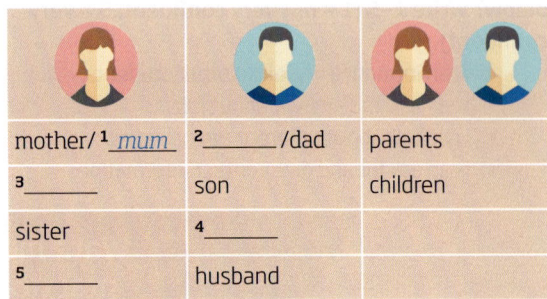

mother/ ¹ _mum_	² _____ /dad	parents
³ _____	son	children
sister	⁴ _____	
⁵ _____	husband	

b 🔊 **2.1** Listen and check your answers. Then listen again and repeat.

3 Look at the family tree again. Complete the sentences.
1 Cristina is Umberto's _____ .
2 José is Luisa's _____ .
3 Esteban is José's _____ .
4 Alonzo is Sierra's _____ .
5 Rafael is Alonzo's _____ .
6 Cristina is Rafael's _____ .
7 Rosalyn and Esteban are José and Luisa's _____ .
8 Umberto and Maria are Cristina and José's _____ .

📱 Go to page 137 or your app for more vocabulary and practice.

Listening

4 a 🔊 2.2 Listen and match speakers 1–4 with photos A–D.

b Listen again and complete the sentences.
1. This is my family. This is **my** _____ , Jon, and **our** _____ . **His** name is James.
2. This is a photo of **my** _____ . **Their** names are Yuriko and Shinya. And this is **our** dog. **Its** name is Aki.
3. This is a photo of **my** _____ . **Their** names are Jan, Karol and Tomasz.
4. This is a photo of **my** _____ . **My** _____ , Tony, is from Canada. **His** family are in Vancouver. My _____ 's name is Lily.

Grammar

5 Complete the grammar box with the words in bold in Exercise 4b.

Possessive 's
name + 's *Rafael is Cristina's husband.*
word + 's *My mother's name is Lily.*

I/my, you/your, etc.

I, you, etc.	possessive adjectives
I	1_____
you	your
he	2_____
she	her
it	3_____
we	4_____
they	5_____

6 a 🔊 2.3 Listen to the sentences. Do the words in blue sound the same or different?
1. a They're from the UK.
   b Their mother is English.
2. a He's an office worker.
   b His sister is a nurse.
3. a Your family is great.
   b You're from a big family.

b Listen again and repeat.

7 🔊 2.4 Choose the correct alternatives. Then listen and check your answers.

Yasemin: This is a photo of ¹*my / you* family.
Tara: Wow! Is this ²*you / your* mother and father? What are ³*they're / their* names?
Yasemin: My ⁴*father's / father is* name is Emir. ⁵*He's / His* from Turkey. My mother's English. ⁶*His / Her* name's Linda.
Tara: OK. So is this ⁷*you / your* brother?
Yasemin: No, it isn't. That's ⁸*our / we* friend from Ankara. This is my brother here. ⁹*Her / His* name's Ali.
Tara: Right. What's your ¹⁰*friends / friend's* name?
Yasemin: Yusuf. He's a student in the UK.

📱 Go to page 118 or your app for more information and practice.

Speaking

PREPARE

8 Draw a picture of your family, or find a photo on your phone.

SPEAK

9 Work in pairs. Tell your partner about your family.
A: *This is a photo of my family. This is my father. His name is Michael. He's an office worker.*

Develop your reading
page 89

2B Everyday things

> **Goal:** talk about everyday objects
> **Grammar:** *this, that, these* and *those*
> **Vocabulary:** everyday objects (1)

Vocabulary

1 a Work in pairs. Look at pictures A and B. Where are the people?

b Match 1–12 in the pictures with a–l.

a a book	g a photo
b a phone	h a computer
c a desk	i a box
d a key	j a chair
e a table	k a cup
f a clock	l a pen

2 🔊 **2.5** Listen and repeat the words in Exercise 1b.

3 Work in pairs. Ask and answer questions about photos 1–8.
  A: *What's number 1?*
  B: *It's a pen.*

4 Say the names of things in your room.
  It's a clock. It's a chair.

Go to page 137 or your app for more vocabulary and practice.

Listening

5 a 🔊 **2.6** Listen and choose the correct picture in Exercise 1, A or B.

b Listen again and complete the conversation.

Max: Hi. Are you Carla?
Carla: Yes, I am.
Max: I'm Max. Nice to meet you.
Carla: Nice to meet you, too.
Max: Welcome to the company. This is our office. And this is your [1]_____ .
Carla: OK.
Max: These are your [2]_____ for the office.
Carla: OK.
Max: This is your [3]_____ and this is the password.
Carla: Great.
Max: And that is my [4]_____ . Please ask me for help.
Carla: Thank you. Are those [5]_____ of your family?
Max: Yes. That's my son and that's my daughter.
Carla: Very nice.
Max: Thank you. OK. Any questions?
Carla: Yes, where's my [6]_____ ?
Max: Oh. Sorry. It's in the meeting room!

8 2.8 Look at pictures 1–4 and complete the conversations with *this, that, these* or *those*. Then listen and check your answers.

1 Monica: Is _____ your cup?
  Davide: Yes, it is.
2 Raquel: Are _____ your books?
  Mario: Yes, they are.
3 Nina: What's in _____ box?
  Paula: _____ 's my new clock.
4 Erik: Are _____ my pens?
  Sara: No, _____ are Jack's pens.

9 a Work in pairs. Student A: Look at picture A in Exercise 1. Student B: Look at picture B. Find the English words for other objects in the pictures. Use your dictionary to help you. Write a list.

b Ask and answer questions about the other objects in the pictures. Make notes.

   A: What's that?
   B: It's a light.
   A: What are those?
   B: They're plants.

Go to page 118 or your app for more information and practice.

Speaking

PREPARE

10 Work in pairs. Look at picture A in Exercise 1. Student A: Prepare to give a new worker a tour of the meeting room. Student B: Ask questions. Use Exercise 5b to help you.

SPEAK

11 Roleplay the tour of the meeting room.

Grammar

6 Complete the phrases with *this, that, these* and *those*. Use Exercise 5b to help you.

this, that, these and *those*

1 _____ key
2 _____ key
3 _____ keys
4 _____ keys

7 a 2.7 Listen and tick the sentence you hear first, a or b.
  1 a This is my key.   b These are my keys.
  2 a These are my books.   b This is my book.
  3 a What's in this box?   b What's in these boxes?

b Listen again and repeat.

Develop your writing
page 90

2c Numbers

- **Goal:** ask questions about other people
- **Grammar:** question words with *be*
- **Vocabulary:** numbers 1–100

Vocabulary

1 a Match the numbers in the photos with the words in the box.

1 one, 2 two

| eight | five | four | nine | ~~one~~ | seven |
| six | ten | three | ~~two~~ | | |

b 🔊 2.9 Listen and repeat numbers 1–19.

11 eleven	12 twelve	13 thirteen
14 fourteen	15 fifteen	16 sixteen
17 seventeen	18 eighteen	19 nineteen

c 🔊 2.10 Listen and repeat the numbers below.

20 twenty	30 thirty	40 forty	50 fifty
60 sixty	70 seventy	80 eighty	90 ninety
100 a hundred			

2 🔊 2.11 Listen and choose the numbers that you hear.

1 13 / 30
2 14 / 40
3 15 / 50
4 16 / 60
5 17 / 70
6 18 / 80
7 19 / 90

3 a Read the numbers. What numbers come next?
twenty-one, twenty-two, *twenty-three, …*

b 🔊 2.12 Listen, check and repeat.

📱 Go to your app for more practice.

Listening

4 a 🔊 2.13 Listen to a conversation. How old are the people in the profiles?

b Listen again and complete the rest of the profiles.

What's her name? Anna Chubb
How old is she? _____
Where is she from? _____
What's her job? _____

What's his name? Bill Gooch
How old is he? _____
Where is he from? _____
What's his job? _____

What's his name? Satoru Goto
How old is he? _____
Where is he from? _____
What's his job? _____

Grammar

5 Read the grammar box and choose the correct alternatives. Use the examples and Exercise 4 to help you.

Question words with *be*

Question words (e.g. *Who, How, What Where, When,* etc.) come ¹*before / after* the verb *be*.
The verb *be* comes ²*before / after* the subject (e.g. *she, they, their names,* etc.)

Who are you?	I'm your new teacher.
How old is he?	He's 99 years old!
What is her name?	Her name is Anna Chubb.
Where are they from?	They're from Canada.
When is your class?	At 9.30 a.m.

6 a 🔊 2.14 Listen to the sentences. Notice the pronunciation of the forms of *be* in blue.

1 What**'s** her name?
2 What**'s** his name?
3 What**'s** her job?
4 What**'s** his job?
5 Where**'s** she from?
6 Where**'s** he from?

b Listen again and repeat.

7 Write questions for answers 1–5.

1 _____ ?
He's from Thailand.
2 _____ ?
He's a doctor.
3 _____ ?
Her name is Lidia Nowicki.
4 _____ ?
She's from Kraków in Poland.
5 _____ ?
They're from the US.

8 a Write the names of three people in your family.

b Work in pairs. Give the names to your partner. Ask and answer questions about the people's ages and jobs.

A: *Who's Felipe?*
B: *He's my brother.*
A: *How old is he?*
B: *He's 19.*
A: *What's his job?*
B: *He's a student.*

📱 Go to page 118 or your app for more information and practice.

Speaking

PREPARE

9 Work in pairs. Student A: Turn to page 151. Student B: Turn to page 152.

SPEAK

10 Ask and answer the questions and complete the information on pages 151/152.

A: *What's Lena's job?*
B: *She's a farmer.*

Develop your listening
page 91

2D English in action

Goal: pay for things in a shop

1 Look at the picture. What objects can you see?

2 a 🔊 2.20 Listen to a conversation in a shop. Which objects in the picture does the man buy?

b Listen again and tick the phrases in the Useful phrases box that you hear.

Useful phrases

Customer's phrases
How much is this book?
How much are those cups?
How much is this?
How much is that?
Can I pay by card?
Here you are.
Here's my card.

Shop assistant's phrases
It's £12 (for four cups).
That's £9.99.
It's £15.99.
That's £27.99, please.
Cash or card?
Here's your change.
Here's your card.

c 🔊 2.21 Listen and repeat the phrases.

3 a Complete the conversation with phrases from the Useful phrases box.

Rosa: Excuse me. ¹_____ that chair?
Assistant: ²_____ £45.
Rosa: And ³_____ this box?
Assistant: That's £14.
Rosa: OK. ⁴_____ these cups?
Assistant: They're £2.
Rosa: OK. Three cups, please.
Assistant: ⁵_____ £6, please. ⁶_____?
Rosa: Card, please. ⁷_____.
Assistant: Thank you. ⁸_____.
Rosa: Thank you.

b Work in pairs and practise the conversation.

4 a Work in pairs. Roleplay conversations in a shop. Student A: You are the customer. Ask about the objects in Exercise 1. Student B: You are the shop assistant. Answer the customer's questions.

 A: *Excuse me. How much is the …?*
 B: *It's …*

b Swap roles and repeat.

Go online for the Roadmap video.

Check and reflect

1 **Complete the sentences with the correct family word.**
   1 Catherine is Michael's wife. Michael is Catherine's _husband_ .
   2 Jim is Hayley's husband. Hayley is Jim's _____ .
   3 Hector is Joe's father. Joe is Hector's _____ .
   4 Jill is Jane's mother. Jane is Jill's _____ .
   5 Sally is David's sister. David is Sally's _____ .
   6 Sam and Ellie are Martin and Kate's children. Martin and Kate are Sam and Ellie's _____ .
   7 Andrew is Beth's brother. Beth is Andrew's _____ .
   8 Pedro is Paulo's son. Paulo is Pedro's _____ .

2 **Correct the phrases. Use the possessive 's.**
   1 the sister of Peter   _Peter's sister_
   2 the family of Julie
   3 the parents of Martin
   4 the dog of my friend
   5 the pen of my teacher
   6 the book of my brother

3 **Choose the correct alternatives.**
   1 We're in Room 211 today. *Our / Their* teacher is Joanna.
   2 This is a photo of my sister. *His / Her* name is Amanda.
   3 This is my brother with *his / her* girlfriend, Lucy.
   4 Misha and Roxana aren't here today. They're with *their / its* mum in London.
   5 Your dog is nice. What's *our / its* name?
   6 This is a photo of *my / their* father. *His / its* name is Andrea and he's a doctor.

4 **Correct the mistakes in the sentences.**
   1 Is this a photo of you're mum?
   2 They're sisters. They're names are Lulu and Beth.
   3 Is your fathers name Eric?
   4 Your from Spain. Your friend is from Mexico.

5 **Put the letters in the correct order to make everyday objects. The first letter is given.**
   1 blate   t_able_
   2 haric   c_____
   3 nophe   p_____
   4 enp   p_____
   5 sked   d_____
   6 petrumoc   c_____
   7 yek   k_____
   8 hotop   p_____
   9 puc   c_____
   10 kobo   b_____
   11 oxb   b_____
   12 lkocc   c_____

6 **Choose the correct alternatives.**
   1 Is *this / that* our classroom here?
   2 *That's / Those are* my husband. His name's Hugo.
   3 Are *this / these* your pens on my table?
   4 Are *that / those* your keys on the teacher's desk?

7 a **Work in pairs. Write and say the correct numbers.**
   1 5 x 5 =   _twenty-five_
   2 6 + 7 =   _____
   3 3 x 10 =   _____
   4 42 + 14 =   _____
   5 10 + 3 + 2 =   _____
   6 2 x 25 =   _____
   7 25 + 17 =   _____
   8 8 x 7 =   _____
   9 17 + 12 =   _____
   10 9 x 9 =   _____
   11 15 + 15 + 6 = _____
   12 9 x 7 =   _____

b **Read the first sentence. Then complete the second sentence.**
   1 My son's 10. He's _ten years old_ .
   2 My mother's 58. She's _____ .
   3 My sister's 19. She's _____ .
   4 My mum's brother is 33. He's _____ .

8 a **Put the words in the correct order to make questions.**
   1 father's / is / What / your / job ?
   2 is / from / Where / teacher / your ?
   3 old / phone / How / is / your ?
   4 old / How / your / parents / are ?
   5 Maradona / are / Messi / Where / from / and ?

b **Work in pairs. Ask and answer the questions in Exercise 8a.**

Reflect

Reflect

How confident do you feel about the statements below? Write 1–5 (1 = not very confident, 5 = very confident).
- I can talk about my family.
- I can talk about everyday objects.
- I can ask questions about other people.
- I can pay for things in a shop.

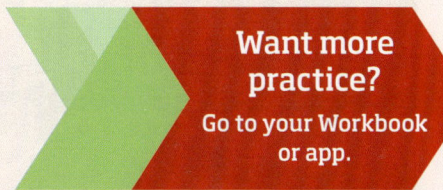

Want more practice? Go to your Workbook or app.

3A My town

> **Goal:** say what's in a town
> **Grammar:** *There is/ There are;* singular and plural nouns
> **Vocabulary:** places in town

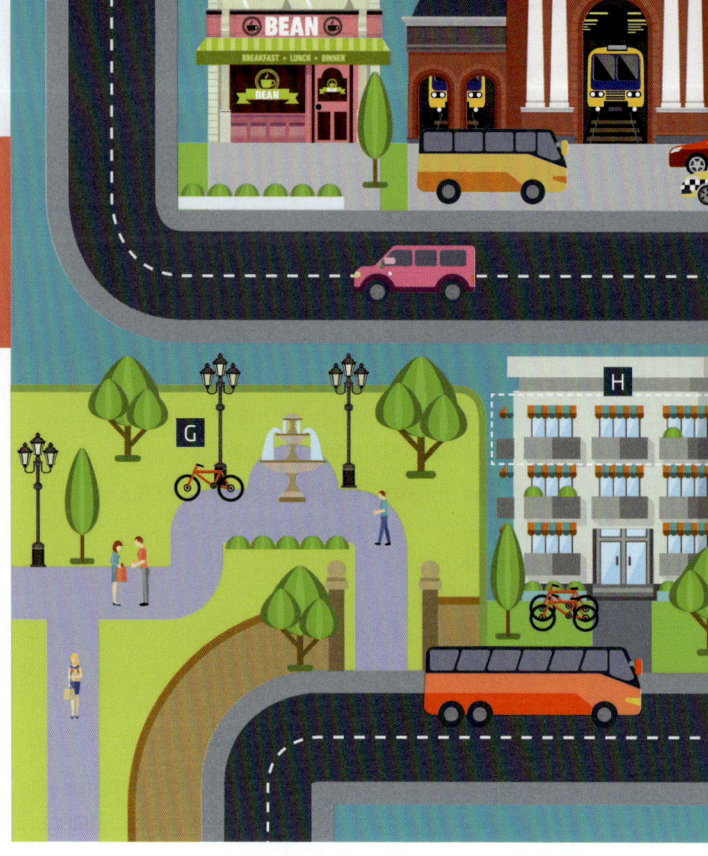

Vocabulary

1 a Work in pairs. Look at the picture. Match A–L with places 1–12.

1 a train station
2 a hotel
3 a café
4 a bank
5 a restaurant
6 a supermarket
7 a cinema
8 a park
9 a market
10 a bookshop
11 a house
12 a flat

b 🔊 3.1 Listen and underline the stressed syllables in the words in Exercise 1a. Listen again and repeat.

2 Cover the words in Exercise 1a. Work in pairs and look at the picture. Ask and answer questions about the places.
  A: *How do you say this in English?*
  B: *That's a cinema.*
  A: *How do you spell that?*
  B: *C-I-N-E-M-A.*

📱 Go to your app for more practice.

Listening

3 🔊 3.2 Listen to three people talking about their town. Match speakers 1–3 with photos A–C.
1 Jack   2 Diana   3 Yuki

4 Listen again. What do the people say? Choose the correct option, a or b.

Jack
1 a There are three restaurants.
  b There are three cafés.
2 a There is a supermarket.
  b There is a market.

Diana
3 a There are three hotels.
  b There aren't any hotels.
4 a There's a supermarket.
  b There's a market.

Yuki
5 a There aren't any shops.
  b There are two restaurants.
6 a There isn't a train station.
  b There isn't a bank.

Grammar

5 Read and complete the grammar box with *There is* and *There are*. Use Exercise 4 to help you.

There is/ There are

	Singular	Plural
+	**There's a** park. ¹_____ **a** park.	²_____ **three** cafés.
–	**There isn't a** bank.	**There aren't any** supermarkets. ³_____ no supermarkets.

6 a 3.3 Listen to the sentences. Notice the sound of *there's*, *there isn't*, *there are* and *there aren't*.

1 There's a park.
2 There are three cafés.
3 There isn't a bank.
4 There are no supermarkets.
5 There aren't any cinemas.

b Listen again and repeat.

7 a Choose the correct alternatives.

1 There *is* / *are* two nice cafés.
2 There is *a* / *any* hotel.
3 There *is* / *are* a big market.
4 There aren't *any* / *a* supermarkets here.
5 There are *no* / *a* hotels in the city.
6 There are *a bookshop* / *two bookshops*.
7 *There's* / *There* a train station.
8 There are *no* / *any* banks here.

b Look at the grammar box again. Complete the lists.

1 one park; two parks; three _____
2 one _____ ; two cafés; three cafés
3 one restaurant; two restaurants; three _____

8 Complete the text.

Uvo is a good town. There ¹_____ two parks, Thorpe Park and Stanley Park. There are no restaurants, but there's ²_____ café – it's really good! ³_____ a train station and ⁴_____ are two bookshops. There ⁵_____ no cinemas, no hotels and ⁶_____ banks, but I love my town!

9 Write six sentences about your town. Use *there is* and *there are*.

There's a train station.
There aren't any hotels.

Go to page 120 or your app for more information and practice.

Speaking

PREPARE

10 Work in pairs. Student A: Turn to page 153. Student B: Turn to page 154.

SPEAK

11 Tell your partner about the town. Find nine differences.

A: There are two cafés in my town.
B: There are three cafés in my town.
A: That's different!

Develop your reading
page 92

3B Is there wifi?

> **Goal:** talk about a flat
> **Grammar:** *Is there a/an ...?/ Are there any ...?*
> **Vocabulary:** rooms and things in a home

Vocabulary

1 Look at photos A–D. What objects can you see?
   There is a table.

2 a Match A–K with the words in the box.

Rooms:	bathroom	bedroom	kitchen	living room
Things:	beds lift	oven shower	toilet	TV wifi

   b 🔊 3.4 Listen and repeat.

CITY FLAT, BRIGHTON ****
£80 per night

In this flat:

3 Work in pairs. Ask and answer the questions about the flat in Exercise 1.
   1 Where is the clock?
   2 What is in the bathroom?
   3 Where is the oven?
   4 What is in the living room?
   5 What is in the bedroom?

4 Close your book and make sentences about the flat.
   There are two beds in the bedroom.

   📱 Go to page 138 or your app for more vocabulary and practice.

Listening

5 a 🔊 3.5 Listen to a conversation between two friends, Jakub and William. Choose the correct flat.

Flat 1
- rooms: two bedrooms, kitchen, living room, bathroom
- shower
- oven
- no wifi

Flat 2
- rooms: bedroom, bathroom
- two beds
- TV
- wifi
- no shower

Flat 3
- rooms: bedroom, bathroom
- two beds
- shower
- TV
- no wifi

   b Listen again. Tick the sentences you hear.
   1 Are there any flats in Berlin for us?
   2 How many beds are there?
   3 There are two beds.
   4 No, there aren't.
   5 Is there a bathroom?
   6 Yes, there is.
   7 No, there isn't.
   8 There isn't an oven.

   c Look at Exercises 5a and 5b again. Complete the sentences with *a* and *an*.
   There is _____ bathroom, _____ shower and _____ TV. There isn't _____ oven.

Grammar

6 Read and complete the grammar box. Use Exercises 5b and 5c to help you.

Is there a/an ...? Are there any ...?

	Singular	Plural
?	¹_____ there a shower?	²_____ there any flats?
+	Yes, there ³_____ .	Yes, there are
−	No, there ⁴_____ . (= No, there is not.)	No, there ⁵_____ . (= No, there are not.)

BUT *Is there* wifi?

with *How many*

How many bedrooms ⁶_____ there?	There ⁷_____ one. There ⁸_____ two.

7 a 🔊 3.6 Listen to the sentences. Does the speaker's voice go up (↑) or down (↓) at the end? Choose the correct alternative.

1 Is there a bathroom? ↑/↓
2 Yes, there is. ↑/↓
3 Are there two beds? ↑/↓
4 Yes, there are. ↑/↓
5 How many rooms are there? ↑/↓
6 There are four rooms. ↑/↓

b Listen again and repeat.

8 Complete the conversation.

William: Look. This flat is £60 per night!
Jakub: Great! How many rooms ¹_____ ?
William: ²_____ five rooms: two bedrooms, a living room, a kitchen and a bathroom.
Jakub: Wow! ³_____ a shower?
William: Yes, ⁴_____ .
Jakub: ⁵_____ wifi?
William: Yes, ⁶_____ .
Jakub: ⁷_____ TVs in the bedrooms?
William: No, ⁸_____ . ⁹_____ a TV in the living room.
Jakub: ¹⁰_____ a lift?
William: No, ¹¹_____ .
Jakub: Oh.

9 a Put the words in the correct order to make questions.

1 your house or flat / is / Where ?
2 are / many / How / there / rooms ?
3 a / Is / shower / there ?
4 there / are / TVs / many / How ?
5 wifi / there / Is ?

b Work in pairs. Ask and answer the questions.

📱 Go to page 120 or your app for more information and practice.

Speaking

PREPARE

10 Look at the table about two holiday flats. Write questions about the flats.

How many beds are there?

	Flat 1	Flat 2
price per night		
number of rooms		
number of bedrooms		
number of beds		
bathroom	Y/N	Y/N
shower/toilet	Y/N	Y/N
living room	Y/N	Y/N
TV	Y/N	Y/N
wifi	Y/N	Y/N
kitchen	Y/N	Y/N
oven	Y/N	Y/N
lift	Y/N	Y/N

SPEAK

11 a Work in pairs. Student A: Turn to page 153. Student B: Turn to page 154.

b Ask and answer the questions and complete the other column in the table.

A: *How many beds are there?*
B: *There are two beds.*

c Choose a flat for your holiday.

Develop your listening
page 93

3c It's expensive!

> **Goal:** describe a town or a city
> **Grammar:** position of adjectives
> **Vocabulary:** describing places

Vocabulary

1 Work in pairs. Look at the pictures. What places can you see?

1 It's busy.

2 It's quiet.

3 It's big.

4 It's small.

5 It's old.

6 It's new.

7 It's cheap.

8 It's expensive.

9 It's good.

10 It's bad.

2 🔊 3.12 Listen and repeat the sentences in Exercise 1.

3 Complete the sentences.
  1 This supermarket isn't good. It's _____ .
  2 This bank isn't small. It's _____ .
  3 This park isn't new. It's _____ .
  4 This hotel isn't cheap. It's _____ .
  5 This café isn't busy. It's _____ .

4 Make sentences about places you know.
  There's a big train station in my city.
  The café in my town is expensive.

📱 Go to page 138 or your app for more vocabulary and practice.

Reading

5 Read the text and match places 1–3 with photos A–C.

WELCOME TO North Norfolk!

1 West Runton
This is a quiet town. There is a café, a good restaurant and six small shops. There are no hotels. There is a small train station.

2 Sheringham
This town is busy. It's big! There is a good market on Saturdays, and there are coffee shops, cheap bookshops and more small shops. There are hotels, restaurants and cafés. There is also a park.

3 Cromer
This town is good for holidays. It isn't expensive. There are cheap shops and restaurants here. There is an old cinema and there is a big hotel in the centre.

6 Read the text again. Are the sentences true (T) or false (F)?
1 Sheringham is a small town.
2 There are six hotels in West Runton.
3 The shops in Cromer are not expensive.
4 There are cheap bookshops in Sheringham.
5 The restaurant in West Runton is bad.
6 The cinema in Cromer isn't new.

Grammar

7 Read the grammar box. Then underline the adjectives in the text in Exercise 5.

Position of adjectives

be + adjective
It's **big**.
It isn't **expensive**.
This town is **busy**.

adjective + noun
This is a **quiet** town.
There's an **old** cinema.
There are **cheap** shops and restaurants.

Cromer

8 a 🔊 3.13 Listen and underline the stressed words.
1 This is a quiet town.
2 There are six small shops.
3 There are no hotels.
4 This town is busy.
5 There's a small cinema.

b Listen again and repeat.

9 Put the words in the correct order to make sentences.
1 expensive / This / restaurant / is
2 small / park / is / There / a
3 are / hotels / cheap / not / These
4 busy / This / station / a / is
5 big / not / is / supermarket / It / a
6 bank / new / Is / this / a ?
7 Is / your / a / station / big / town / in / there ?
8 restaurants / good / town / your / there / any / in / Are ?

10 a Complete the questions about places in your town. Use adjectives.
1 Is there a _____ ?
2 Is the _____ ?
3 Is there a _____ ?
4 Are there any _____ in your town?
5 Is your town's _____ ?
6 Is the _____ in your town _____ ?

b Work in pairs. Ask and answer the questions.
A: *Is there a big hotel?*
B: *Yes, the City Hotel is big./No, there are no big hotels.*
A: *Is the cinema good?*
B: *Yes, it is./No, it isn't.*

📱 Go to page 120 or your app for more information and practice.

Speaking

PREPARE

11 Work in groups. Choose three towns or cities and make notes about them. Think about:
• shops
• restaurants
• parks
• hotels
• cinemas
• markets

Use Exercise 5 to help you.

SPEAK

12 Describe your towns/cities to the class.

Develop your writing
page 94

3D English in action

> **Goal:** ask for and give directions

1 Look at the map. What buildings can you see?

2 a 🔊 3.14 Listen and answer the questions.
1 Where is the woman?
2 Where is her friend, David?

b Listen again and number the pictures in the order that you hear them.

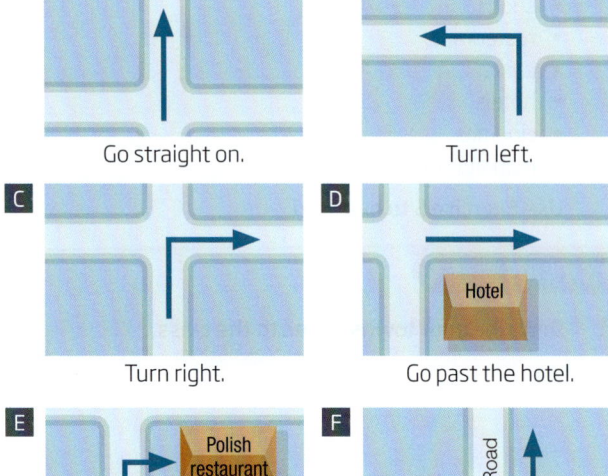

c Work in pairs. Draw the woman's route on the map in Exercise 1.

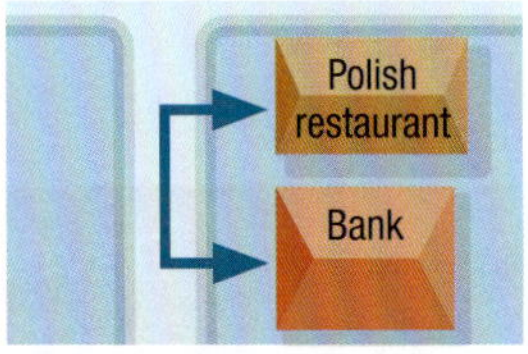

3 🔊 3.15 Listen and number the sentences in the order that you hear them. Listen again and repeat.

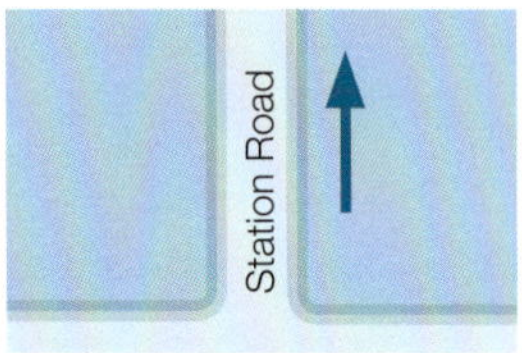

Useful phrases
Is there a (supermarket) near here?
Yes, there's one on (Station Road).
Excuse me. Where's the (cinema), please? 1
It's on (Park Street).
Go past the (bank).
Go straight on.
Go down (Main Street).
Turn left (at the bookshop).
Turn right (after the big house).
It's next to (a restaurant).
It's on the right.
(The supermarket) is on the right.

4 a 🔊 3.16 Look at the map in Exercise 1. Complete the conversations. Use the Useful phrases box to help you. Then listen and check your answers.

1 **A:** Excuse me. _____
   D: Yes, there's one on Station Road. _____ , go past the Turkish restaurant and the supermarket is on the left.
   A: Thank you.
   B: You're welcome.

2 **A:** Excuse me. _____
   B: It's on Park Street. Go down Station Road, _____ , go past the school and the cinema is on the left.
   A: Thanks.
   B: No problem.

3 **A:** Excuse me. Is there a bookshop near here?
   B: Yes, there's one on Market Street. Go straight on, _____ and turn right onto Market Street. _____
   A: Thank you.
   B: No problem.

b Work in pairs. Practise the conversations in Exercise 4a.

5 a Look at the map in Exercise 1. Choose a place. You are at this place now. Prepare to give directions from the station to this place.

b Work in pairs. Take turns giving directions. Can your partner guess where you are?
   A: Go down Station Road and turn right at the hotel.
   B: Turn right at the hotel?

Go online for the Roadmap video.

Check and reflect

1 a Complete the places in town.
1. t_ _ _ n s _ _ _ _ _ n
2. c _ n _ _ a
3. c _ _ é
4. s _ p _ _ _ _ _ k _ _
5. p _ _ k
6. h _ _ e _
7. h _ u _ _
8. f _ _ t
9. b _ _ k
10. r _ _ _ a _ _ a _ t
11. m _ _ k _ _
12. b _ _ k _ _ _ p

b Work in pairs. Ask and answer about the places in your town.
A: Is there a bank? **B:** Yes, there is.

2 Complete the sentences with *is*, *isn't*, *are* or *aren't*. Use short forms.
1. There _are_ six good cafés in this town.
2. There _____ a hotel in Baker Street.
3. Sorry, no, there _____ a bank near here.
4. There _____ two football teams in our town.
5. No, there _____ any shops near here.
6. No, there _____ no expensive restaurants.
7. There _____ three or four supermarkets in the centre.
8. Oh no, there _____ a lift in our hotel!

3 Correct the mistakes in the sentences.
1. There aren't no dogs in the park today.
2. There's three keys in the kitchen.
3. There's box in the living room.
4. There aren't a teacher in our class today!

4 Choose the correct alternatives.
1. The oven is in the *kitchen* / *bedroom*.
2. There's a table in the *living room* / *bathroom*.
3. There are three *kitchens* / *bathrooms* in our house.
4. There are two *beds* / *ovens* in my bedroom.
5. There's a *shower* / *lift* in the bathroom.
6. There's a big *wifi* / *TV* in the bathroom!

5 a Complete the questions about your classroom with the words in the box. You will need to use the words more than once.

| any | Are | are | How | Is | many | there |

1. _Is_ _there_ a TV in our classroom?
2. _____ _____ books?
3. _____ _____ desks _____ _____ ?
4. _____ _____ a computer?
5. _____ _____ _____ photos?
6. _____ _____ chairs _____ _____ ?

b Work in pairs. Ask and answer the questions in Exercise 5a.
A: Is there a TV in our classroom?
B: No, there isn't.

6 Complete the sentences with an adjective.
1. It's a s<u>mall</u> town. There are no hotels or restaurants.
2. My flat isn't new. It's o_ _ .
3. There are five bedrooms. It's a b_ _ house.
4. There aren't any people in the café. It's q_ _ _ _ .
5. The flat in Berlin is £500 per night. It's e_ _ _ _ _ _ _ _ .
6. This is a b_ _ _ town. There are big shops, a market and a train station.
7. This clock isn't expensive. It's c_ _ _ _ .

7 Rewrite the sentences.
1. This is a busy café.
   This _café is busy_ .
2. This _is an expensive car_ .
   This car is expensive.
3. This is a cheap shop.
   This _____ .
4. They _____ .
   The houses are new.
5. This is a quiet street.
   This _____ .
6. It _____ .
   The station is busy.
7. They are new computers.
   The _____ .
8. He _____ .
   The man is old.

8 a Put the words in the correct order to make questions.
1. your / computer / Is / new ? *Is your computer new?*
2. busy / town / Is / your ?
3. park / Is / a / there / near / house / quiet / your ?
4. your / big / Is / small / house / or ?
5. in / expensive / hotels / Are / town / or / your / cheap ?

b Work in pairs. Ask and answer the questions in Exercise 8a.
A: Is your computer new?
B: No, it isn't. It's old.

Reflect

How confident do you feel about the statements below? Write 1–5 (1 = not very confident, 5 = very confident).
- I can say what's in a town.
- I can talk about a flat.
- I can describe a town or a city.
- I can ask for and give directions.

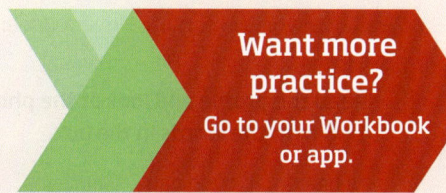

Want more practice?
Go to your Workbook or app.

4A You've got a friend

> **Goal:** describe people
> **Grammar:** *have/has got*
> **Vocabulary:** describing people

Reading and vocabulary

1 Read the profile and look at the photos below. Which person is Luca? Which person is Mehmet?

OK, so my name is Luca and this is my good friend, Mehmet. I'm from Italy. He's from Turkey. We live in Rome. I'm a taxi driver and Mehmet's a student here. He's got a daughter. I haven't got any children.

I've got **blonde hair** and **blue eyes**. He's got **brown hair**, **brown eyes** and **a beard**. I'm **in my 20s** and Mehmet is **in his 30s**.

We're very different, but we're good friends!

2 Read the profile and look at the photos again. Match 1–6 with the words in the box.

a beard   blonde hair   blue eyes   brown eyes
brown hair   in his 30s   in his 20s

3 a Match descriptions 1–4 with photos A–D.
  1 She's got **blonde hair** and **blue eyes**. She's **in her 50s**.
  2 He's got **red hair**. He's **in his 40s**.
  3 She's got **brown hair** and **green eyes**. She's **in her 20s**.
  4 He's got **grey hair** and **a beard**.

b 🔊 4.1 Listen and repeat the words in bold in Exercise 3a.

c Work in pairs. Add more words to the word map.

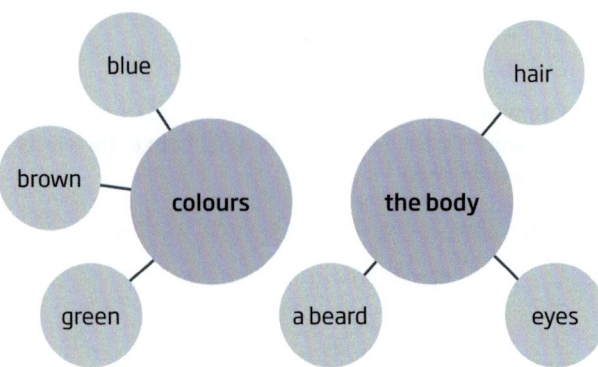

4 a Think of another student in the room. Complete the sentences.
  1 He/She's got _____ hair.
  2 He/She's got _____ eyes.
  3 He/She is in his/her *20s / 30s / 40s /* _____

b Work in pairs. Read your sentences. Your partner guesses the student.

📱 Go to page 139 or your app for more vocabulary and practice.

Grammar

5 Read and complete the grammar box.

have/has got

+	I/You/We/They	¹_____ **got** brown hair.
	He/She/It	²_____ **got** green eyes.
−	I/You/We/They	**haven't got** blue eyes.
	He/She/It	³_____ **got** red hair.

6 a 🔊 4.2 Listen to the sentences. Notice the pronunciation of the words in blue.

1 I've got brown hair.
2 You've got red hair.
3 We've got blue eyes.
4 They've got blue eyes.
5 He's got a beard.
6 She's got grey hair.

b Listen again and repeat.

7 Choose the correct alternatives.

1 I *has / have* got red hair.
2 My friend *has / have* got a son and a daughter.
3 They *has / have* got two children.
4 She *hasn't / haven't* got a dog.
5 We *hasn't / haven't* got a car.
6 He *has / have* got brown hair.
7 I *hasn't / haven't* got any children.
8 They *has / have* got grey hair.

📱 Go to page 122 or your app for more information and practice.

8 Look at the picture and make sentences using the prompts.

1 Sofia / be / an office worker
2 She / have got / a son
3 She / have got / blonde hair / brown eyes
4 She / be / 30s
5 Her son / have got / brown hair / blue eyes
6 He / be / eight years old
7 They / live / in Paris

Speaking

PREPARE

9 You're going to talk about a friend. Think about:
- their job
- where they are from/live
- their age/hair/eyes

SPEAK

10 a Work in pairs. Describe yourself. Then describe your friend from Exercise 9.

A: *OK, my name is Piotr. My friend's name is Basia. We're from Poland. I'm a teacher. I've got …*

b Is your partner very different from his/her friend?

B: *Piotr is very different from his friend Basia. Piotr is a teacher, but Basia is …*

Develop your reading
page 95

4B Have you got it?

> **Goal:** prepare for a trip
> **Grammar:** have/has got: questions
> **Vocabulary:** everyday objects (2)

Vocabulary and listening

1 a Match photos 1–12 with the words in the box.

| bag   bottle of water   camera   coat |
| credit card   food   keys   money |
| passport   phone   sunglasses   tickets |

b 🔊 4.3 Listen and repeat.

2 a Match photos A–D with activities 1–4.
1 a day in the office
2 a holiday in a cold country
3 a long walk
4 a holiday in a hot country

b Which things from Exercise 1a do you need for the activities in Exercise 2a?
1 bottle of water, phone …

3 a 🔊 4.4 Listen to a conversation. Where is Sam going?

b Listen again. Tick the things Sam has got.

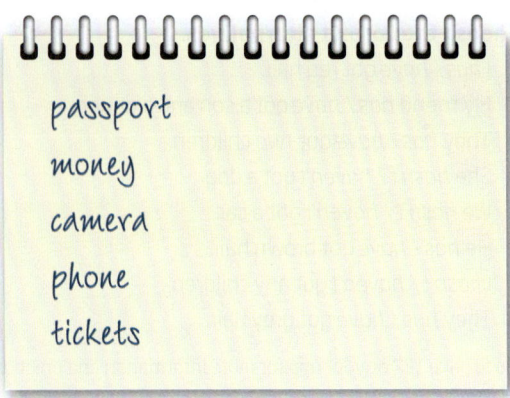

passport
money
camera
phone
tickets

Go to your app for more practice.

Grammar

4 Read part of the conversation from Exercise 3a. Underline the questions.

Zara: OK ... Have you got your camera?
Sam: No, I haven't – but I've got my phone. And Fifi has got a good camera.
Zara: OK. You're ready. Oh, have you got your tickets?
Sam: Tickets, tickets ...
Zara: Has Fifi got your tickets?
Sam: Oh, yes, she has! Phew!

5 Read and complete the grammar box. Use Exercise 4 to help you.

have/has got: questions

Question		Short answer
¹_____ I/we/you/they **got** a ticket?	+	Yes I/we/you/they ² _____.
	–	No, I/we/you/they **haven't**.
³_____ he/she/it **got** a phone?	+	Yes, he/she/it ⁴ _____.
	–	No, he/she/it ⁵ _____.

6 a 🔊 4.5 Listen to two conversations. Do the words in blue sound the same or different?

1 A: <u>Have</u> you got your ticket?
B: Yes, I <u>have</u>.
2 A: <u>Has</u> it got a restaurant?
B: Yes, it <u>has</u>.

b Listen again and repeat.

7 a Make questions using the prompts.
1 you / food / in your bag
   Have you got food in your bag?
2 sister / a camera
3 friend / a good job
4 you / sunglasses
5 you / a big family
6 you / a new phone

b Work in pairs. Ask and answer the questions in Exercise 7a.

8 Put the conversation in the correct order.
a Rose: Yes, we are.
b Rose: Tickets ... Yes, I've got them.
c Rose's mum: Have you got your tickets?
d Rose: Yes, we've got money.
e Rose's mum: Hi Rose. Are you and your brother ready for your trip? *1*
f Rose's mum: And your money?

📱 Go to page 122 or your app for more information and practice.

Speaking

PREPARE

9 Work in pairs. Student A: Turn to page 155. Student B: Turn to page 156.

SPEAK

10 What's in your partner's bag? Ask and answer questions. Then complete the checklist in Exercise 9b on page 155/156 with your partner's answers.

A: *OK, this is my bag for Canada.*
B: *OK. Have you got your passport?*
A: *Yes, I have.*

Develop your listening
page 96

4C Dos and don'ts

> **Goal:** give advice
> **Grammar:** imperatives
> **Vocabulary:** common verbs

Reading and vocabulary

1 Work in pairs. What places in London do you know?
Notting Hill, Buckingham Palace

2 a Read the text messages. Why is Lydia going to London?

I have a work trip to London next week! Have you got any *dos* and *don'ts* for London? Lydia xx

Ben: Don't **go to** Oxford Street. It's very busy.

Carla: **Visit** The British Museum. It's really interesting.

Vitor: Don't **take** taxis! They're expensive.

Jemima: **Go to** Greenwich and **take** photos.

Juana: **Try** Indian food. Indian food in the UK is really good.

Alexis: **Drink** English tea, Lydia. It's cheap x

Theresa: **See** a show, Lydia. There are lots of good shows in London.

Toni: **Take** a coat!

b Read the text messages again. Complete 1–5 with the verbs in bold.
1 _try_ Japanese food, British food
2 _____ , _____ New York, Rome, The British Museum
3 _____ a taxi, a bus, a train, photos, a coat
4 _____ tea, coffee
5 _____ a film, a show

c 🔊 4.9 Listen and repeat the verbs in Exercise 2b.

3 Complete 1–6 with phrases from Exercise 2b.

1 _drink tea_ 2 _____

3 _____ 4 _____

5 _____ 6 _____

📱 Go to your app for more practice.

Grammar

4 Read the messages in Exercise 2a again. Tick the things that are good to do in London.
1 go to Oxford Street
2 visit The British Museum
3 take taxis
4 go to Greenwich
5 take photos
6 try Indian food
7 drink tea
8 see a show
9 take a coat

5 Read and complete the grammar box. Use Exercise 2a to help you.

Imperatives

+	−
Visit Greenwich.	¹_____ **visit** Greenwich.
Take photos.	²_____ **take** photos.
³_____ a show.	**Don't see** a show.

6 a 🔊 4.10 Listen and choose the correct stress pattern.
1 <u>Don't</u> go to <u>Notting Hill</u>. / <u>Don't</u> go to <u>Notting Hill</u>.
2 <u>Try Polish</u> food. / Try <u>Polish</u> food.
3 <u>Drink</u> coffee <u>in</u> a <u>café</u>. / <u>Drink coffee</u> in a <u>café</u>.
4 <u>Don't take</u> photos. / <u>Don't</u> take <u>photos</u>.

b Listen again and repeat.

7 Look at the pictures and the symbols. Make sentences about a trip to Rome.

1 <u>Drink coffee.</u>   2 _____

3 _____   4 _____

5 _____   6 _____

📱 Go to page 122 or your app for more information and practice.

Speaking

PREPARE

8 Your friend wants to visit your city. Complete the table of dos and don'ts.

Dos	Don'ts

SPEAK

9 a Work in pairs. Tell your partner your dos and don'ts for your city. Then complete the table with your partner's dos and don'ts for their city.

Go to the Eiffel Tower. Take photos. Don't have coffee there. It's expensive!

Dos	Don'ts

b Has your partner's city got more dos or more don'ts?

Develop your writing
page 97

4D English in action

> **Goal:** tell the time

1 Read the times on the clocks.
Six forty-five.

A
B
C
D
E
F
G
H

2 🔊 4.11 Listen and match conversations 1–4 with the correct clocks from Exercise 1.

3 Listen again and complete the conversations.
1 **A:** Excuse me. What time is it?
  B: _____ o'clock.
  A: Thank you.
2 **A:** What time is it?
  B: It's quarter past six.
  A: Quarter to six?
  B: No, _____ .
3 **A:** What time is it, Alex?
  B: Er, it's half past eleven.
  A: Sorry, _____ ?
  B: Yeah.
  A: Oh no! I'm late.
4 **A:** What time is our train?
  B: It's at quarter to eleven.
  A: Quarter past eleven?
  B: No, _____ .
  A: Oh OK.

4 🔊 4.12 Find times 1–7 in the Useful phrases box. Then listen and repeat the Useful phrases.

1 4.15   5 4.45
2 4.55   6 4.30
3 4.00   7 4.05
4 4.40

Useful phrases

Asking for the time
What time is it?

Saying the time
It's four o'clock.
It's five past four.
It's quarter past four.
It's half past four.
It's twenty to five.
It's quarter to five.
It's five to five.

Asking for the time of things
What time is the (train to London)?

Saying the time of things
It's at (seven forty-five).

5 Work in pairs. Ask and answer questions about the clocks in Exercise 1. Use the Useful phrases to help you.
  A: *What time is it?*
  B: *It's quarter to seven.*

6 Work in pairs. Student A: Turn to page 156. Student B: Turn to page 155.

Go online for the Roadmap video.

Check and reflect

1 Complete the word map with the words in the box.

| a beard | blonde | brown | eyes | grey | hair |
| in her 20s | in his 50s | red | | | |

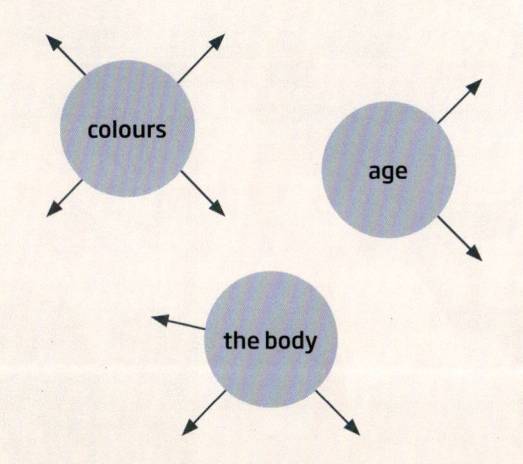

- colours
- age
- the body

2 Complete the sentences with the words in the box.

| a beard | blonde | eyes | in his 80s | in her 20s |

1. No, her hair isn't red. It's _____ .
2. I'm in my 30s, and my wife is _____ .
3. My brother's got blonde hair and _____ .
4. My father is _____ .
5. My sister's got green _____ .

3 Complete the sentences with the positive (+) or negative (-) form of *have got*.

1. I _'ve got_ a beard. (+)
2. We _haven't got_ a big house. (-)
3. John _____ two sisters. (+)
4. Sarah _____ blue eyes. (-)
5. Our flat _____ a big kitchen. (-)
6. They _____ three children. (+)
7. You _____ grey hair! (-)
8. Our town _____ two restaurants. (+)

4 Complete the sentences so they are true for you.

1. I've got _____ .
2. My friend hasn't got _____ .
3. My house/flat has got _____ .
4. My parents have got _____ .
5. My teacher has got _____ .
6. My town has got _____ .

5 a Put the words in the correct order to make questions.

1. you / got / a / Have / phone ?
2. Has / your / green / teacher / eyes / got ?
3. Have / blonde / your / hair / parents / got ?
4. you / food / your / bag / in / Have / got ?
5. camera / good / your / phone / Has / a / got ?
6. bottle / of / Have / a / got / water / you ?
7. How / credit cards / you / many / got / have ?

b Work in pairs. Ask and answer the questions in Exercise 5a.

6 Choose the correct alternatives.

1. *Go to / Take* Spain – it's very nice.
2. *Take / Visit* Tokyo. It's amazing!
3. *Go to / Take* some photos of the park.
4. *Try / Take* a coat. It's cold.
5. *Don't take / Don't go to* the bus. It's slow.
6. *Drink / Try* French food.
7. *Drink / Take* coffee from Brazil, it's very good.
8. *See / Take* the new Star Wars film.

7 Look at the photos and the symbols. Write sentences.
On your holiday to the UK:

1. _Take your passport_
2. _____
3. _____
4. _____
5. _____
6. _____

Reflect

How confident do you feel about the statements below? Write 1–5 (1 = not very confident, 5 = very confident).

- I can describe people.
- I can prepare for a trip.
- I can give advice.
- I can tell the time.

Want more practice?
Go to your Workbook or app.

5A My week

> **Goal:** describe part of your week
> **Grammar:** present simple: *I/you/we/they*
> **Vocabulary:** days of the week, everyday activities

Vocabulary

1. Match pictures A–J with sentences 1–10.
   1. **I get up** at six thirty.
   2. **I have breakfast** at 7 o'clock.
   3. **I go to work** at seven forty-five.
   4. **I work** from nine to five thirty.
   5. **I have lunch** at twelve thirty.
   6. **I go home** at half past five.
   7. **I have dinner** at 7 o'clock.
   8. **I watch TV** at seven thirty.
   9. **I study** at 9 o'clock.
   10. **I go to bed** at half past ten.

2. Write five sentences about your day.
   I get up at 7 o'clock.

3. a ♪ 5.1 Look at the table. Listen and repeat the days of the week.

Monday	bookshop
Tuesday	university
Wednesday	lunch with class
Thursday	dinner at my mum's house
Friday	English homework
Saturday	sleep until midday!
Sunday	TV

   b Look at the table again. Complete the sentences with the verbs in bold in Exercise 1.
   1. On Mondays, I _____ in a bookshop.
   2. On Tuesdays, I _____ university.
   3. On Wednesdays, I _____ lunch with my class.
   4. On Thursdays, I _____ dinner at my mum's house.
   5. On Fridays, I _____ at home.
   6. On Saturdays, I _____ late.
   7. On Sundays, I _____ TV.

   c ♪ 5.2 Listen, check and repeat.

4. Write three sentences about your week.
   On Mondays, I work in a café.

   📱 Go to page 140 or your app for more vocabulary and practice.

Reading

5. a Read about Mari's week and answer the questions.
   1. What is her job?
   2. Are the week and the weekend very different for her?

   From Monday to Friday, I get up at <u>7 o'clock</u>. I have breakfast at <u>seven thirty</u> and I go to <u>work</u> at <u>8 o'clock</u> by <u>bus</u>. I'm a <u>nurse in the San Juan Hospital</u>. I have lunch at <u>1 o'clock</u> and I go home at <u>five forty-five</u>. In the evening, I have dinner at home and <u>watch TV</u> or <u>study English</u>. I go to bed at <u>eleven</u>. At the weekend, I <u>don't work</u>. On Saturdays, I get up at <u>10 o'clock</u>. I have breakfast and <u>go to my sister's flat</u>. <u>We have lunch and talk</u>. Later, I <u>go to the shops</u>. At 6 or 7 o'clock, I <u>have dinner with friends at a restaurant</u>. I go to bed at <u>12</u>. I love the weekend!

   b Change the underlined information so it's true for you.
   From Monday to Friday, I get up at 6 o'clock.

   c Work in pairs. Read your description to your partner. Are your weeks very different?

5A | My week

9 a Write three true and three false sentences about your week.

  b Work in pairs. Take turns reading your sentences. Guess your partner's false sentences.
   A: *I get up at 6 o'clock on Mondays.*
   B: *That's not true!*
   A: *You're right. I get up at 7 o'clock on Mondays.*

  Go to page 124 or your app for more information and practice.

Speaking

PREPARE

10 What do you do on Fridays, Saturdays and Sundays? Make notes.

Friday	
Saturday	
Sunday	

SPEAK

11 a Work in pairs. Student A: Describe your routine. Student B: Make notes. Then swap roles and repeat.
    On Fridays, I get up at …

Friday	
Saturday	
Sunday	

  b Are your routines the same or different? Report back to the class.
   A: *We don't go to university on Saturdays.*
   B: *You have lunch at home on Saturdays. I have lunch in a café.*

Grammar

6 Read the grammar box and choose the correct alternatives. Use Exercise 5a to help you.

Present simple: *I/ you/ we/ they*

Use the present simple to talk about routines.

+	I/You/We/They	**go**	to work.
–	I/You/We/They	**don't work**.	

Use ¹*on / at* + times: *I go to work* ²*on / at 8 o'clock.*
Use ³*on / at* + days: ⁴*On / At Saturdays, I get up at 10 o'clock.*
Use *from … to …* for days and times:
From Monday to Friday, I get up at 7 o'clock. On Wednesdays, I work from 2 o'clock to 10 o'clock.

7 a 🔊 5.3 Listen and underline the stressed words.
   1 On <u>Fridays</u>, I have <u>breakfast</u> at <u>ten</u>.
   2 I go to work at eight thirty.
   3 At twelve o'clock, I have lunch.
   4 I watch TV from seven thirty to eight thirty.
   5 From ten to twelve, I play football with my friends.

  b Listen again and repeat.

8 Put the words in the correct order to make sentences.
   1 get up / six / Mondays / I / at / on
    I get up at six on Mondays./On Mondays, I get up at six.
   2 breakfast / I / seven thirty / have / at
   3 work / go to / I / half past eight / at
   4 work / nine / five / to / from / I
   5 have / dinner / with / I / at / seven / my family
   6 bed / late / go / I / don't / to
   7 Saturdays / don't / I / and / Sundays / work / on
   8 watch TV / on / and read books / I / Saturdays

Develop your reading
page 98

39

5B A long journey

> **Goal:** talk about how you travel to work/university
> **Grammar:** present simple questions: *I/you/we/they*
> **Vocabulary:** travel and transport

Vocabulary and listening

1 a Match photos A–G with sentences 1–7.
   1 I go to work by bus.
   2 I take a boat to work.
   3 I cycle to work. I love my bike!
   4 I drive to my parents' house.
   5 I travel to work by taxi.
   6 I go to the office by train.
   7 I walk home.

b 🔊 5.4 Listen and repeat.

c Work in pairs. Which sentences in Exercise 1a are true for you? Tell your partner.

2 a Complete transport phrases 1–3 with verbs a–c. Use Exercise 1a to help you.
   a cycle/drive/walk
   b go/travel
   c take
   1 _____ to work by bike/car/boat/taxi/train/bus
   2 _____ a boat/a train/a taxi/a bus to my house
   3 _____ to work/my parents' house/the café

b Complete the sentences.
   1 I go _____ work by bus. I leave home at about 6.30.
   2 I go to work _____ bus and train. I arrive at 8 o'clock.
   3 I live in Hong Kong. I _____ a boat to work. I leave the house at 7.00 and arrive at work at 8.00.
   4 I _____ to work by bus. I leave home at 6.30.
   5 I drive _____ work on Mondays and Tuesdays.

c Read the sentences in Exercise 2b again. What is the opposite of *leave*?

3 a 🔊 5.5 Listen and complete the table.

Tim	Donna
travels to work by ¹_____ .	travels to work by ⁴_____ .
leaves home at ²_____ .	leaves home at ⁵_____ .
arrives at work at ³_____ .	

b Listen again. Tick the questions you hear.
   1 Do you drive to work?
   2 Do you cycle to work every day?
   3 What time do you arrive at work?
   4 What time do you leave home?
   5 How do you travel to work?

📱 Go to your app for more practice.

Grammar

4 Read and complete the grammar box. Use Exercise 3b to help you.

Present simple questions: *I/you/we/they*

Question	Short answer
¹_____ I/you/we/they **drive** to work?	+ Yes, I/you/we/they ²_____ .
	− No, I/you/we/they ³_____ .

with question words

How	⁴_____ you travel to work?	I cycle.
What time	⁵_____ you leave home?	At 6.00.
What time	⁶_____ you arrive at work?	At 8.00.

5B | A long journey

7 a Put the words in the correct order to make questions.

1. do / leave home / you / What time ?
   What time do you leave home?
2. travel to work / you / by bus / Do ?
3. you / do / in your office / have lunch / What time ?
4. travel / home / you / do / How ?
5. people / at your office / to work / drive / Do ?
6. cycle / on Saturdays / you / and Sundays / Do ?

b Work in pairs. Ask and answer the questions in Exercise 7a.

A: What time do you leave home?
B: I leave home at 8.00 from Monday to Friday.

Go to page 124 or your app for more information and practice.

Speaking

PREPARE

8 a Read the questions and guess the answers.

1. How many people in the class drive to work/university?
2. How many people in the class leave home at 8 o'clock?
3. How many people have got a long journey to work/university?
4. How many people take two different forms of transport?
5. How many people have got a short journey to work/university?

b How can you find the answers to the questions in Exercise 8a? Write questions.

1 Do you drive to work/university?

SPEAK

9 a Ask other students your questions from Exercise 8b. Make notes about their answers.

b Work in pairs. Tell your partner what you learnt in Exercise 9a.

5 5.6 Listen to the conversations. Do the words in blue sound the same or different?

1. **A:** Do you go to work by bus?
   B: Yes, I do.
2. **A:** Do they walk to work?
   B: Yes, they do.

6 Choose the correct alternatives.

1. **A:** How ¹ *you travel / do you travel* to work?
   B: I ² *cycle / do cycle.* ³ *Do you go / Do you* by bike?
   A: No, ⁴ *we don't / we aren't.* We walk to work.
2. **A:** What time ⁵ *leave / do you leave* home?
   B: At about eight o'clock. ⁶ *I walk / I am walk* to the station and ⁷ *I take / I do take* the train to work.
   A: What time ⁸ *you do / do you* arrive?
   B: At 8.30.
3. **A:** How ⁹ *your children travel / do your children travel* to school?
   B: ¹⁰ *Go / They go* by bus. They ¹¹ *leave / are leave* home at eight.
   A: What time ¹² *they arrive / do they arrive*?
   B: At 8.45.

Develop your listening
page 99

5c Food and drink

> **Goal:** take part in a survey about being healthy
> **Grammar:** present simple with frequency adverbs
> **Vocabulary:** food and drink

Vocabulary

1 a Match photos 1–14 with the words in the box.

bread	cakes	cheese	chicken	chocolate
coffee	eggs	fish	meat	milk	salad
sandwiches	sugar	tea		

b 🔊 5.10 Listen and repeat.

2 🔊 5.11 Listen to the words. Do the sounds in blue sound the same or different?

1. m**ea**t/br**ea**d *different*
2. s**a**lad/s**a**ndwiches
3. coff**ee**/t**ea**
4. c**o**ffee/ch**o**colate
5. m**i**lk/f**i**sh
6. s**a**lad/s**u**gar
7. chocol**a**te/c**a**kes

3 Work in pairs. Make a list of food and drink which is:
- good for you (healthy). *salad*
- bad for you (unhealthy). *chocolate*

📱 Go to page 140 or your app for more vocabulary and practice.

Listening

4 a 🔊 5.12 Listen to a radio programme. Tick the food and drink they talk about.

- tea
- coffee
- sandwiches
- sugar
- bread
- cakes
- chocolate
- eggs
- meat
- fish
- cheese
- salad
- chicken
- milk

b Listen again. What does Tom eat and drink?

5 Read sentences a–d from the radio programme. Complete the diagram with the words in bold.

0% ————————————————— 100%
↓   ↓   ↓   ↓   ↓   ↓
1_____ 2_____ often usually 3_____

a I **never** drink coffee, I don't like it, but I **always** drink tea in the morning.
b I often eat cakes. Chocolate cakes are so good!
c I usually eat chocolate at work. Maybe three times a week?
d Well, Basil, I **sometimes** eat fish or salad, but I often eat meat.

Grammar

6 Read the grammar box and choose the correct alternatives.

Present simple with frequency adverbs

Use frequency adverbs to say how often you do things.
I **always** drink tea in the morning.
I **usually** eat chocolate at work.
I **often** eat cakes.
I **sometimes** eat fish or salad.
I **never** drink coffee.
Frequency adverbs go [1] *before / after* most verbs (e.g. *eat, have, drink*).
Ask questions about frequency with
[2] *How often / How many*:
How often do you eat meat?
How often are you late for work?

7 a 🔊 5.13 Listen and underline the stressed syllables in the words in blue.

1. I never drink tea.
2. I'm sometimes late home for dinner.
3. I often eat sandwiches for lunch.
4. I usually have lunch in a café.
5. I always have milk and sugar in my coffee.

b Listen again and repeat.

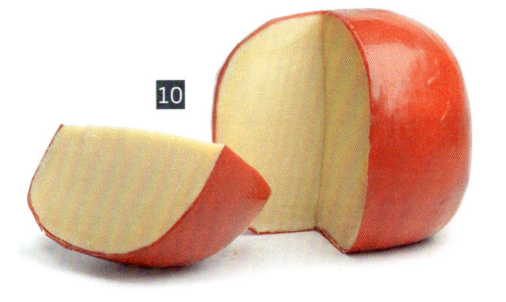

8 a Complete the sentences with frequency adverbs so they are true for you.

1. I _____ eat meat.
2. I _____ have chocolate at work.
3. I _____ drink milk.
4. I _____ have sugar in my coffee or tea.
5. I _____ have cakes for breakfast.
6. I _____ have fish for dinner.
7. I _____ eat cheese and bread.
8. I _____ eat sandwiches for dinner.

b Work in pairs and compare your answers.
I sometimes have cakes for breakfast!

9 a Put the words in the correct order to make questions.

1. have / How often / breakfast / at work / do / you ?
   How often do you have breakfast at work?
2. eggs / for breakfast / How often / you / do / have ?
3. How often / you / do / buy / for lunch / sandwiches ?
4. coffee / drink / How often / do / or tea / you ?
5. have / dinner / at home / you / How often / do ?
6. How often / sweet food / do / eat / you ?

b Work in pairs. Ask and answer the questions in Exercise 9a.

A: *How often do you have breakfast at work?*
B: *I never have breakfast at work. I always have breakfast at home.*

Go to page 124 or your app for more information and practice.

Speaking

PREPARE

10 Turn to page 154.

SPEAK

11 Work in pairs. Take turns asking the questions in Exercise 10a. Complete the table on page 154 with your partner's answers. Are they healthy?

Develop your writing page 100

5D English in action

> **Goal:** order food and a drink

1 Look at the menu. What food and drinks has the café got?

MENU

Food
- £3.50
- £3.25
- £4.95
- £3.25
- £2.50
- £2.50

Drink
- £1.50
- £1.50
- £1.50

2 🔊 5.14 Listen and tick Ela's food and drink on the menu in Exercise 1.

3 Listen again and complete the conversation.

Café worker: What would you like?
Ela: A ¹_____ sandwich, please.
Café worker: Would you like white bread or brown ²_____?
Ela: ³_____ bread, please.
Café worker: Here you are. Would you like a drink?
Ela: Yes. I'd like a cup of ⁴_____, please.
Café worker: Would you like ⁵_____?
Ela: No, thank you. How much is that?
Café worker: That's ⁶_____, please.
Ela: Thank you.
Café worker: You're welcome.

4 a 🔊 5.15 Match 1–5 with a–e in the Useful phrases box. Then listen and check your answers.

Useful phrases

Café worker
1. What would you like?
2. Would you like (black coffee) or (white coffee)?
3. Would you like (a drink)?
4. Would you like (sugar)?
5. That's (£5.50), please.

Customer
a. I'd like (a chicken sandwich), please.
b. No, thank you.
c. Yes, please. I'd like (a bottle of water).
d. (Black), please.
e. How much is that?

b Listen again and repeat.

5 a 🔊 5.16 Put the conversation in the correct order. Then listen and check your answers.

a. **Café worker:** Thank you.
b. **Customer:** Thank you. How much is that?
c. **Customer:** I'd like a chocolate cake, please.
d. **Café worker:** That's £4.00, please.
e. **Café worker:** OK, great. And would you like a drink?
f. **Customer:** Yes, please. I'd like a cup of black coffee.
g. **Café worker:** What would you like? 1
h. **Customer:** Here you are.
i. **Café worker:** OK. Here's your cake and your coffee.

b Work in pairs. Practise the conversation.

6 Work in pairs. Roleplay a conversation in a café. Order food and a drink. Use the menu in Exercise 1.

Go online for the Roadmap video.

Check and reflect

1 Complete the days of the week.
1 M_____
2 T_____
3 W_____
4 Th_____
5 F_____
6 Sa_____
7 Su_____

2 Match 1–6 with a–f.
1 get up
2 have
3 go
4 study
5 work
6 watch

a TV/a film/football
b English/at home
c breakfast/lunch/dinner
d to school/to work/home/to bed
e in an office/at a hospital
f late/early/at 6 o'clock

3 Put the words in the correct order to make sentences.
1 Sundays / late / I / up / on / get
   I get up late on Sundays.
2 have / o'clock / We / 7 / at / breakfast
3 every / They / day / work / don't
4 on / You / Saturdays / don't / study
5 TV / Saturdays / watch / We / Sundays / and / on
6 5 / home / go / They / o'clock / at

4 Make the sentences negative.
1 They play football on Sundays.
   They don't play football on Sundays.
2 We have lunch at one thirty.
3 They go to bed at 10 o'clock.
4 I work from Monday to Friday.
5 They study at home on Wednesdays.
6 I get up late on Mondays.

5 Complete the crossword with seven travel and transport words.

6 Complete the sentences with the verbs in the box.

| arrive | ~~cycle~~ | drive | leave | take |
| travel | walk | | | |

1 I've got a new bike. I _cycle_ to school.
2 My sister has got a car, but she doesn't _____ to work.
3 I usually _____ the bus to university.
4 I _____ home at 8 o'clock and _____ at the office at eight forty-five.
5 I haven't got a car or a bike. I always _____ to work.
6 People usually _____ to work by bus in my city.

7 a Correct the mistakes in five of the sentences.
1 How do you travel to work?
2 What time arrive you at your office?
3 Do have you a big breakfast every day?
4 Do your parents drive to work?
5 Do get up early Simon and Lucy?
6 What time leave you the house in the morning?
7 What time do we have our English class?
8 How do travel to university your friends?

b Work in pairs. Ask and answer questions with *How* and *What time*.
   A: *How do you travel to school?* B: *By bus.*

8 a Put the letters in the correct order to make food words. The first letter is given.
1 hifs   f_____
2 eschee   c_____
3 gasur   s_____
4 heccatolo   c_____
5 dwinsechas   s_____
6 dalsa   s_____
7 nekcich   c_____

b Cross out the incorrect alternatives.
1 chocolate cake / sugar cake / coffee cake
2 a cup of meat / a cup of tea / a cup of coffee
3 a chicken sandwich / a milk sandwich / a cheese sandwich
4 chicken salad / egg salad / bread salad

9 a Put the words in the correct order to make sentences.
1 at 8.30 / have dinner / usually / in the evening / We
2 hungry / am / I / in the morning / never
3 have / I / meat or fish / for lunch / always
4 chicken / eat / you / often / Do ?
5 you / do / buy / How often / in a coffee shop / coffee ?
6 your / for class / Are / sometimes / late / friends ?
7 parents / your / Do / always / on Mondays / work ?

b Work in pairs. Ask and answer the questions in Exercise 9a.

Reflect
How confident do you feel about the statements below? Write 1–5 (1 = not very confident, 5 = very confident).
- I can describe part of my week.
- I can talk about how I travel to work/university.
- I can take part in a survey about being healthy.
- I can order food and a drink.

Want more practice? Go to your Workbook or app.

6A Good and bad habits

> **Goal:** talk about another person's habits
> **Grammar:** present simple: *he/she/it*
> **Vocabulary:** time expressions

Vocabulary

1 a Match pictures A–G with sentences 1–7.
  1 I start work **in the morning**.
  2 I have coffee **every day**.
  3 I watch TV **in the evening**.
  4 I drive to the park **at the weekend**.
  5 I take the bus **in the afternoon**.
  6 I study **at night**.
  7 I go to the gym **every week**.

b 🔊 6.1 Listen and repeat the phrases in bold in Exercise 1a.

2 Work in pairs. Which sentences in Exercise 1a are true for you?

Number 3 is true. I watch TV in the evening.

3 a Complete the sentences so they are true for you. Use the phrases in the box.

| in the morning | in the afternoon | in the evening |
| at night | at the weekend | every day | every week |

  1 I don't go to work _____.
  2 I sometimes have dinner _____.
  3 I never study English _____.
  4 I usually see my family _____.

b Work in pairs and compare your answers. Are any of them the same?

📱 Go to your app for more practice.

Reading

4 a Read the texts and match Erica and Tina with photos A and B.

My friend Erica has lots of good habits:
She doesn't take the bus or the train to work in the morning, she walks or cycles.
She doesn't drink tea or coffee, she drinks water.
She doesn't eat chocolate or cakes and often has salad for lunch.
She goes to the gym every day.
She always sees a show at the weekend or meets friends for dinner.

My friend Tina has lots of bad habits:
She eats chocolate every day and drinks a lot of coffee.
She even drinks coffee at night!
She always watches TV in the evening and goes to bed at 1 o'clock in the morning.
She always takes the bus. She doesn't walk or cycle.
She's at university, but she never studies.

b Read the texts again. What is a *habit*? Choose the correct option, a or b.
  a something people often do
  b something people never do

c Work in pairs. Think of more examples of good and bad habits.

5 Rewrite the sentences using *she*. Use the texts in Exercise 4a to help you.
  1 I don't take the bus.
     She doesn't take the bus.
  2 I don't eat chocolate or cakes.
  3 I go to the gym.
  4 I watch TV.
  5 I never study.

Grammar

6 Read and complete the grammar box. Use Exercises 4a and 5 to help you.

Present simple: *he/she/it*

+	He	gets up	early.
	She	works	at home.
	It	starts	at nine.
−	He	doesn't have	dinner at home.
	She	doesn't work	every day.
	It	doesn't leave	at 6 o'clock.

For most verbs, + ¹_____. *He arrives home late.*
For verbs ending in *-y*, ~~y~~ and + ²_____. *She studies Spanish.*
For verbs ending in *-ch, -o, -s, -sh, -x,* + ³_____. *She watches TV.*

7 a 🔊 6.2 Listen to the endings of the verbs in the box. Put the verbs into three categories: /s/, /z/ and /ɪz/.

| arrives | finishes | goes | puts | starts | studies |
| uses | walks | watches | wears | | |

b 🔊 6.3 Listen and check your answers. Then listen again and repeat.

8 Complete the sentences with the correct form of the verbs in brackets.
  1 Carla _____ (not cycle) to work every day. She sometimes _____ (take) the bus.
  2 Ethan _____ (not eat) sandwiches for lunch. He often _____ (have) salad.
  3 Ahmed _____ (work) at the weekend. He _____ (not work) on Monday and Tuesday.
  4 Yuriko _____ (not study) English on Sunday. She _____ (teach) Japanese classes.
  5 Claudia _____ (not read) the newspaper on the train. She _____ (study) English.

Go to page 126 or your app for more information and practice.

Speaking

PREPARE

9 Choose a friend or a person from your family. Make notes about his/her good and bad habits.

SPEAK

10 a Work in pairs. Take turns telling your partner about your friend or family member.

b Work in groups. Which bad and good habits have lots of people got?

Develop your writing page 101

6B Jobs around the house

> **Goal:** ask and answer about things people often do
> **Grammar:** present simple questions: *he/she/it*
> **Vocabulary:** jobs around the house

Vocabulary

1 a Match pictures A–H with phrases 1–8.
1. clean the bathroom
2. cook dinner
3. feed the dog
4. go to the supermarket
5. make the beds
6. walk the dog
7. do the washing
8. wash the dishes

b 🔊 6.4 Listen and repeat.

2 Look at the pictures in Exercise 1a again. Make sentences about the jobs each person does around the house.

Thomas cleans the bathroom and …

Thomas   Masaru   Isabella   Milada

3 Complete the phrases. Use verbs from Exercise 1a.
1. _____ the bath/the toilet/the house
2. _____ chicken/fish
3. _____ the children
4. _____ the car/the cups

📱 Go to your app for more practice.

Listening

4 a 🔊 6.5 Listen to the conversation and look at the table. Who does the jobs around the house? Tick *Albert* or *Bella*.

	Albert	Bella
cleans the bathroom		
cooks dinner		
washes the dishes		
does the washing		
walks the dog		

b Listen again and complete the questions.
1. _____ you live with your family, Bella?
2. Well, _____ he cook dinner?
3. OK, but _____ he wash the dishes?
4. What _____ Albert do?
5. Or _____ you wash his clothes?

7 🔊 **6.7** Read the conversation and choose the correct alternatives. Then listen and check your answers.

Nicholas: Hi, Chloe. What's your dog's name?
Chloe: Ronaldo.
Nicholas: Good name! ¹ *Do / Does* you ² *walk / walks* him every day?
Chloe: No, I ³ *don't / doesn't*. My dad usually ⁴ *walk / walks* him.
Nicholas: Where ⁵ *do / does* they ⁶ *go / goes*?
Chloe: To the park.
Nicholas: ⁷ *Do / Does* Ronaldo ⁸ *run / runs* in the park?
Chloe: Yes, he ⁹ *do / does*! And he ¹⁰ *play / plays* with his ball.
Nicholas: What time ¹¹ *do / does* he ¹² *have / has* dinner?
Chloe: About seven.
Nicholas: ¹³ *Do / Does* your dad ¹⁴ *feed / feeds* Ronaldo?
Chloe: Yes, he ¹⁵ *do / does*.

8 a Make questions using the prompts.
1 Where / your friend / live?
2 your friend / live / in a house or a flat?
3 Who / your friend / live with?
4 Where / your friend / work?
5 your friend / have / a dog?
6 How often / you / talk to / your friend?

b Choose a friend to talk about. Work in pairs. Ask and answer the questions in Exercise 8a.
   A: *What's your friend's name?*
   B: *Jasper.*
   A: *Where does Jasper live?*

📱 Go to page 126 or your app for more information and practice.

Speaking

▶ **PREPARE**

9 Turn to page 157.

▶ **SPEAK**

10 a Work in pairs. Ask the questions in Exercise 9a. Complete the table on page 157 with your partner's answers.

b Change partners. Tell your new partner about your old partner.
   Diego's father usually cooks dinner. Diego sometimes cooks dinner.

Grammar

5 Read and complete the grammar box. Use Exercise 4b to help you.

Present simple questions: he/she/it

Yes/No questions

?	¹_____ she **clean** the bathroom?
+	Yes, she ²_____.
–	No, she ³_____.

Wh- questions

What	jobs ⁴_____ he **do** around the house?
How often	⁵_____ he **clean** the kitchen?
Where	⁶_____ he **walk** the dog?
When	⁷_____ it **open**?
Who	**does** Bonnie **live** with?

6 a 🔊 **6.6** Listen to the conversations. Notice the pronunciation of the words in blue.
1 **A:** **Does** she clean the bathroom?
  B: Yes, she **does**.
2 **A:** When **does** he go to the supermarket?
  B: On Saturdays.
3 **A:** What jobs around the house **does** he do?
  B: He makes the beds.

b Listen again and repeat.

> **Develop your listening**
> page 102

49

6c Skills

> **Goal:** ask and answer about things you can and can't do
>
> **Grammar:** can/can't for ability
>
> **Vocabulary:** skills

Vocabulary

1 a Match photos A–L with skills 1–12.

1. build a website
2. dance
3. draw pictures
4. fly a plane
5. make a cake
6. make clothes
7. play football
8. ride a horse
9. sing
10. sleep on a train
11. speak two languages
12. swim

b 6.13 Listen and repeat.

c 6.14 Work in pairs. Which of the activities in Exercise 1a do you hear?

1 play football

Go to page 141 or your app for more vocabulary and practice.

Reading and listening

2 a Look at the website. What does it do?

ChooseYourJob.com

1. Add your personal details (e.g. name, email address, etc.).
2. Answer the questions.
3. See which jobs we think are right for you!

b 6.15 Listen to Yusuf and Gloria. Which job does the website think is right for Gloria?

c Listen again and tick the things Gloria can do.

use a computer	✓
build a website	
speak two languages	
drive	
cook	
draw	
sing	
dance	

Grammar

3 Read the grammar box and choose the correct alternatives.

can/can't for ability

+	I/You/He/She/It/We/They	can	¹ *sing / sings*.
−	I/You/He/She/It/We/They	can't	² *drive / drives*.

Yes/No questions

Question	Short answer	
Can you ³ *use / uses* a computer?	+	Yes, I **can**.
	−	No, I **can't**.
Can he ⁴ *play / plays* football?	+	Yes, he **can**.
	−	No, he **can't**.

with question words

What	**can** you ⁵ *cook / cooks*?	I can cook fish.
How many	languages **can** you ⁶ *speak / speaks*?	Two. English and Spanish.

50

4 a 🔊 **6.16** Listen to the conversations. Do the words in blue sound the same or different?

1 **A:** I can't speak Spanish, can you?
   B: No, I can't.
2 **A:** Can you drive?
   B: Yes, I can.
3 **A:** Can he swim?
   B: Yes, he can.

b Listen again and repeat.

5 Read the interview for a computer club teacher and choose the correct alternatives.

Sara: ¹ *Can you / You can* use a computer?
Rodrigo: Yes, ² *can / I can*. I use my computer every day.
Sara: ³ *You can / Can you* build a website?
Rodrigo: Yes, ⁴ *I can / I can build*.
Sara: ⁵ *You can / Can you* speak two languages?
Rodrigo: ⁶ *Can I / I can* speak three languages.
Sara: What languages ⁷ *can you / you can* speak?
Rodrigo: I ⁸ *am / can* speak English, Spanish and Japanese.
Sara: ⁹ *Can you / Can* work at the weekend?
Rodrigo: Yes, I ¹⁰ *can / can work*.

6 a Write three questions with *can* for each of the jobs.

1 taxi driver
   Can you drive?
2 office worker
3 hotel worker

b Work in pairs. Ask and answer the questions in Exercise 6a. What is a good job for your partner?

📱 Go to page 126 or your app for more information and practice.

Speaking

PREPARE

7 Work in pairs. Read the information. Write questions for the club teachers.

Questions for club teachers
Ask these questions to choose good teachers:
Sports club
1 *Can you run?*
2 _____
3 _____
Food club
1 _____
2 _____
3 _____
Travel club
1 _____
2 _____
3 _____
Computer club
1 _____
2 _____
3 _____

SPEAK

8 Work with another pair. Ask and answer the questions in Exercise 7. Who is a good teacher for the clubs?

A: *Can you run?*
B: *Yes, I can.*

Develop your reading
page 103

6D English in action

> **Goal:** make requests

1 Look at the pictures of Tom and Ana's flat. What jobs around the house can you see?

A B C
D E F

2 🔊 6.17 Listen and match conversations 1–6 with pictures A–F in Exercise 1.

3 Listen again. Who agrees to do the jobs in Exercise 1, Tom or Ana? Write *T* or *A*.

4 a Read the Useful phrases box. Then listen again. How many requests do the speakers make?

Useful phrases

Making requests
Can I (use your bike), (please)?
Can you (walk the dog), (please)?

Saying yes to requests
Yes, you can.
Yes, I can.
Sure.
No problem.

Saying no to requests
I'm sorry, I can't.
I'm sorry, you can't.

b 🔊 6.18 Listen and repeat.

5 a Complete the conversations with phrases from the Useful phrases box.
1. A: _____ clean the living room, please?
   B: _____ . I can do it now.
2. A: _____ use your computer, please?
   B: _____ . It's on my desk.
3. A: _____ watch TV at 8 o'clock?
   B: _____ . I study in the living room from seven to nine.
4. A: _____ cook dinner on Monday, please? I can't do it.
   B: _____ . I play football on Monday evening.

b Work in pairs. Practise the conversations in Exercise 5a.

6 a Think of some requests for these situations.
- a teacher and a student
- a customer and a café worker
- a customer and a shop assistant
- two friends in their flat
- an office worker and a manager

b Work in pairs. Roleplay conversations for the situations in Exercise 6a.

Go online for the Roadmap video.

Check and reflect

1 Match time phrases 1–6 with a–f.

1 in the morning
2 in the afternoon
3 in the evening
4 at night
5 at the weekend
6 every day

a from 11.00 p.m. to 5.00 a.m.
b on Saturdays and Sundays
c from 6.00 a.m. to 12.00 p.m.
d from 6.00 p.m. to 9.00 p.m.
e from 12.00 p.m. to 5.00 p.m.
f from Monday to Sunday

2 Complete the text with the phrases in the box.

at the weekend   in the afternoon   in the evening
in the morning

I get up at 6 or 7 o'clock ^{1}_____ , then I go to work. I finish work at 4 o'clock ^{2}_____ . ^{3}_____ I have dinner with my family, usually at 8 o'clock. I don't work ^{4}_____ .

3 Complete the text with the correct form of the verbs in brackets.

My brother ^{1} _works_ (work) in London. He ^{2}_____ (get up) very early and ^{3}_____ (travel) to work by train. He ^{4}_____ (not talk) to people on the train – he ^{5}_____ (draw) or ^{6}_____ (read) the newspaper. He ^{7}_____ (not have) lunch in a café – he ^{8}_____ (buy) a sandwich from a shop and ^{9}_____ (eat) it in the park. In the evening, he ^{10}_____ (have) dinner at home and ^{11}_____ (watch) TV. He ^{12}_____ (go) to bed at 11.00 p.m.

4 Make the sentences negative.

1 Julio studies French.
   Julio doesn't study French.
2 She works in an office.
3 Aleksi listens to music on the train.
4 Linda teaches at the university.
5 Amy takes the bus to work.
6 Juan works in the evening.
7 Lizzie studies in the evening.
8 Luke works in the morning.
9 Jane has lunch at home.
10 Danny watches a lot of TV.

5 Match verbs 1–7 with a–g.

1 clean
2 feed
3 cook
4 wash
5 do
6 make
7 go to

a breakfast/lunch/dinner
b the dishes/the car
c the dog/the children
d the kitchen/your bedroom
e the supermarket/the shops
f the washing
g the beds

6 a Complete 1–6 with *do* or *does*. Then match the sentence halves.

1 Where _____ you
2 How _____ your classmates
3 What time _____ your mother
4 Who _____ your best friend
5 What sports _____ your father
6 How often _____ your parents

a go to work?
b watch?
c go to a restaurant?
d travel to school?
e live with?
f do your homework?

b Work in pairs. Ask and answer the questions.

7 a Complete the questions with the verbs in the box.

build   cook   draw   fly   play   ride   ~~sing~~   sleep
speak   use

1 Do you _sing_ in the shower?
2 Do you _____ dinner every evening?
3 Do you _____ video games at the weekend?
4 Can you _____ three languages?
5 Can you _____ a plane?
6 Can you _____ a website?
7 Can you _____ a horse?
8 Do you _____ a computer every day?
9 Do you sometimes _____ pictures in your classes?
10 Do you sometimes _____ on the train?

b Work in pairs. Ask and answer the questions.

8 a Choose the correct alternatives.

1 Dogs *can / can't* swim.
2 A fish *can / can't* walk.
3 Horses *can / can't* run.
4 Children *can / can't* drive.
5 Children *can / can't* sing.
6 A dog *can / can't* fly.

b Work in pairs. Ask and answer the questions.
   A: *Can dogs swim?*   **B:** *Yes, they can.*

Reflect

How confident do you feel about the statements below? Write 1–5 (1 = not very confident, 5 = very confident).

- I can talk about another person's habits.
- I can ask and answer about things people often do.
- I can ask and answer about things another person can do.
- I can make requests.

Want more practice?
Go to your Workbook or app.

7A Questions

> **Goal:** ask and answer about a place
> **Grammar:** *wh-* questions
> **Vocabulary:** places

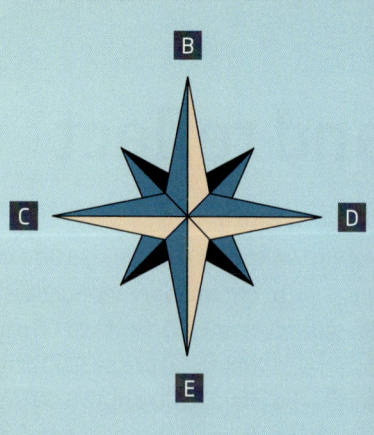

Vocabulary

1 a Match photos A–O with the words in the box.

clouds	east	a field	flowers	a hill	an island
a lake	a mountain	north	a river	the sea
the sky	south	trees	west

b 🔊 7.1 Listen and repeat.

2 Complete the table with the words in Exercise 1a.

water	land	plants	air	directions

3 Choose the correct alternatives.
1 There are three black *clouds / sky* in the *clouds / sky*.
2 I live in the *south / flowers* of my country.
3 We have a *river / hill* and a *lake / mountain* near my house. We swim a lot.
4 People take photos of the red *flowers / trees* and the high *fields / mountains*.
5 People sit on the *river / hill* and eat lunch.
6 Milan is in the *north / hill* of Italy.

4 Complete the sentences about your town or city. Use the words in Exercise 2 to help you.
1 My city/town is in the _____ of my country.
   My town is in the south of my country.
2 There are beautiful _____ there.
3 There aren't any _____ there.
4 There is a famous _____ – its name is _____ .

📱 Go to your app for more practice.

Listening

5 a 🔊 7.2 Listen to Fatma and Dan. Where is the place that Dan talks about?

b Listen again. Match questions 1–8 with answers a–h.
1 What's the name of the place?
2 How do you spell that?
3 Where is it?
4 What do you like about it?
5 How many lakes are there?
6 When do you usually go there?
7 Who do you go with?
8 How much is a train ticket from London?

a In June or July.
b In the north of England.
c L-A-K-E D-I-S-T-R-I-C-T
d The Lake District.
e Sometimes with my friends, sometimes with my wife.
f There are mountains and lakes. It's very beautiful.
g Ah, quite expensive!
h Um, sixteen, I think.

7 a 🔊 **7.3** Listen to the questions. Notice the intonation (when the speaker's voice goes up ↑ and down ↓).
1 When do you go there?
2 Do you go there in June?
3 How much is it?
4 Is it £10?
5 Is it old?

b Listen again and repeat.

8 a Make questions using the prompts.
1 What / name of the place?
   What is / What's the name of the place?
2 Where / it?
3 When / you / usually / go there?
4 What / you / usually / do / there?
5 How much / a train ticket / from here?
6 How many / cafés / there?
7 it / a quiet place?

b Work in pairs. Think of a nice place in your country. Ask and answer the questions in Exercise 8a.

9 Make questions for the underlined answers.
1 My parents are from <u>Izmir, in Turkey</u>.
   Where are your parents from?
2 I go <u>with Tina</u>.
3 It's <u>in the east</u>.
4 I visit in <u>January or February</u>.
5 There are <u>five lakes</u> there.
6 A ticket is <u>£10.50</u>.
7 It's <u>R-O-M-E</u>.

📱 Go to page 128 or your app for more information and practice.

Speaking

PREPARE

10 a Think of another nice place to visit in your country. Make notes about it.
   flowers, mountains, beautiful, visit with parents

b Work in pairs. Ask and answer questions about the places. Use the prompts to help you.
- What (is the name of the place)?
- Where (is it)?
- When (do you visit)?
- Who (do you go with)?
- How many (rivers are there)?
- How much (is a train ticket)?
- How do you spell (it)?

SPEAK

11 Work in groups. Tell your group about your partner's place.

Develop your writing page 104

Grammar

6 Read the grammar box and choose the correct alternatives. Use Exercise 5b to help you.

Wh- questions

Wh- question word	Example
Use **what** for ¹*things / people*.	**What's** the name of the place?
Use **how** for the ²*way / time* you do something.	**How** do you spell that?
Use **when** for ³*places / days, months and times*.	**When** do you usually go there?
Use **who** for ⁴*prices / people*.	**Who** do you go with?
Use **where** for ⁵*places / times*.	**Where** is it?
Use **how much** for ⁶*prices / people*.	**How much** is a ticket?
Use **how many** for ⁷*prices / the number of things*.	**How many** lakes are there?

55

7B A good day

> **Goal:** talk about good days
> **Grammar:** was/were, there was/were
> **Vocabulary:** months, dates

Reading and listening

1 a Read the text. Then match photos 1–5 with paragraphs A–E.

David's year

These were my five very good days this year:

A • **12th February** was the first day in our new flat. It's great. We've got a new table and chairs and a big sofa.

B • **5th April** was my birthday. I was 31 this year. There was a party with great music – it was amazing!

C • **7th August** was the first day of our holiday. We usually go to a big city, but this year was different. Our hotel was near a lake, and there were mountains and fields. There weren't any cars or buses. It was really quiet.

D • **On 14th October** in the evening we were at the Spanish restaurant near Liverpool Street. Mike, Junko, Wes and Trin were there. The food wasn't cheap … but it was really good.

E • **8th December** was my first day at my new job. I work for a video games company in London and I often travel to other countries. It's a really good job.

b 🔊 7.4 Listen to David and find five things that are different from the text in Exercise 1b.

Vocabulary

2 a 🔊 7.5 Look at the calendar. Listen and repeat the months of the year.

January	February	March	April	May	June
July	August	September	October	November	December

b Rewrite the sentences so they are true for you.
1 My birthday is in **April**.
2 My best friend's birthday is in **December**.
3 My teacher's birthday is in **November**.
4 The weather is good in my country in **May**.
5 My favourite month is **July**.

3 a 🔊 7.6 Match numbers a–q with the words in the box. Then listen and check your answers.

> eleventh   fifth   fifteenth   first   fourth   fourteenth
> second   third   thirteenth   thirtieth   thirty-first
> twelfth   twentieth   twenty-first   twenty-fourth
> twenty-second   twenty-third

a	1	f	11	k	20	p	30
b	2	g	12	l	21	q	31
c	3	h	13	m	22		
d	4	i	14	n	23		
e	5	j	15	o	24		

b Listen again and repeat.

4 Write sentences about your family's birthdays. Work in pairs and tell your partner.

My brother's birthday is on the nineteenth of April.

7B | A good day

8 Choose the correct alternatives.
1 My birthday party *was / were* on 12th March.
2 There *was / were* a big party near the hotel last week.
3 Our holiday *was / were* from 7th July to 15th July.
4 There *was / were* six people on the train.
5 The restaurants *wasn't / weren't* busy.
6 The plane tickets *was / were* really cheap.
7 Norma and Shelley *was / were* at the party yesterday.
8 There *was / were* a big cake in the living room.

9 a Complete the sentences so they are true for you.
1 I _____ on the train at 8 a.m. on Monday.
2 My bus/train _____ late on Tuesday.
3 There _____ five people in my office/my class on Wednesday.
4 Yesterday _____ a good day.
5 There _____ fish for lunch at work/at school/at university on Friday.
6 My family _____ at home on Saturday.
7 My friends and I _____ at the cinema on Sunday evening.

b Work in pairs. Compare your sentences. How many are the same?

Go to page 128 or your app for more information and practice.

Speaking

PREPARE

10 Think of five very good days from last year. Make notes in the table.

	when	where	who with	what
1				
2				
3				
4				
5				

SPEAK

11 a Work in pairs. Tell your partner about your good days. Listen and make notes.

On 18th June, I was on holiday in Paris with my friend Ulrika. There were lots of great places to visit. It was amazing!

b Change partners. Tell your new partner about your old partner's good days.

On 18th June, Gina was in Paris with her friend. They were on holiday. There were lots of great places to go to. It was amazing!

5 a Complete the sentences with the words in the box.

last ~~today~~ week weekend yesterday

1 *Today* is Wednesday 14th.
2 _____ was Tuesday 13th.
3 _____ Friday was the 9th.
4 Last _____ was Saturday 10th and Sunday 11th.
5 Last _____ was Monday 5th to Sunday 11th.

b 🔊 7.7 Listen, check and repeat.

Go to your app for more practice.

Grammar

6 Read and complete the grammar box. Use Exercise 1a to help you.

was / were

+	I/He/She/It	¹ *was*	thirty-one this year.
-		² _____	quiet.
+	You/We/They	³ _____	great.
-		⁴ _____	there.

there was / were

+	There	⁵ _____	a party.
-	There	⁶ _____	a lift.
+	There	⁷ _____	mountains and fields.
-	There	⁸ _____	any buses or cars.

7 a 🔊 7.8 Listen to the sentences. Notice the pronunciation of the words in blue.
1 The food wasn't cheap.
2 Bill and Jane weren't there.
3 There wasn't a lift.
4 There weren't any cars or buses.

b Listen again and repeat.

Develop your listening page 105

7C How was it?

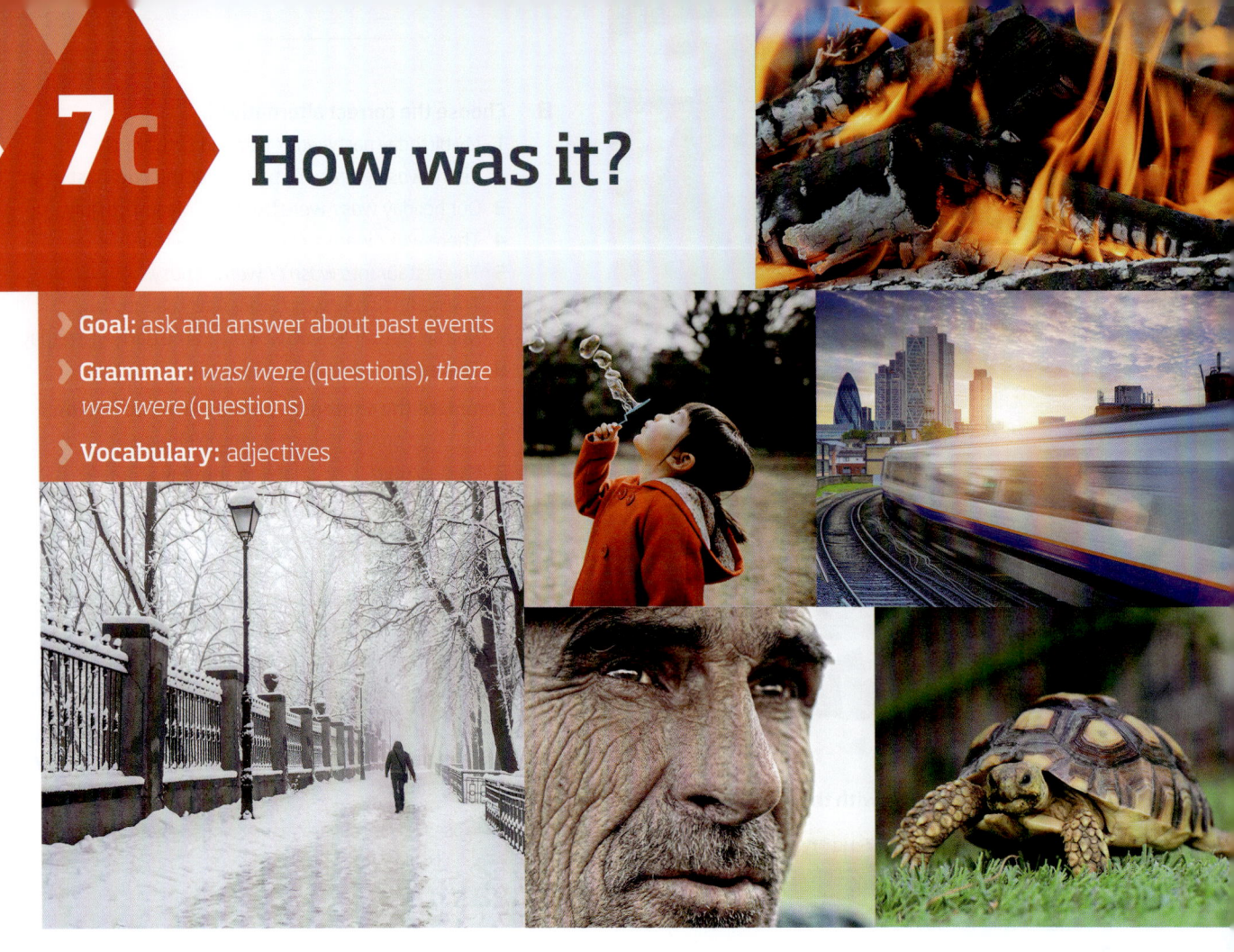

> **Goal:** ask and answer about past events
> **Grammar:** *was/were* (questions), *there was/were* (questions)
> **Vocabulary:** adjectives

Vocabulary

1 Match adjectives 1–8 with their opposites, a–h.

1 cold	a easy
2 dark	b sad
3 difficult	c hot
4 fast	d young
5 happy	e short
6 high	f slow
7 long	g low
8 old	h light

2 🔊 7.12 Listen and repeat.

3 Complete the sentences with words from Exercise 1.

1 In December, I don't have lunch in the park. It's _____ .
2 **A:** Has that building got a lift?
   B: Yes! The building is very _____ .
3 It's her ninety-seventh birthday today. She's _____ .
4 Don't take the bus. It's _____ . It arrives at 9. Take the train. It arrives at 8.30.
5 This book is _____ . The words are long.
6 There aren't any lights here. It's really _____ at night.
7 My daughter hasn't got homework this week. She's really _____ .
8 It's a _____ film. It's only an hour!

4 Make similar sentences with the other words from Exercise 1.

In August, I have lunch in the park. It's hot.

📱 Go to page 142 or your app for more vocabulary and practice.

Listening

5 a 🔊 7.13 Listen and match conversations 1–3 with photos A–C.

b Listen again and choose the correct alternatives.

1 a The meeting today was about new *computers / phones*.
  b It was a *difficult / long* meeting.
2 a The mountain was really *high / short*.
  b They were *slow / cold*.
3 a The train was *dark / busy*.
  b It was really slow and *hot / old*.

Grammar

6 Read the grammar box and choose the correct alternatives.

was/were (questions)

Yes/No questions

?	¹ **Was** / **Were**	he/she/it	OK?	+	Yes, he/she/it **was**.
				-	No, he/she/it **wasn't**.
?	**Were**	you	cold?	+	Yes, I **was**.
				-	No, I ² **weren't** / **wasn't**.
?	**Were**	we/they	with you?	+	Yes, we/they **were**.
				-	No, we/they **weren't**.

Wh- questions

Where	³ **was** / **were**	they?
What	**was**	it about?
How much	⁴ **was** / **were**	it?

there was/were (questions)

Yes/No questions

?	**Was**	there	a meeting?	+	Yes, there ⁵ **was** / **wasn't**.
				-	No, there **wasn't**.
?	⁶ **Was** / **Were**	there	a lot of people?	+	Yes, there **were**.
				-	No, there **weren't**.

Wh- questions

| What food | **was there** | at the party? |

7 a 🔊 7.14 Listen to four conversations. Notice the pronunciation of the words in blue.
1. **A:** Was the hotel good?
   B: Yes, it was. It was great.
2. **A:** Were they expensive?
   B: Yes, they were. They were about £50.
3. **A:** Were there drinks?
   B: Yes, there were. There were cups of tea and coffee.
4. **A:** Was there a restaurant?
   B: Yes, there was. It was really good.

b Listen again and repeat.

8 Choose the correct alternatives.

Hank: How ¹*was* / *were* your weekend?
Donna: Great. It ²*was* / *were* my dad's sixtieth birthday party on Saturday night.
Hank: ³*Was* / *Were* it good?
Donna: Yes, it was.
Hank: Where ⁴*was* / *were* the party?
Donna: It ⁵*was* / *were* in the restaurant near the park.
Hank: How many people ⁶*was* / *were* there?
Donna: About 50.
Hank: Wow! ⁷*Was* / *Were* there a cake?
Donna: No, there ⁸*wasn't* / *weren't*. Dad doesn't like it!

9 a Make questions using the prompts.
1. your last test / easy or difficult?
2. you / at home / on Saturday night?
3. you / at 10.00 p.m. last night?
4. there a swimming pool / at your school?
5. it cold / this morning?
6. your favourite / class at school?

b Work in pairs. Ask and answer the questions in Exercise 9a.
> **A:** Was your last test easy or difficult?
> **B:** It was difficult.

📱 Go to page 128 or your app for more information and practice.

Speaking

PREPARE

10 a Make notes about past events in the table.

	your day	your weekend	your holiday
good or bad?			
where?			
who with?			

b Think of questions to ask your partner about their day/weekend/holiday.
> How was your holiday?
> Was it hot?
> Was it expensive?

SPEAK

11 Work in pairs. Ask and answer the questions in Exercise 10b.

> **A:** How was your holiday?
> **B:** It was great. I was in Spain.
> **A:** Was it hot?
> **B:** Yes, it was.
> **A:** Was it expensive?
> **B:** No, it wasn't. It was cheap.

7C | How was it?

Develop your reading page 106

7D English in action

> **Goal:** buy travel tickets

Welcome to Paddington Station

9.13 platform 3	9.17 platform 2	9.20 platform 7	9.25 platform 5	9.30 platform 7	9.45 platform 1	9.53 platform 5
Cardiff	**Oxford**	**Bath**	**Heathrow**	**Bath**	**Swansea**	**Heathrow**
(Arrives 10.25)	(Arrives 10.05)	(Arrives 12.15)	(Arrives 10.25)	(Arrives 10.55)	(Arrives 12.25)	(Arrives 10.15)
1	2	3	4	5	6	7

1 Look at the information board above. What information can you see?

2 a 🔊 7.15 Listen to Jeff buy a train ticket. Which train from Exercise 1 does he take?

b Listen again and choose the correct ticket A–D.

A Return £08.20

B Single £16.80

C Return £107.00

D Single £15

3 a Listen again and number the sentences in the order that you hear them. The speakers do not use one sentence.

Useful phrases

Customer
A ticket (for the fast train) to (Bath), please.
What time is the next train to (Bath), please?
What time does it arrive in (Bath)?
Which platform is the (fast) train to (Bath), please?
How much is a ticket to (Bath), please?

Assistant
Is that a single or a return?
The next train leaves at (9.20).
It arrives at (12.15).
It leaves from platform (7).
That's (£68.20), please.

b 🔊 7.16 Listen and repeat.

4 a 🔊 7.17 Read the prompts and make a conversation. Helena's train is to Heathrow. Use the information board in Exercise 1, the Useful phrases and the ticket prices below. Then listen and check your answers.

Helena:	(next train time?)
Assistant:	(answer)
Helena:	(when arrive at Heathrow?)
Assistant:	(answer, give information about fast train)
Helena:	(ask for ticket)
Assistant:	(single or return?)
Helena:	(single)
Assistant:	(say the price)
Helena:	(say thank you; platform for fast train?)
Assistant:	(answer)
Helena:	(say thank you)

b Work in pairs. Practise the conversation.

TRAINS TO HEATHROW
Single: £15
Return: £27.50

5 Work in pairs. Student A: Turn to page 157. Student B: Turn to page 158.

Go online for the Roadmap video.

Check and reflect

1 a Look at the compass and complete the words.

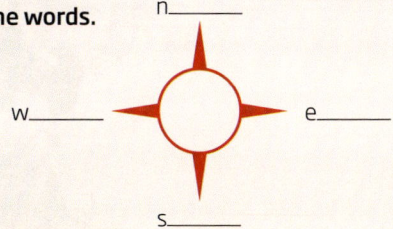

n_____
w_____   e_____
s_____

b Choose the correct alternatives.
1. It's a nice day. There isn't a *sky / cloud* in the *sky / cloud*.
2. We swim in the *lake / fields* and walk in the *lake / fields*.
3. There's *an island / a hill* in *the sea / the mountain*. You can go there by boat.
4. You can see the high *mountains / flowers* in the north.

2 a Put the words in the correct order to make questions.
1. does / What / do / a taxi driver ?
2. is / the / White House / Where ?
3. was / Pelé / Who ?
4. is / Valentine's Day / When ?
5. in August / many / How / days / are / there ?
6. got / How / rooms / the Taj Mahal / many / has ?

b Work in pairs. Match questions 1–6 in Exercise 2a with answers a–f.
a. 120
b. 31
c. It's in Washington DC.
d. 14th February
e. He/She drives a car.
f. a footballer

3 a Complete the words with the months of the year in the correct order.
1. J_____
2. F_____
3. M_____
4. A_____
5. M_____
6. J_____
7. J_____
8. A_____
9. S_____
10. O_____
11. N_____
12. D_____

b Rewrite the dates as words.
1. 2nd _second_
2. 11th _____
3. 23rd _____
4. 19th _____
5. 30th _____
6. 12th _____
7. 8th _____
8. 27th _____
9. 5th _____
10. 31st _____

c Complete the sentences with the words in the box.

| last | today | weekend | yesterday |

1. There was a big party in our office _____ .
2. It was my birthday _____ Tuesday. It was my 21st!
3. Is there a train to Brussels _____ ?
4. There was a Ryan Gosling film at the cinema last _____ . It was great!

4 Complete the text with *was, were, wasn't* or *weren't*.

I ¹ _was_ on holiday last week with my friend Kate. We ² _____ in Spain and our hotel ³ _____ really good. There ⁴ _____ a lot of people at the hotel – six or seven – and it ⁵ _____ quiet. There ⁶ _____ a restaurant at the hotel but there ⁷ _____ really good restaurants in the town centre. The town ⁸ _____ never quiet. It ⁹ _____ always busy.

5 Chose the correct alternatives.
1. My friend has got a new car. It's really *fast / slow*!
2. My father is 89. He's *a young / an old* man.
3. The homework wasn't *easy / difficult*, but it was OK.
4. In Canada, it's really *hot / cold* in January and February.
5. It was a really *short / long* meeting! We were there for nine hours!
6. Mount Everest is 8,848 metres. It's a *high / low* mountain.
7. It was late at night and it was *light / dark*.
8. We've got *hot / cold* drinks; tea and coffee.
9. The dog's *happy / sad*. It's got a ball.

6 a Put the words in the correct order to make questions.
1. last / Were / night / you / home / at ?
   Were you at home last night?
2. name / your / was / What / first teacher's ?
3. expensive / Was / your / phone ?
4. were / Where / you / 8.00 a.m. / at ?
5. there / a / difficult / Was / question / in class ?
6. students / there / last week / were / How / in class / many ?

b Work in pairs. Ask and answer the questions.

Reflect

How confident do you feel about the statements below? Write 1–5 (1 = not very confident, 5 = very confident).

- I can ask and answer about a place.
- I can talk about good days.
- I can ask and answer about past events.
- I can buy travel tickets.

Want more practice?
Go to your Workbook or app.

8A When I was young

> **Goal:** give a talk about when you were young
> **Grammar:** past simple (regular verbs)
> **Vocabulary:** verb phrases

Vocabulary

1 a Work in pairs. Look at the photos. What can you see?
In this photo, there's a girl on a bike.

b Read the text and look at the photos again. Match the text with the correct photo, A–C.

> When I was young, I lived in a village in Norway – its name was Nostrum. I travelled to school by bus every day. The school bus was old, but I liked it. On the bus I talked to my friends about football. Every week I watched a game on the computer. I loved Manchester United and I wanted to play for them! I played football every day with my friends after school. I was happy then.

2 a Look at the word map. Then read the text in Exercise 1b again. Add more words to the word map.

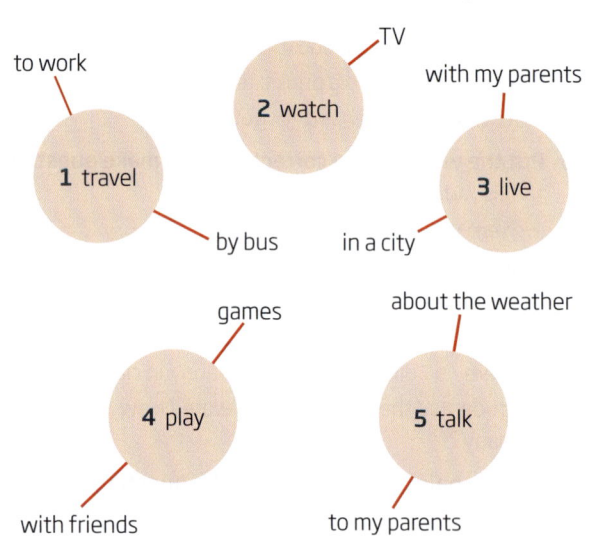

- 1 travel — to work, by bus
- 2 watch — TV, with my parents
- 3 live — in a city
- 4 play — games, with friends
- 5 talk — about the weather, to my parents

b 🔊 8.1 Listen, check and repeat.

3 a Add the words/phrases in the box to the word map in Exercise 2a.

> in a town   to my teacher   a film   tennis
> to my grandparents' house   by car
> about my weekend   with my family   in a house

b Work in pairs. Add more words to the word map.

4 a Make sentences about yourself. Use the phrases in Exercises 2a and 3a.
I often play football.

b Work in pairs and compare your sentences. Are any sentences the same?

📱 Go to your app for more practice.

Reading

5 Read the text and complete the table. Tick *Nanami*, *Michal* or *Lucy*.

Who ...	Nanami	Michal	Lucy
1 liked school?			
2 travelled every year?			
3 went to a new country?			
4 lived in a small place?			
5 doesn't talk about games?			

School days

Nanami: When I was young, I lived in a small town. I walked to school every day with my friends, and we usually talked about the other girls in our class. We studied every day. I didn't like my school, but I liked my friends. We lived in Hokkaido, in the north, but every year my family travelled to Fukuoka in the south. We played games on the beach there. It was a happy time.

Michal: My first school was in Poland – my parents are Polish. I lived in Poland for six years in a village. Later, we lived in a big city in the UK because of my dad's job. In Poland I walked to school, but in England I travelled to school by bus. My English was not good, and I didn't understand British children. School was very difficult, too. I didn't like it.

Lucy: I lived in a town called Uxbridge when I was young. I travelled to school by train every day with my best friend, Josh. School was great. My teacher was called Mrs Harrison. She played games with us, but she also helped us a lot. I lived with my parents and my sister. At night we watched TV together.

8 a 🔊 **8.4** Complete the sentences with the correct form of the verbs in brackets. Then listen and check your answers.
1 At school my lessons _____ (start) at 9 o'clock in the morning.
2 I _____ (travel) to school by train.
3 I _____ (clean) my dad's car every weekend.
4 I _____ (not like) my English teacher at school.
5 At school I _____ (play) sports every day.
6 I often _____ (study) in a café after school.

b Change the sentences in Exercise 8a so they are true for you.

At school, my lessons started at ten in the morning.

9 a Write two true and two false sentences about when you were a child. Use the verbs in the box.

arrive	clean	cycle	finish	listen to	like
live	love	play	study	talk to	travel	use
visit	walk	watch	work

I watched Pokémon on TV every day.

b Work in pairs. Read your sentences. Guess your partner's false sentences.

A: *I watched Pokémon on TV every day.*
B: *That's false.*
A: *No, it's true!*

📱 Go to page 130 or your app for more information and practice.

Grammar

6 Read and complete the grammar box. Use the text in Exercise 5 to help you.

Past simple (regular verbs)

| + | I/You/He/She/It/We/They | **lived** in a village. |
| - | | **didn't live** in a city. |

Spelling

	Rule	Example
most verbs	+ -ed	walk → 1_____
verbs ending in -e	+ -d	like → 2_____
verbs ending in consonant + -y	y + -ied	study → 3_____
many verbs ending in consonant + vowel + consonant	double the final consonant + -ed	travel → 4_____

Speaking

PREPARE

10 Prepare a short talk about when you were young. Make notes about:
- village, town or city?
- big or small school?
- travelled to school by bus, train – or walked?
- liked school/teacher?
- TV/games/travel?
- friends?

SPEAK

11 Tell your classmates about when you were young.

I went to a big school in Madrid. ...

7 a 🔊 **8.2** Listen to the words. Notice the pronunciation of the verb endings.
1 work<u>ed</u> (sounds like /t/)
2 stay<u>ed</u> (sounds like /d/)
3 start<u>ed</u> (sounds like /ɪd/)

b Listen again and repeat.

c 🔊 **8.3** Listen and choose the correct pronunciation of the verb endings, a–c.
1 visit<u>ed</u> **a** /t/ **b** /d/ **c** /ɪd/
2 play<u>ed</u> **a** /t/ **b** /d/ **c** /ɪd/
3 watch<u>ed</u> **a** /t/ **b** /d/ **c** /ɪd/
4 cook<u>ed</u> **a** /t/ **b** /d/ **c** /ɪd/
5 want<u>ed</u> **a** /t/ **b** /d/ **c** /ɪd/

Develop your reading page 107

8B You had a bad day

> **Goal:** talk about a bad day
> **Grammar:** past simple (irregular verbs)
> **Vocabulary:** irregular verbs

A I **took** a taxi to work. It was expensive.

B I arrived at work. I was late for a meeting with my boss. I **ran**!

C Yesterday, I **got up** at eight. I was late for work!

D After work I **met** my friend at the cinema but it was closed. I **had** a bad, bad day!

Vocabulary and reading

1 a Look at the pictures. Are they about a good day or a bad day?

b Look at the pictures again and read the captions. Put the pictures in the correct order.
  1 C

c 🔊 8.5 Listen and repeat the verbs in the box.

| ate | bought | broke | felt | forgot | got up | had |
| lost | met | ran | saw | spoke | took | went |

2 a Match infinitives 1–14 with the past simple verbs in bold in the captions in Exercise 1a.

1 get up *got up*
2 break
3 take
4 buy
5 meet
6 lose
7 feel
8 speak
9 have
10 go
11 run
12 eat
13 forget
14 see

b Complete the sentences with verbs from Exercise 1c.

1 I _____ an advert for one online.
2 I _____ really bad because I was late.
3 We _____ the train back home in the evening.
4 She _____ to Tokyo last summer.
5 You _____ a lot of food at at the party!
6 I _____ my wife at a work party.
7 I _____ my dad's birthday again!
8 I _____ my keys on the way to work.
9 She _____ to her teacher about it yesterday.
10 He _____ me a cup of coffee from the cafe next door.

3 a Read the text about Carla's day and match with the correct photo, A–C.

Yesterday I was busy. I didn't have time for breakfast. I didn't speak to my colleagues about football or the weekend. I didn't buy lunch. I didn't eat anything! I worked and worked and worked.
I usually walk home from work, but yesterday I felt very tired and I took the train. I arrived home. It was nine o'clock. I ate chips and I watched TV. The really bad thing? I forgot my mum's birthday.

b Which things did Carla do? Which things didn't she do?
  She worked.
  She didn't have time for breakfast.

📱 Go to page 143 or your app for more vocabulary and practice.

8B | You had a bad day

E I **ate** the sandwich at my desk. It was really bad.

F and I **forgot** an important meeting.

G I **went** to a restaurant for lunch, but I **saw** lots of people there.

H I didn't have lunch at the restaurant. I **bought** a sandwich.

I He wasn't happy. I **felt** bad.

J ... my computer **broke** ...

K In the afternoon, there were more bad things: I **lost** my phone,

L My boss **spoke** to me about my work.

Grammar

4 Read the grammar box and choose the correct alternatives.

Past simple (irregular verbs)

Regular past simple verbs usually end in ¹ *-ed / -ing*.
I watched TV.
I walked to the office.
Irregular past simple verbs have different forms:
feel ➜ felt
go ➜ went
lose ➜ lost
➜ Irregular verbs list page 160
The negative of irregular past simple verbs is ² *didn't / don't* + verb:
+ *I went to work.*
- *I didn't go to work.*
+ *He ate soup in the kitchen.*
- *He didn't eat soup in the kitchen.*

5 a 🔊 8.6 Listen to the sentences. Which letter in *didn't* is not pronounced?

1 I <u>didn't</u> buy lunch.
2 I <u>didn't</u> take the train.
3 I <u>didn't</u> go to work today.
4 I <u>didn't</u> feel good.

b Listen again and repeat.

6 🔊 8.7 Complete the text with the correct form of the verbs in brackets. Then listen and check your answers.

I ¹ <u>didn't get up</u> (not get up) at 7 o'clock today. I stayed in bed. I ² _____ (have) a cup of coffee and I ³ _____ (feel) really good. I left my house at 12 o'clock and ⁴ _____ (meet) a friend. We ⁵ _____ (go) to the park and we ⁶ _____ (run) for half an hour. Then we ⁷ _____ (have) lunch and we ⁸ _____ (speak) about our holidays. I ⁹ _____ (not take) the bus. I ¹⁰ _____ (not go) to work. I ¹¹ _____ (not see) my boss. It was a nice Saturday!

7 a Complete the sentences so they are true for you.

1 _____ yesterday.
2 _____ last night.
3 _____ last week.
4 _____ last Saturday.
5 _____ last month.
6 _____ last year.

b Work in pairs and compare your sentences.

📱 Go to page 130 or your app for more information and practice.

Speaking

PREPARE

8 Think of a bad day you had. It can be real or imagined. Make notes in the table.

When?	
Where?	
What?	

SPEAK

9 Work in groups. Tell your group about your bad day. Who had a very bad day?

I had a bad day last week. I went to a café with my friend ...

Develop your writing
page 108

8c Good places

> **Goal:** talk about a holiday
> **Grammar:** past simple (questions)
> **Vocabulary:** holiday activities

Vocabulary

1 a Match photos A–H with the words and phrases in the box.

go for a walk	go shopping	go to restaurants
have a good time	relax	stay in a hotel
swim in the sea	visit a museum	

b 🔊 8.8 Listen and repeat.

c Which things do you usually do on holiday?
I often go to restaurants.

2 a Read the text. What is the present tense of the verbs in bold? Use Exercise 1a to help you.
had – have

> We **had** a good time in Greece last month. Sometimes we **relaxed** at the beach and **swam** in the sea. Some days we were very busy – we **visited** museums, we **went** to a restaurant for lunch or dinner or we went shopping. One day we went for a nice walk outside the city. It was very hot! We **stayed** in a good hotel – it was called 'The Lux'.

b Which verbs in bold are irregular?

📱 Go to your app for more practice.

Listening

3 a 🔊 8.9 Listen to a conversation. What does Megan talk about – a party, her holiday or the weekend?

b Listen again. Tick the questions you hear.
1. Did you have a nice holiday, Megan?
2. Did you relax?
3. How did you get there?
4. What did you do there?
5. Where did you stay?
6. When did Josh arrive?

Grammar

4 Read and complete the grammar box. Use Exercise 3b to help you.

Past simple (questions)

Yes/No questions

Question		Short answer
¹_____ you **have** a good weekend?	+	Yes, I **did**.
	–	No, I **didn't**.
²_____ they have fun?	+	Yes, they **did**.
	–	No, they **didn't**.

***Wh-* questions**

Where	³_____	Emily	**go**?
When	⁴_____	she	**visit** Tokyo?
How	⁵_____	you	**get** there?
What	⁶_____	you	**do**?

5 a 🔊 **8.10** Listen to the sentences. Notice how the two words join together.

1 Did you have a good holiday?
2 Where did you go?
3 What did you do?
4 Who did you go with?
5 Did you have lunch there?
6 When did you leave?

b Listen again and repeat.

6 a Make questions using the prompts.

1 you / have a good weekend?
   Did you have a good weekend?
2 what time / you get up / on Saturday?
3 where / you go?
4 who / you go with?
5 where / you have lunch / on Sunday?
6 what / you eat?
7 what / do / in the evening?
8 you / study English?
9 your best friend / text you?

b Work in pairs. Ask and answer the questions in Exercise 6a.

   A: Did you have a good weekend?
   B: Yes, I did.

📱 Go to page 130 or your app for more information and practice.

Speaking

PREPARE

7 a Make past simple questions about a holiday using the prompts in the table.

Where?	
When?	
How / get there?	
Who / go with?	
What food / eat?	
What / do?	

b Make notes in the table about your favourite holiday.

SPEAK

8 a Work in pairs. Ask and answer the questions in Exercise 7a.

   A: Where did you go on holiday?
   B: I went to Bergen, in Norway.
   A: When did you go there?

b Tell the class about the place your partner visited.

   Mikael went to Bergen in Norway. He went there last month with his family. He ate fish every day. It was really good.

Develop your listening page 109

8C | Good places

8D English in action

> **Goal:** greet people

1 a Look at the photos. Where are the people? How do you think they know each other (e.g. friends, colleagues, etc.)?

b 🔊 8.15 Listen and match conversations 1 and 2 with photos A and B.

c Listen again. What did the people do at the weekend?
   1 Sara _____ . Mike _____ .
   2 Erica _____ . Duncan _____ .

2 a Listen again. Tick the phrases in the Useful phrases box that you hear.

Useful phrases

Starting a conversation
Hello/Hi, (Mike).
Good morning/afternoon/evening, (Erica).

Questions for greetings
How are you?
How are things?
Are you OK?

Answers for greetings
(I'm) OK, thank you. (And you?)
(I'm) not bad, thanks. (And you?)
(I'm) great, thanks. (And you?)
(I'm) very well, thank you. (And you?)
(I'm) fine, thanks. (And you?)
(I'm) good, thank you. (And you?)

Ending a conversation
Goodbye/Bye.
See you/See you later.

b 🔊 8.16 Listen and repeat.

3 a Complete the conversations with phrases from the Useful phrases box.

1 Simon: Good morning, Magda.
  Magda: ¹_____ , Simon.
  Simon: How are things?
  Magda: ²_____
  Simon: I'm great, thank you. Did you have a good weekend?
  Magda: Yes, thanks. I had lunch with my parents on Saturday. How about you?
  Simon: I stayed at home all weekend and watched TV.
  Magda: Sounds good!
  Simon: Yeah, it was. Well, bye, Magda.
  Magda: ³_____ .

2 Cassie: Hi, Jun.
  Jun: ⁴_____ , Cassie.
  Cassie: How are you?
  Jun: ⁵_____
  Cassie: Good, thanks. How was your weekend?
  Jun: It was OK. I cleaned my flat. How about you?
  Cassie: I visited a friend.
  Jun: Sounds good!
  Cassie: It was! OK, see you later.
  Jun: ⁶_____ .

b Work in pairs. Practise the conversations in Exercise 3a.

4 Walk around the classroom and greet your classmates. Ask about their weekend.
Hello, Haruka. How are you?

Go online for the Roadmap video.

Check and reflect

1 a Complete the sentences with the correct verbs.
   1 I _____ in a village/in a town/in a city.
   2 I _____ tennis/video games with friends/football.
   3 I _____ to my parents every day/to my neighbour about the weather/my friends every week.
   4 I _____ a film once or twice a week/TV every day.
   5 I _____ to work/by bus/to my parents' house every weekend.

   b Tick the sentences that are true for you. Work in pairs and compare your answers.

2 Complete the text with the past simple form of the verbs in brackets.

   My school was near my house. I [1] _walked_ (walk) to school but my friends [2] _____ (travel) by bus. One or two children [3] _____ (cycle) to school. I usually [4] _____ (arrive) at 8.45 and lessons [5] _____ (start) at 9 o'clock. We [6] _____ (study) all day and [7] _____ (play) sports on Wednesday afternoon. I [8] _____ (like) my lessons but I [9] _____ (not like) the sports. Lessons [10] _____ (finish) at 3.45.

3 Find the twelve irregular verbs in the wordsearch.

   | ~~ate~~ | broke | felt | forgot | got up | had | lost | met |
   | ran | spoke | took | went | | | | |

X	F	A	T	E	K	R	A	N	M
Q	O	S	H	K	S	P	O	K	E
R	R	W	K	W	L	J	G	J	T
B	G	P	G	E	I	T	O	O	K
R	O	J	O	N	H	K	K	L	F
O	T	N	T	T	A	O	B	O	E
K	L	M	U	H	D	D	F	S	L
E	O	U	P	H	T	E	K	T	T

4 Complete the sentences with the verbs in the box.

   | broke | bought | forgot | got up | met | spoke |

   1 Yesterday, I _____ my sandwiches. I wasn't happy!
   2 I _____ to my parents on the phone last night.
   3 They _____ a big house in the mountains.
   4 He _____ at 11.00 a.m. today!
   5 My wife and I _____ at university.
   6 She _____ another cup last night.

5 a Complete the sentences with the past simple form of the verbs in brackets.
   This morning …
   1 I _got up_ (get up) at 7.30.
   2 I _____ (have) a shower.
   3 I _____ (make) my breakfast.
   4 I _____ (eat) breakfast.
   5 I _____ (drink) two cups of tea with my breakfast.
   6 I _____ (buy) coffee in a coffee shop.
   7 I _____ (read) a book.
   8 I _____ (take) a bus to work.

   b Tick the sentences that are true for you. Work in pairs and compare your answers.

6 Complete the phrases with infinitive verbs.
   1 _____ in the sea
   2 _____ a museum
   3 _____ for a walk/shopping/to restaurants
   4 _____ a good time
   5 _____ in a hotel

7 a Read the answers and complete the questions.
   1 Q: What time _did you get up_ this morning?
      A: I got up at 7.30.
   2 Q: _____ a shower this morning?
      A: No, I didn't. I had a shower last night.
   3 Q: How _____ to work?
      A: I travelled by bus.
   4 Q: _____ TV last night?
      A: No, I didn't. I read a book.
   5 Q: _____ to anyone on the phone?
      A: Yes, I did. I spoke to my friend.
   6 Q: Where _____ dinner?
      A: I ate dinner at home.

   b Work in pairs. Ask the questions and answer them so they are true for you.

Reflect

How confident do you feel about the statements below? Write 1–5 (1 = not very confident, 5 = very confident).

- I can give a talk about when I was young.
- I can talk about a bad day.
- I can talk about a holiday.
- I can greet people.

Want more practice?
Go to your Workbook or app.

9A Family photos

> **Goal:** talk about the people in a photo
> **Grammar:** object pronouns (*me, him, her,* etc.)
> **Vocabulary:** prepositions of place

Vocabulary

1 a Look at the pictures. What can you see?

b 🔊 9.1 Where are the red things? Match sentences 1–9 with pictures A–I in Exercise 1a. Then listen and check your answers.

1. The man is **at** the hotel.
2. The table is **below** the picture.
3. The flowers are **in** the bag.
4. The bag is **next to** the chair.
5. The cup is **in front of** the cake.
6. The bag is **on** the table.
7. The picture is **above** the table.
8. The clock is **between** the computer and the books.
9. The cake is **behind** the cup.

c Listen again and repeat.

2 a Write sentences about objects in your classroom. Don't write the name of the object. Use *it*.
   It's on the table.

b Work in pairs. Read your sentences and guess your partner's objects.
   A: *It's on the table.*
   B: *Is it a book?*

Listening

3 a 🔊 9.2 Look at the photo and listen to Tony and Camilla. Label 1–4 *Tony, Agnes, Carol* and *Pat*.

b Listen again. Who says a–e, Tony (T) or Camilla (C)?

   a Well, that's ¹**me** behind the chair, next to my wife, Carol.
   b Yeah, I know that's ²**you**!
   c And, in front of ³**us**, that's my sister and her family.
   d Wow, how often do you see ⁴**her**?
   e We visit ⁵**them** once a year, but Pat comes to the UK for work sometimes, so we see ⁶**him** three times a year, maybe.

c Look at the words in bold in Exercise 3b. Which people are they?

   1 me *Tony*   4 her
   2 you   5 them
   3 us   6 him

📱 Go to your app for more practice.

Grammar

4 Read the grammar box and choose the correct alternatives.

Object pronouns (*me*, *him*, *her*, etc.)

- Use subject pronouns ¹*before / after* the verb:
  I live in London.
- Use object pronouns ²*before / after* the verb:
  *My parents visit **me** at the weekend.*

subject pronouns	object pronouns
I	me
you	you
he	him
she	her
it	it
we	us
they	them

5 a 🔊 9.3 Listen to the sentences. Are the pronouns in blue stressed or unstressed?

1 Do you often visit them?
2 Who's next to him?
3 He works with her.

b Listen again and repeat.

6 Choose the correct alternatives.

Jenna: Where does your family live, Miguel?
Miguel: ¹*They / Them* live in Acapulco in Mexico.
Jenna: Wow! Do you often talk to ²*they / them*?
Miguel: ³*I / Me* often talk to my mum. ⁴*I / Me* talk to ⁵*she / her* on my computer every weekend. My dad doesn't like computers, so I don't often talk to ⁶*he / him*.
Jenna: Have you got a photograph of your family?
Miguel: Yeah, I've got a photo of ⁷*we / us* on my phone.
Jenna: Oh yeah. Is this your dad?
Miguel: Yeah.
Jenna: Who's this in front of ⁸*him / he*?
Miguel: That's my sister. ⁹*She / Her* is a teacher. ¹⁰*She / Her* sometimes calls ¹¹*me / I*, but ¹²*we / us* usually just send emails.

7 Work in pairs. Ask and answer the questions. Use object pronouns in your answers.

1 Do you often talk to your parents?
   *Yes, I usually talk to **them** every week. I call **them** after my English class.*
2 Do you often send emails to your family?
3 Do you like family parties?
4 How often do you visit your grandmother?
5 Do you always meet your friends at the weekend?
6 Who always calls you at the weekend?

📱 Go to page 132 or your app for more information and practice.

Speaking

PREPARE

8 Find a photo of your family or friends, or choose one of these photos. Prepare to talk about the people in the photo.

SPEAK

9 Work in pairs. Take turns talking about your photo. Ask questions about your partner's photo.
   A: *This is my father.*
   B: *What's his name?*
   A: *Ivan.*
   B: *How often do you see him?*

Develop your reading
page 110

9B Hobbies

> **Goal:** ask and answer about things you and I like doing
>
> **Grammar:** like/enjoy/love/hate + -ing
>
> **Vocabulary:** hobbies

Vocabulary

1 a Match photos A–F with phrases 1–6.
   1 do exercise
   2 listen to music
   3 play cards
   4 use the internet
   5 read a book
   6 watch a film

   b 🔊 9.4 Listen and repeat.

2 a 🔊 9.5 Complete the phrases with verbs from Exercise 1a. Then listen and check your answers.
   1 _____ a play
   2 _____ a TV programme
   3 _____ a game
   4 _____ the radio
   5 _____ a newspaper
   6 _____ / _____ some sport
   7 _____ a video game
   8 _____ a song
   9 _____ / _____ a story

   b Listen again and repeat.

3 Complete the sentences with the correct verbs.
   1 I usually _____ a book on the train in the morning.
   2 We usually _____ to music at work.
   3 Can you _____ cards?
   4 I _____ video games with my friends last Friday.
   5 I _____ a good programme on TV last night.
   6 I don't _____ newspapers.
   7 She _____ the internet in the evening.
   8 They _____ plays every week.

4 Work in pairs. Ask and answer questions using the phrases in Exercise 1a.
   1 How often do you … ?
   2 Did you … last night?
   3 Where do you usually … ?
   4 Do you sometimes … on the train?
   5 Do you usually … at dinner time?

📱 Go to page 144 or your app for more vocabulary and practice.

Listening

5 a 🔊 9.6 Listen to two interviews about the weekend. Complete the tables.

1 Tania	loves	likes/enjoys	doesn't like	hates
going to restaurants				
reading books				
running in the park				

2 Kristoff	loves	likes/enjoys	doesn't like	hates
walking the dog				
watching TV				
playing video games				

b Listen again. Choose the correct option, a or b.
   1 Tania enjoys going to restaurants with her …
      a friends.   b parents.
   2 Tania likes doing …
      a homework.   b sports.
   3 Tania's sister doesn't like …
      a dancing.   b running.
   4 Kristoff likes walking the dog …
      a in the park.   b near the sea.
   5 Kristoff's sons love …
      a watching TV.   b listening to music.
   6 Kristoff's sons like …
      a doing exercise.   b playing video games.

7 a 🔊 **9.7** Listen to the sentences. Notice the pronunciation of *-ing*.
1 I like watching films.
2 I don't like reading newspapers.
3 I hate cleaning the bathroom.
4 I enjoy taking photos.
5 Do you like playing football?
6 What do you like doing at the weekend?

b Listen again and repeat.

8 Complete the sentences with the correct form of the verbs in brackets.
1 I don't like _____ (stay) at home at the weekend.
2 I enjoy _____ (make) dinner for my friends.
3 I hate _____ (study) in the evening.
4 I like _____ (clean) my flat on Sundays.
5 My children don't like _____ (travel) by car, so we never go anywhere.
6 She loves _____ (eat) food from different countries.

9 Work in pairs. Ask and answer questions with *Do you like ...?* and the phrases in Exercise 8.
A: Do you like staying at home at the weekend?
B: No, I don't. I never stay at home at the weekend. I always go somewhere.

📱 Go to page 132 or your app for more information and practice.

Grammar

6 Read and complete the grammar box. Use Exercise 5 to help you.

like/enjoy/love/hate + -ing

Statements

+	I/You/We/They	like/enjoy/love/hate	1_____ the dog.
-		don't like	2_____ TV.
+	He/She/It	likes/enjoys/loves/hates	3_____ books.
-		doesn't like	4_____ in the park.

Yes/No questions

Do	I/you/we/they **like**	5_____ books?
Does	he/she/it **like**	6_____ exercise?

Wh- questions

What	**do** you **like**	7_____ at the weekend?
	does she **like**	8_____ at the weekend?

-ing form

do - doing	verb + *-ing*
make - making	Drop the final *-e* in verbs ending in *-e*.
travel - travelling	Double the final consonant in verbs ending in consonant + vowel + consonant. BUT visit → visiting

Speaking

PREPARE

10 Read questions 1–3 in an entertainment survey. Write six more questions. Use Exercises 1 and 2 to help you.

What do you like doing?
1 Do you like reading the newspaper?
2 Do you like listening to music?
3 Do you like playing cards?

SPEAK

11 a Work in pairs. Ask and answer the questions in Exercise 10. Make notes about your partner's answers.
A: Do you like reading the newspaper?
B: Yes, I do. I often read the newspaper on the train to work.

b Tell the class about your partner.
Fernando likes reading the newspaper. He often reads it on the train to work.

Develop your listening
page 111

9c Study habits

> **Goal:** ask and answer about study habits
> **Grammar:** *why* and *because*
> **Vocabulary:** learning a language

Vocabulary

1 a Match pictures A–L with phrases 1–12.

1. write on the board
2. take a course
3. use a dictionary
4. take an exam
5. do my homework
6. go to the library
7. make notes
8. do online practice
9. pass an exam
10. fail an exam
11. know the answer
12. can't remember a word

b 🔊 9.12 Listen and repeat.

2 Complete the sentences with the correct form of the words in Exercise 1.

1. I haven't got a _____ . I use a website on my phone.
2. What does *important* mean? I can't _____ !
3. The _____ is 12 weeks long.
4. Our teacher often writes on the _____ .
5. The _____ in our town is very good.
6. He didn't study, so he _____ the exam.
7. I took an English _____ last week. It was very difficult.
8. She got 90 percent, so she _____ the exam.

3 Work in pairs. Student A: Turn to page 153. Student B: Turn to page 158.

Go to your app for more practice.

Reading

4 a 🔊 9.13 Read the text. Match questions 1–5 with answers A–E. Then listen and check your answers.

Because …

Every week we ask a student about their reasons for studying English. This week we talked to **Bianca Costa**.

❶ Why do you study English?
❷ Why is English difficult for you?
❸ Why didn't you study English at school?
❹ Why have you got four lessons this week?
❺ Why do you study here?

Ⓐ Because the teacher is very good. He knows about my exam.
Ⓑ Because I didn't like my English teacher!
Ⓒ Because there is an English exam on Saturday.
Ⓓ Because I can't remember all the new words. And I didn't study English at school.
Ⓔ Because I use it for my work. I often talk to people from other countries.

b Read the text again and complete the answers.

1 Q: Why does Bianca use English for work?
   A: Because _____ .
2 Q: Why is Bianca busy on Saturday?
   A: Because _____ .
3 Q: Why does Bianca like her English teacher?
   A: Because _____ .

Grammar

5 Read and complete the grammar box. Use Exercise 4a to help you.

why and *because*

Ask for reasons with *why*

Question	Example
Why + *be*	**Why** is English difficult for you?
Why + *do* + subject + verb	1 _____ 2 _____ 3 _____
Why + *have* + subject + *got*	4 _____

Give reasons with *because*

Statement + *because* + reason

Bianca studies English **because** she uses it for her work.
English is difficult for Bianca **because** she can't remember all the new words.

---

6 a 🔊 9.14 Listen to the sentences. Notice the pronunciation of the words in blue.

1 I study English because I need it for my job.
2 I study English because I want to travel.
3 I study English because I'd like to take an exam.

b Listen again and repeat.

7 a 🔊 9.15 Complete the conversation with the words in the box. Then listen and check your answers.

| because (x3) | do | do you | I | it's | where |
| why (x2) | | | | | |

Esma: Why ¹_____ study English, Pierre?
Pierre: ²_____ I like watching films in English. How about you?
Esma: I study because ³_____ like travelling and I can use English in lots of countries.
Pierre: ⁴_____ do you study?
Esma: I take a course at the university.
Pierre: ⁵_____ do you study there?
Esma: Because ⁶_____ near my house. ⁷_____ you go to a class?
Pierre: No, ⁸_____ I'm very busy at work.
Esma: How do you study?
Pierre: I often play games in English on my phone. Do you know any good games?
Esma: Yes, I often play 'Language Crab'.
Pierre: ⁹_____ do you like that game?
Esma: I like it ¹⁰_____ it helps me with my vocabulary.

b Work in pairs. Practise the conversation in Exercise 7a.

📱 Go to page 132 or your app for more information and practice.

Speaking

PREPARE

8 Work in pairs. Write five questions about study habits.

When do you study?
Do you study at home?

SPEAK

9 Change partners. Ask your questions from Exercise 8. Answer your partner's questions. Use *because*.

A: When do you study?
B: I study at the weekend.
A: Why do you study at the weekend?
B: Because I've got a busy job and I'm tired in the evening.

Develop your writing page 112

9D English in action

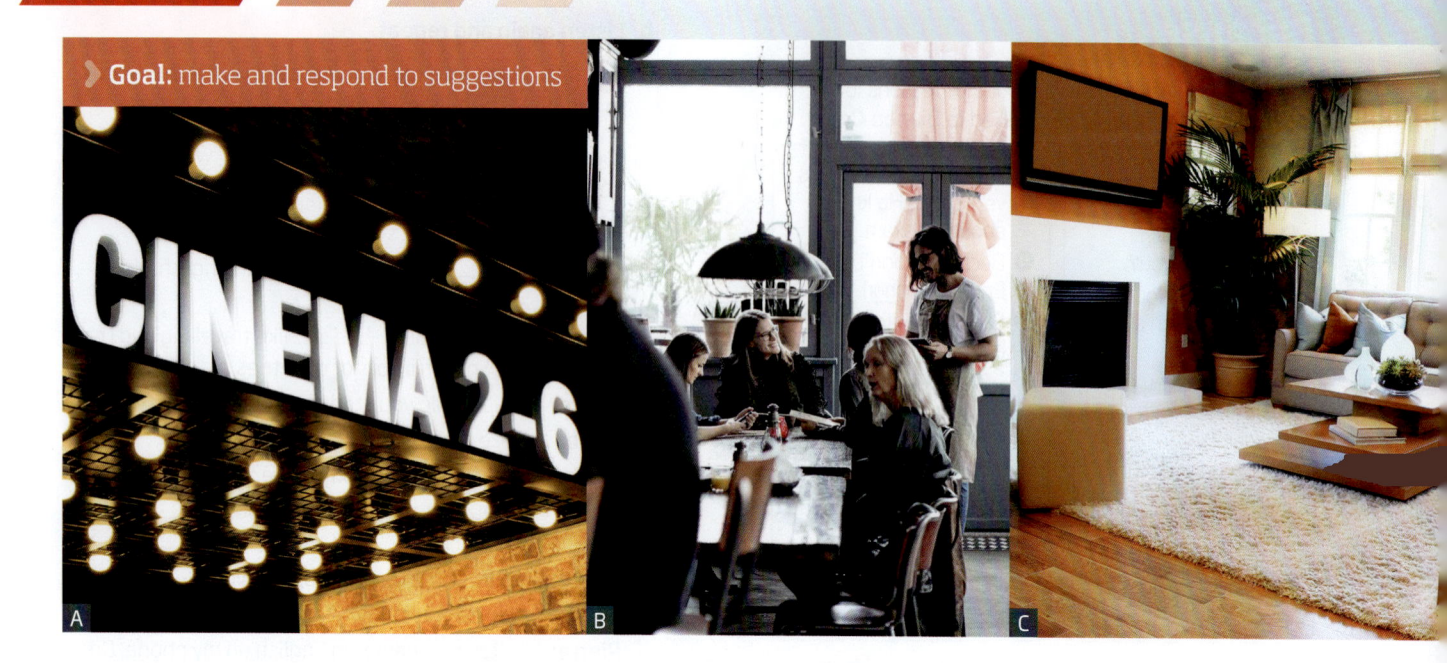

> **Goal:** make and respond to suggestions

A B C

1 a Look at the photos. What can you do there?

   b 🔊 **9.16** Listen to three conversations and match them with photos A–C in Exercise 1a.

2 a Listen again and choose the correct alternatives.
   1 They choose to watch a *football* / *music* programme.
   2 The film starts at *7.30* / *8.00*.
   3 They choose to go to a *Spanish* / *Thai* restaurant.

   b Listen again. Which conversation do the phrases in the Useful phrases box come from: 1, 2 or 3?

   > **Useful phrases**
   >
   > **Making suggestions**
   > Let's do something!
   > Shall we go at 7.30?
   >
   > **Saying yes to suggestions**
   > That's a great idea!
   > Good idea.
   >
   > **Saying no to suggestions**
   > Sorry, I don't like it.
   > Hmm. I went there last week.
   >
   > **Making plans**
   > When shall we go?
   > Where shall we go?
   > What shall we watch?

   c 🔊 **9.17** Listen and repeat.

3 a 🔊 **9.18** Put the conversation in the correct order. Then listen and check your answers.
   a **Dylan:** Hmm. It's very cold today.
   b **Dylan:** OK. Shall we play a video game?
   c **Olivia:** The library?
   d **Olivia:** Shall we walk to the lake?
   e **Dylan:** No, they haven't got any good films today. Let's go to the library.
   f **Olivia:** Hmm. I don't like reading.
   g **Olivia:** Let's do something. *1*
   h **Dylan:** Yeah, let's read some books.
   i **Olivia:** Great idea! What shall we play?
   j **Dylan:** OK. What shall we do?
   k **Dylan:** Let's play this game. You can fly a plane.
   l **Olivia:** Yeah, you're right. Shall we go to the cinema?

   b Work in pairs. Practise the conversation.

4 Work in groups. Decide on six activities to do together at the weekend. Decide where and when to do them. Then complete the table.

	morning	afternoon	evening
Saturday			
Sunday			

   A: *Let's go to the library on Saturday morning.*
   B: *That's a great idea.*
   C: *Hmm. I don't like the library. Shall we go to the park?*
   A: *OK, that's a good idea.*

Go online for the Roadmap video.

Check and reflect

1 Look at the pictures. Then complete the sentences with the prepositions in the box.

| above | at | behind | below | between | in |
| in front of | next to | ~~on~~ | | | |

1 It's _on_ the table.
2 It's _____ the table.
3 It's _____ the door.
4 He's _____ the bus stop.
5 It's _____ the window.
6 He's _____ the TV.
7 He's _____ the window.
8 It's _____ the tables.
9 It's _____ the cup.

2 Complete the sentences with the words in the box.

| her | him | it | me | them | us |

1 My grandfather is 82. I speak to _____ on the telephone every day.
2 My mum is great. I visit _____ all the time!
3 Two of my good friends are Irina and Davide. I see _____ every weekend.
4 I didn't like a girl at school. She didn't talk to _____ .
5 At school, we didn't like Mr Clarkson. He gave _____ difficult homework.
6 This is a photo of my dog. Do you like _____ ?

3 a Complete the sentences with the correct form of the verbs in the box.

| do | listen to | play | read | use | watch |

1 I often _____ music on the bus.
2 I usually _____ a book in the evening.
3 I _____ exercise in the morning.
4 I _____ a good film last night.
5 I often _____ the internet on the train.
6 I _____ video games every day.

b Tick the sentences that are true for you. Work in pairs and compare your answers.

4 Complete the sentences with the correct form of the verbs in brackets.

1 I _love reading_ (love/read) books at the weekend.
2 I _____ (hate/do) exercise on Sundays.
3 What sports _____ you _____? (enjoy/watch)
4 Jason _____ (love/listen to) music.
5 Sally _____ (not enjoy/work) at the weekend.
6 What radio programmes _____ you _____ (like/listen to)?
7 My children _____ (not like/get up) early for school.

5 Complete the sentences with the correct form of the verbs in the box.

| do | fail | go to | know | pass | ~~take~~ |
| use | write | | | | |

1 All the students _take_ exams in June.
2 You look happy. Did you _____ the exam?
3 This exam is really difficult. A lot of students _____ it.
4 Please _____ the homework for tomorrow.
5 You can _____ a dictionary for difficult words.
6 We always _____ the library on Friday.
7 Sorry, I don't _____ the answer to Question 6.
8 The teacher _____ jobs on the board yesterday.

6 a Put the words in the correct order to make questions.

1 you / are / hungry / Why ?
2 eat / Why / salad / you / don't / your ?
3 doesn't / the / Leo / answer / Why / know ?
4 week / last / Why / you / go / didn't / to work ?
5 late / morning / was / this / Why / Sam ?
6 can / Sara / Why / Portuguese / speak ?
7 new / have / a / teacher / Why / got / we ?

b Match answers a–g with questions 1–7 in Exercise 6a.

a Because she studied it in Brazil.
b Because he wasn't in the lesson yesterday.
c Because I don't like it.
d Because I was in Spain.
e Because Mrs Lewis is on holiday.
f Because his train was late.
g Because I didn't have breakfast.

Reflect

How confident do you feel about the statements below? Write 1–5 (1 = not very confident, 5 = very confident).

- I can talk about the people in a photo.
- I can ask and answer about things you and I like to do.
- I can ask and answer about study habits.
- I can make and respond to suggestions.

Want more practice?
Go to your Workbook or app.

10A Goals

> **Goal:** ask and answer about dreams and wishes
>
> **Grammar:** would like/love to
>
> **Vocabulary:** collocations

Listening and vocabulary

1. Work in pairs. Look at the photos. Where are the people?

2. a 🔊 10.1 Listen and match the speakers with photos A–E. There are ten speakers but only five photos.

   b Listen again and read the text. Complete phrases 1–10.

   c 🔊 10.2 Listen and repeat phrases 1–10.

What are your goals?

Natalie: I'd like to ¹ **start** _____ . I like making clothes and I'd love to open a shop and sell them to people.

Andy: I love reading, so I'd like to ² **join** _____ and talk to people about books. My friends don't like reading!

Matthew: I moved to a new city last month, so I'd like to ³ **make** some _____ . I love talking to friends!

Lars: I'd love to ⁴ **change** _____ . My job is very difficult, and my manager is never happy. I don't like working there.

Denise: My office is far from our flat. I leave home at 7 in the morning and arrive home at 9 in the evening. I'd like to ⁵ **spend** more time with _____ , because I never see them from Monday to Friday!

Maria: I always eat unhealthy food and I never exercise. I'd like to ⁶ **try a new** _____ and get healthy.

Brad: We'd love to ⁷ **have** _____ , but our flat is very small, so we're going to buy a house.

Justine: Our new flat is very small, so we need to ⁸ **sell** _____ . Maybe our old books?

Stella: I hate living in the city. I'd love to ⁹ **build** _____ near a lake and walk in the mountains every day!

Hilal: I live in a small village and I hate it. There isn't a cinema and there are no restaurants. I'd love to ¹⁰ **move** to _____ .

3. a 🔊 10.3 Complete the phrases with the highlighted verbs in Exercise 2b. Listen and check your answers.

   1. _____ my small car for a big car
   2. _____ something different
   3. _____ friends with someone at work
   4. _____ some books on the internet
   5. _____ a sports team
   6. _____ time with my parents
   7. _____ a son or a daughter
   8. _____ a small company
   9. _____ to a small village
   10. _____ a desk for my bedroom

   b Listen again and repeat.

4. Write five sentences using phrases from Exercises 2 and 3.

   I changed jobs last year.

   📱 Go to page 145 or your app for more vocabulary and practice.

Grammar

5 Read and complete the grammar box. Use Exercise 2b to help you.

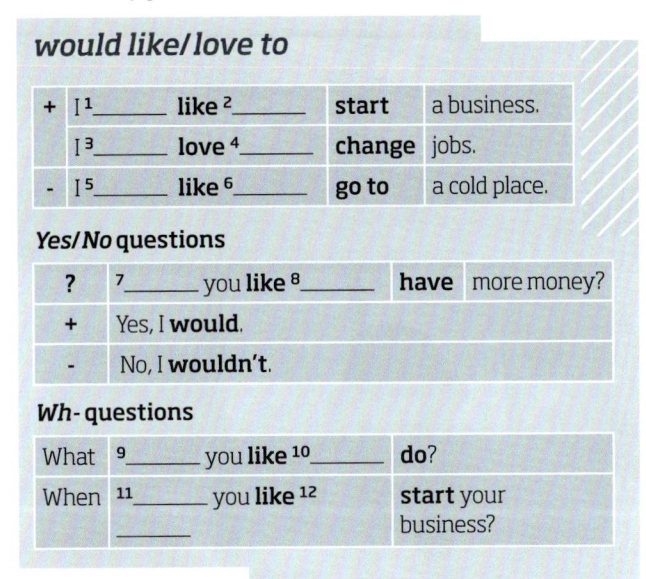

would like/love to

+	I ¹_____ like ²_____	start	a business.
	I ³_____ love ⁴_____	change	jobs.
-	I ⁵_____ like ⁶_____	go to	a cold place.

Yes/No questions

?	⁷_____ you like ⁸_____	have	more money?
+	Yes, I **would**.		
-	No, I **wouldn't**.		

Wh- questions

What	⁹_____ you like ¹⁰_____	do?
When	¹¹_____ you like ¹²_____	start your business?

6 a 🔊 **10.4** Listen to the sentences. Which sentence do you hear, a or b?

1. a I like being a nurse.
   b I'd like to be a nurse.
2. a What would you like to do at the weekend?
   b What do you like doing at the weekend?
3. a We love living in the city.
   b We'd love to live in the city.
4. a I'd like to live near the sea.
   b I like living near the sea.

b Listen again and repeat.

7 🔊 **10.5** Choose the correct alternatives. Then listen and check your answers.

1. **Interviewer:** What ¹*do / would* you like to do in the future?
   Wayne: ²*I like / I'd like* to start a business. I ³*love / would love* cooking, so I'd love ⁴*to have / having* a restaurant.
   Interviewer: What food ⁵*would / are* you like to make at your restaurant?
   Wayne: I would like to ⁶*make / making* Italian food. My family is from Italy, so ⁷*I'd love / I love* Italian food.
2. **Interviewer:** What would you like ⁸*do / to do* in the future?
   Vanessa: ⁹*I love / I'd love* travelling, so ¹⁰*I like / I'd like* to travel around the world for six months.
   Interviewer: Where ¹¹*would you / you would* like to go?
   Vanessa: I'd like ¹²*to go / go* to lots of countries! But ¹³*I love / I'd love* eating Chinese food, so I'd like ¹⁴*go / to go* to China.

8 a Complete the sentences with *I'd like to …*, *I'd love to …* or *I wouldn't like to …* so they are true for you.

1. _____ sing and dance on TV.
2. _____ have more brothers and sisters.
3. _____ play video games after class.
4. _____ be a doctor.
5. _____ travel around the world by boat.
6. _____ learn another language.

b Work in pairs. Read your sentences and compare your answers.

📱 Go to page 134 or your app for more information and practice.

Speaking

PREPARE

9 a Look at the table and think about your answers to Questions 1–4.

Would you like to …	Name/Notes
1 start a business?	
2 travel around the world?	
3 write a book?	
4 learn to dance?	
5 _____ ?	
6 _____ ?	
7 _____ ?	
8 _____ ?	

b Write questions for 5–8.

SPEAK

10 a Ask your classmates the questions in Exercise 9a. Makes notes about their answers in the table. Ask follow-up questions for more information.

A: *Would you like to start a business?*
B: *Yes, I would. I'd like to open a bookshop.*
A: *Where would you like to open a bookshop?*
B: *In my home town.*

b Report back to the class.

Elena would like to open a bookshop.

Develop your reading
page 113

10A | Goals

79

10B Party time

> **Goal:** talk about plans for a class party
> **Grammar:** be going to
> **Vocabulary:** party vocabulary

Vocabulary

1 a Work in groups. Look at photos 1–5. Which of the activities do you often do?
I often listen to music.

b Look at photos 6–11. Which food and drink do you like? Which don't you like?
I really like chicken sandwiches!

6 snacks
7 drinks
8 a dessert
9 sandwiches
10 salad
11 fruit

1 talk to friends
2 play games
3 listen to music

2 a 🔊 10.6 Listen and repeat the words and phrases in Exercises 1a and 1b.

b Work in pairs. Make a list of more party activities or party food and drink.

📱 Go to your app for more practice.

Listening

3 🔊 10.7 Listen to Charlie and Leo. Tick the food, drink and activities that you hear.

1 listen to music
2 dance
3 talk to friends
4 play games
5 sing songs
6 snacks
7 drinks
8 a dessert
9 sandwiches
10 salad
11 fruit

dance 4

sing songs 5

4 a 🔊 **10.8** Listen to Charlie talking to his class. When does he use *be going to*?
1 to talk about a future plan
2 to talk about a past action

b Listen again and complete the sentences.
1 We're going to _____ a party next week.
2 Leo's going to _____ sandwiches.
3 I'm not going to _____ songs!
4 She isn't going to _____ music!

c Listen again. Can you hear any other sentences with *be going to*?

Grammar

5 Read and complete the grammar box. Use Exercise 4b to help you.

+	I'm	going to	**talk** to Teri.
-	I ¹_____	going to	**buy** small snacks.
+	You/We/They ²_____	going to	**watch** a film.
-	You/We/They ³_____	going to	**meet** my friends.
+	He/She/It ⁴_____	going to	**be** at the restaurant.
-	He/She/It ⁵_____	going to	**be** at my house.

6 a 🔊 **10.9** Listen to the sentences. Notice the pronunciation of *going to*.
1 I'm going to buy drinks for the party.
2 You're going to come to my house.
3 He's going to make sandwiches.

b Listen again and repeat.

7 Complete the sentences with the *be going to* form of the verbs in brackets.
1 He _____ (eat) a dessert.
2 You _____ (buy) snacks.
3 She _____ (sing) a song.
4 I _____ (cycle) to your house.
5 They _____ (arrive) at 6 o'clock.
6 I _____ (make) a cake.
7 He _____ (not come) to the party.
8 She _____ (not play) football.

8 a Complete the sentences with the correct form of *be going to* so they are true for you.
1 After class, we _____ .
2 At the weekend, my family _____ .
3 Next week, I _____ .
4 In the next class, we _____ .
5 For dinner today, I _____ .
6 On Saturday, I _____ .

b Work in pairs and compare your answers. How many are the same?

📱 Go to page 134 or your app for more information and practice.

Speaking

PREPARE

9 Work in pairs. Imagine you are going to have a class party. Make notes about:
• food and drink
• music
• where/when to have the party
• things to do at the party

A: *Let's get some pizzas from that restaurant in town.*
B: *Good idea! I love pizza.*

SPEAK

10 Present your party plan to the class. Which is your favourite plan? Why?

OK, we're going to have a party at 'La Chaise' restaurant. We're going to ...

Develop your listening
page 114

10c My plans

> **Goal:** ask and answer about plans for the year
> **Grammar:** *be going to*: questions
> **Vocabulary:** seasons, time expressions

Vocabulary

1 a Match photos A–D with the seasons in the box.

| autumn | spring | summer | winter |

b 🔊 10.13 Listen and repeat.

c Work in pairs. When are the different seasons in your country? Mark them on the calendar.

Calendar

January	February	March	April
Today: 15th	22nd travel to Osaka office work in Osaka office 23rd, 24th, 25th, 26th, 27th, 28th		

May	June	July	August
		1st take Jake to summer school Jake at summer school 2nd–23rd	

September	October	November	December
3rd–17th stay with Olga's mother			31st meet old school friends

2 Look at the calendar in Exercise 1c again. Complete the sentences.

1 Next month, I'm going to ___*travel to Osaka*___ .
2 I'm going to stay for _____ days.
3 In July, I'm going to _____ .
4 He's going to stay for _____ weeks.
5 In September, we're going to stay with _____ for a fortnight.
6 I'm going to meet my old school friends on 31st _____ .

3 a Look at the sentences in Exercise 2. Complete the phrases with the correct prepositions.

1 ___*in*___ + **season:**
   I'm going to visit Tim ___*in*___ the autumn.
2 _____ + **month:** _____ March, I'm going to take a trip to Dubai.
3 _____ + **month/week/year:** _____ year, I'm going to study French.
4 _____ + **date:** I'm going to stay with my family _____ 23rd December.
5 _____ + **days/weeks/months:** I'm going to stay with her _____ three days.

b 🔊 10.14 Listen, check and repeat the sentences.

4 Complete the sentences so they are true for you.

1 Next week, _____ .
   Next week, I am going to have lunch with my friends.
2 Next year, _____ .
3 Next month, _____ .
4 In _____ , I _____ for _____ .
5 On _____ , I _____ .

📱 Go to your app for more practice.

Listening

5 🔊 10.15 Listen to a conversation and choose the correct option, a–c, to answer the questions.

1 Where is the woman going to go on holiday?
   a England
   b Norway
   c New Zealand
2 Where is the man going to go on holiday?
   a He isn't going to go on holiday.
   b his parent's house
   c the mountains

10C | My plans

6 Match questions 1–4 with answers a–d. Then listen again and check your answers.
1 Are you going to go on holiday next year?
2 When are you going to go?
3 What are you going to do there?
4 Are your parents going to visit you again?
a Yes, they are.
b My friend lives in Auckland, so we're going to visit him.
c In August.
d Yes, we are.

Grammar

7 Read and complete the grammar box. Use Exercise 6 to help you.

be going to: questions

Yes/No questions

Question				Short answer	
Am	I	going to	drive?	+	Yes, you **are**.
				-	No, you **aren't**.
¹____	you	going to	go on holiday?	+	Yes, I **am**.
				-	No, ²____.
Is	he/she	going to	cycle?	+	Yes, he/she **is**.
				-	No, he/she **isn't**.
Is	it	going to	be at the café?	+	Yes, it **is**.
				-	No, it **isn't**.
³____	we/they	going to	visit?	+	Yes, we/they ⁴____.
				-	No, we/they **aren't**.

Wh- questions

When	⁵____ you	going to	go?
What	**are** you	going to ⁶____	**do** there?
Where	**are** you	going to	**take** them?

8 a 🔊 10.16 Listen and underline the words that are linked.
1 What are you going to do in the summer?
2 When are you going to go?
3 Where are you going to stay?
4 How are you going to travel?
5 What are you going to do every day?

b Listen again and repeat.

9 Add one word to complete the questions.
1 What time are you going to finish work?
2 Where you going to take your parents?
3 Jane going to come with you next month?
4 Are you going to do in the summer?
5 Are all of the students to come to the party?
6 When we going to take a trip?
7 Are you going go to the Moscow office for a fortnight?
8 Pam and John going to drive?

10 a Make questions using the prompts and *be going to*.
1 what / do / autumn?
   What are you going to do in the autumn?
2 where / go / next weekend?
3 study / on Sunday?
4 when / go / on holiday?
5 who / have dinner with / on Saturday?
6 you / take a trip / next month?

b Work in pairs. Ask and answer the questions in Exercise 10a.

📱 Go to page 134 or your app for more information and practice.

Speaking

PREPARE

11 Make notes about your plans for the year. Think about:
• what you are going to do
• when you are going to do it
• how long you are going to do it for
Visit parents - next month - two days

SPEAK

12 a Turn to page 159.

b Show the calendar to your partner. Is the information correct?

Develop your writing
page 115

10D English in action

> **Goal:** make and respond to invitations

1 a Look at the photos. Where are the people? How often do you do these things?

b 🔊 10.17 Listen to three conversations and match them with photos A–C in Exercise 1a.

c Listen again and answer the questions.
1. Where is the man going to go?
2. What is Kenny going to do at 7.30?
3. What time are they going to meet?

2 a Listen again. Which conversation do the phrases in the Useful phrases box come from: 1, 2 or 3? Two phrases are not used.

> **Useful phrases**
>
> **Making invitations**
> Would you like to come?
> Would you like to have dinner with us?
> Would you like to come with me?
> Would you like to come with us?
>
> **Responding to invitations**
> I'd love to, thanks.
> That would be great.
> Sorry, I can't, because I work on Saturdays.
> Thank you, but I can't, because I'm going to have dinner with my parents.

b 🔊 10.18 Listen and repeat.

3 a 🔊 10.19 Complete the conversation. Use the Useful phrases to help you. Then listen and check your answers.

Anna: Hi, Laurence. How are you?
Laurence: I'm good, thanks. And you?
Anna: Fine, thanks. Listen, we're going to have a small party on Friday night. ¹_____ ?
Laurence: Sorry, ²_____ I'm going to have dinner with some friends.
Anna: Oh, OK.
Laurence: But I'm going to have lunch at the new café on Sunday. ³_____ and Greg ⁴_____ to join me?
Anna: Thanks. That ⁵_____ great. What time shall we meet?
Laurence: Let's meet at 12.
Anna: OK. See you then.
Laurence: See you then.

b Work in pairs. Practise the conversation.

Speaking

4 a Think about your schedule for the weekend. When are you busy?

b Think of something good to do at the weekend. Choose a time, a place and an activity.

c Talk to your classmates. Make invitations and respond to their invitations. How many people are going to join you?

> Go online for the Roadmap video.

Check and reflect

1 Complete the sentences with the correct form of the verbs in the box.

| build | change | have | join | make | move |
| sell | start | | | | |

1 I'd like to _change_ my job and spend more time at home.
2 My brother _____ his car last week. He got £2,500.
3 I'd like to _____ more friends.
4 I _____ a gym last week.
5 My parents _____ a small business last month.
6 Is there a right time to _____ children?
7 I'd love to _____ a house by the sea one day.
8 Jenny would like to _____ to the US.

2 a Choose the correct alternatives.

1 I'd like to *see* / *seeing* you again.
2 She would *like* / *likes* to study in the US.
3 *Do you* / *Would you* like to see my photos?
4 *I'd* / *I'm* love to go to Tokyo one day.
5 **A:** Would you like to come?
   B: Yes, I *do* / *would*.
6 I *don't would* / *wouldn't* like to live there.
7 I'd like to do more exercise *next* / *last* year.
8 I'd love *talk* / *to talk* to you about the project.

b Work in pairs. Ask and answer questions with *Would you like to* and the phrases in the box.

drive a fast car   eat salad every day
have four or five children   live in the US
play football with Lionel Messi

3 Put the letters in the correct order to make party vocabulary.

1 ypla gsaem
   play games
2 leistn ot umsic
3 deanc
4 swchandies
5 ltak to ienfrds
6 skcnas
7 rdniks
8 a tdesrse
9 isng osngs
10 saald
11 fritu

4 Complete the sentences with the correct form of *be going to*. Use the short form where possible.

1 I start university next year. _I'm going to_ study Italian.
2 Liz and Eddie _____ move to France in March.
3 I _____ go travelling around Southeast Asia.
4 We _____ buy a house next to a lake.
5 Sit down! I _____ tell you again!
6 It's late. We _____ have time now.

5 Correct the mistakes in five of the sentences.

1 I'm going to change jobs on May.
2 In the summer, we're going to visit my friends in Canada.
3 Next years, I'm going to study at university.
4 In 25th September, we're going to have a big party.
5 We're going to be in Italy for a week.
6 Next month, I'm not going to eat any cakes.
7 On July, I'm going to have a holiday.
8 In the summer, she's going to stay with her father for four weeks.
9 I'm not going to talk to you when you're angry.
10 What you are going to do when you get there?

6 a Make questions using *be going to* and the prompts.

1 When / Emma / start her new business ?
   When is Emma going to start her new business?
2 Where / you / have lunch today ?
3 What time / this train / arrive ?
4 Who / Tim / visit next month ?
5 Fred / change his job ?
6 we / take a taxi next week ?
7 you / finish early on Friday?
8 Where / you / buy your new phone?

b Work in pairs. Are you going to …

1 walk home after class?
2 watch a film tonight?
3 go on holiday this year?
4 get up early on Sunday?
5 live in another country in the future?
6 get a new job this year?

c Change partners. What/Where/When are you going to ….

1 do in the summer?
2 go on Sunday?
3 change your job?
4 learn to drive?
5 have a holiday?
6 do this weekend?

Reflect

How confident do you feel about the statements below? Write 1–5 (1 = not very confident, 5 = very confident).

- I can ask and answer about dreams and wishes.
- I can talk about plans for a class party.
- I can ask and answer about plans for the year.
- I can make and respond to invitations.

Want more practice? Go to your Workbook or app.

1A Develop your reading

> **Goal:** understand a simple online profile
> **Focus:** understanding capital letters

1 Match photos A–D with sentences 1–4.
1. John Smith is from Liverpool in the UK.
2. Maria Fernandez is from Granada in Spain.
3. Toru Yamashita is from Osaka in Japan.
4. Natalia Mazur is from Poznań in Poland.

2 Read the Focus box. Underline the capital letters in Exercise 1.

Understanding capital letters

People's names start with CAPITAL letters:
- *John Smith*
- *Maria Fernandez*

Place names start with CAPITAL letters:
- *Granada in Spain*
- *Poznań in Poland*

3 a Look at the website. Underline the people's names. Circle the place names.

International Student Conference
London University

Listen to these people:
- ☐ Marco Silva: he's from Buenos Aires in Argentina.
- ☐ Monika Lewandowski: she's from Warsaw in Poland.
- ☐ Benjamin Carter: he's from Auckland in New Zealand.
- ☐ Mariko Sato: she's from Fukuoka in Japan.
- ☐ Sang Mai: he's from Hanoi in Vietnam.

b Read the website again. Answer the questions.
1. Is Benjamin from the UK?
2. Where is Marco from?
3. Is Mariko from Tokyo?
4. Where is Monika from?
5. Where is Sang from?

4 Read the messages and complete the table. Use the capital letters to help you.

1 Hello. Nice to meet you. I'm Antoni Bakula. I'm an English teacher at a language school in Berlin in Germany. I'm from Lublin in Poland. Are you an English teacher? Where are you from?

2 Hi. I'm Billy Davies. I'm from Chicago in the US. I'm an English teacher at a university in Moscow in Russia. It's nice to meet you.

3 Hi! Nice to meet you. I'm Josefina Flores. I'm from Acapulco in Mexico. I'm an English teacher at a school in San Juan in Mexico.

	Name	From	Place of work
1			
2			
3			

1B Develop your listening

> **Goal:** understand short conversations about personal details
>
> **Focus:** understanding answers to questions

1 a Match questions 1–3 with answers a–c.
1 What's your name?
2 Where are you from?
3 What's your job?
a I'm a farmer.
b Jason.
c the US.

b 🔊 1.9 Listen to four conversations. How does Jason answer the questions?
1 _I'm called Jason._
2 _____
3 _____
4 _____

2 Read the Focus box. Where is the important information in answers, at the beginning or end?

Understanding answers to questions

What's your name?
*It's **Jason**.*
*My name's **Jason**.*
***Jason**.*
*I'm called **Jason**.*
Where are you from?
*I'm from **the US**.*
*I come from **the US**.*
***The US**.*
What's your job?
*I'm a **farmer**.*
*My job? I'm a **farmer**.*

3 Match questions 1–3 with answers a–h.
1 What's your name?
2 Where are you from?
3 What's your job?
a It's Pamela.
b Spain.
c Steven.
d I'm called Trudy.
e I'm a taxi driver.
f My job? I'm a teacher.
g My name's Anna.
h I come from Argentina.

4 🔊 1.10 Listen to three conversations and complete the information about the people.

1
Name: _____
Country: _____
Job: _____

2
Name: _____
Country: _____
Job: _____

3
Name: _____
Country: _____
Job: _____

1c Develop your writing

> **Goal:** write a short personal profile
>
> **Focus:** using capital letters and full stops

1 Match photos A–C with profiles 1–3.
1. Hi. I'm Pedro. I'm from Barcelona in Spain. I'm a doctor.
2. Hello. My name is Benjamin Turner. I'm from Vancouver in Canada. I'm an English teacher.
3. Hello. I'm Raquel Jimenez. I'm from Mexico City in Mexico. I'm an office worker.

2 Read the Focus box. Circle the capital letters and full stops in Exercise 1.

Using capital letters and full stops
Use capital letters (A, B, C, etc.):
- for *I*: **I**'m a football player.
- for names: My name is **H**elen **M**artin.
- for places: I'm from **N**agasaki in **J**apan.
- for languages: I'm an **E**nglish student.

Use full stops (.) and capital letters in sentences:
I'm a teacher. **A**re you a teacher?
No, **I**'m not. **I**'m an office worker.

3 Correct the mistakes. Use capital letters and full stops.

1. Hello. I'm louisa west. i'm from London I'm an english teacher.
2. hello. i'm Marek Kowalski. i'm from Lodz in poland. i'm a nurse. 
3. Hi. I'm christine chen. I'm from Beijing in china. I'm an office worker 
4. Hello. i'm Tamara Gonzalez. i'm from valencia in Spain. i'm a football player. 
5. hi. i'm stefano pomesano. i'm from Bergamo in italy. i'm a farmer. 

4 Write a profile for this student. Use capital letters and full stops.

Name	Jonas weber
City	berlin
Country	germany
Job	taxi driver

Prepare

5 Complete the table with your information.

Name	
City	
Country	
Job	

Write

6 a Write your profile.

b Work in pairs. Read and check the capital letters and full stops in your partner's profile.

2A Develop your reading

> **Goal:** read a description of a photo
> **Focus:** understanding subject pronouns and possessive adjectives

1 Read the social media posts. What is the competition about?

a jobs   b families   c countries

LL Language Learn

Win a family holiday to London!
Tell us about your family

Nina Fischer
I'm Nina and this is my brother Kristof. We're students. Our university is in London. It's called SOAS.

Emir Arslan
This is my mum Seyhan and my dad Hakan. They are from Turkey.

Ewa Wójcik
I'm Ewa and this is John. He's my brother. This is his wife. Her name is Julia. They live in Berlin.

2 Read the Focus box and choose the correct alternatives. Then read the texts in Exercise 1 again and check your answers.

Understanding subject pronouns and possessive adjectives

I'm Nina and this is my brother Kristof. [1] **We / They**'re students.

Our university is in London. [2] **Its / It's** called SOAS.

This is my mum Seyhan and my dad Hakan. [3] **They / We** are from Turkey.

I'm Ewa and this is John. [4] **He / She**'s my brother. This is his wife. [5] **His / Her** name is Julia. They live in Berlin.

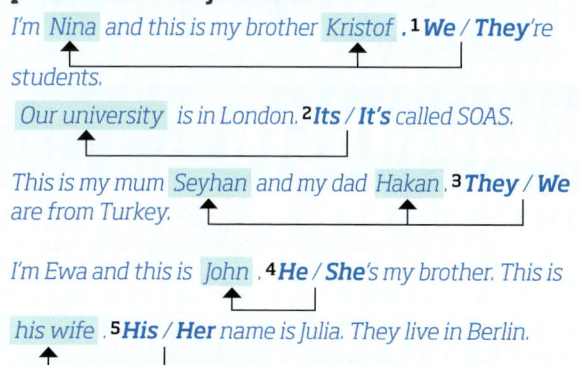

3 Read the sentences. Write the correct names for the pronouns in bold.

1 I'm Helena and this is **my** husband Walter.
   my = Helena's
2 This is Robin. **He**'s a doctor. **He**'s from Canada.
3 I'm Susan and this is Pedro. **We**'re English teachers.
4 This is Yulia and this is her son. **He**'s a student.
5 This is a photo of my family. **They** are from Mexico.
6 Hello, Viola. Is this a photo of **your** parents?
7 Gus is my husband. This is a photo of **our** children.

4 a Read the social media post and circle the names.

Gloria Martínez
I'm Gloria and this is a photo of my family. My husband's name is Joe. He's from the UK. Our son's name is Javier and our daughter's name is Sofia. My brother's name is Raul. He's a pilot. My dad's name is Miguel and my mother's name is Rosa. Their house is in Monterrey, in Mexico. He's a doctor and she's an office worker. Joe's parents are in London. Their names are Tony and Regina. They are teachers.

b Read the text again. Complete the sentences with the correct names.

1 _____'s children's names are Javier and Sofia.
2 _____ is a pilot.
3 _____'s house is in Monterrey, in Mexico.
4 _____'s father is a doctor.
5 _____ is an office worker.
6 _____ are teachers.

2B Develop your writing

> **Goal:** complete a form
> **Focus:** completing forms

1 Read the form and answer the questions.
1 What is the person's full name?
2 Where does he live?

GOLDMAN'S GYM
APPLICATION FORM

First name: William
Surname: Sterling
DOB: 03/05/95
Address: 12 Station Road, London, NW1 2PP
Phone number: 0181 5553455
Email address: w.sterling@rmail.com
Occupation: Office Manager

2 Read and complete the Focus box with words from Exercise 1.

Completing forms
- ¹_Surname_ = family name
- ²_____ = date of birth
- ³_____ = job
- Write your ⁴_____ in this order: house number + street name, city, postcode
- Write your ⁵_____ in this order: DD/MM/YY = date/month/year

3 Match 1–7 with a–g.
1 first name
2 surname
3 address
4 phone number
5 email address
6 DOB
7 occupation

a 12 London Road, Leeds, LS1 BR3
b Doctor
c 0113 5552398
d Jones
e v.jones@abcmail.com
f Vanessa
g 09/12/89

Prepare

4 Complete the form with the information in the box.

07700 900 077   22.10.91   65 Cherry Road
Cambridge   Isobel   Martinez   i.martinez
Teacher

Four Seasons Hotel | Guest information

First name: 1_____
Surname: 2_____
DOB: 3_____
Address: 4_____,
         5_____, CB1 2PP
Phone number: 6_____
Email address: 7_____@abcmail.com
Occupation: 8_____

Write

5 a Complete the form with your information.

Fairbanks School of English
Application form

First name: _____
Surname: _____
DOB: _____
Address: _____
Phone number: _____
Email address: _____
Occupation: _____

b Work in pairs. Read and check your partner's form.

2C Develop your listening

> **Goal:** understand a description of classmates
>
> **Focus:** understanding numbers

1 🔊 **2.15** Listen and match speakers 1–4 with pictures A–D.

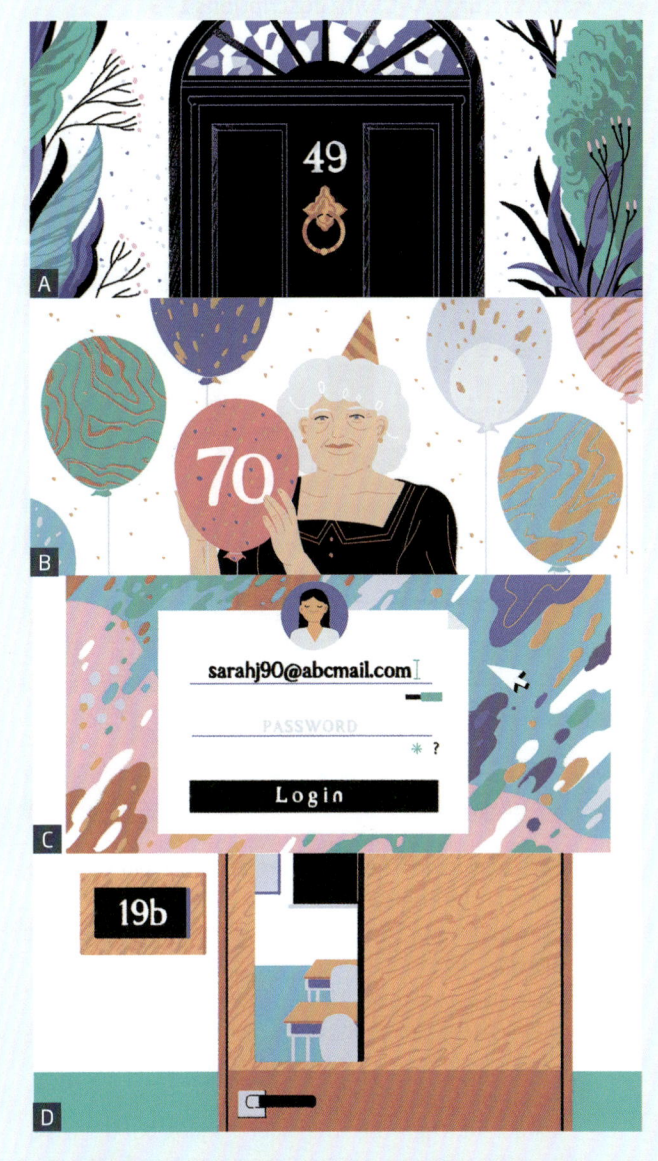

A
B
C
D

2 a 🔊 **2.16** Read the Focus box and look at the stressed syllables. Then listen and underline the stressed syllables in the other numbers.

Understanding numbers

- 13 = thir<u>teen</u>
- 14 = four<u>teen</u>
- 15 = fifteen
- 16 = sixteen
- 17 = seventeen
- 18 = eighteen
- 19 = nineteen
- 30 = <u>thir</u>ty
- 40 = <u>for</u>ty
- 50 = fifty
- 60 = sixty
- 70 = seventy
- 80 = eighty
- 90 = ninety

b Listen again and repeat.

3 🔊 **2.17** Listen and choose the correct alternatives.
1. 15 / 50
2. 17 / 70
3. 13 / 30
4. 19 / 90
5. 14 / 40
6. 16 / 60
7. 18 / 80

4 🔊 **2.18** Listen and complete the sentences with the correct numbers.
1. This is my brother, Simon. He's _____ .
2. Your class is in Room _____ b.
3. My sister is _____ years old.
4. My name's George and I'm _____ .
5. This hospital is _____ years old
6. My address is _____ London Road.

5 🔊 **2.19** Look at the photos. Then listen and complete the captions with the correct ages.

Lucia
_____

Yuri
_____

Ahmed
_____

Azra
_____

Petra
_____

Marco
_____

3A Develop your reading

> **Goal:** read a description of a place
> **Focus:** understanding *and* and *but*

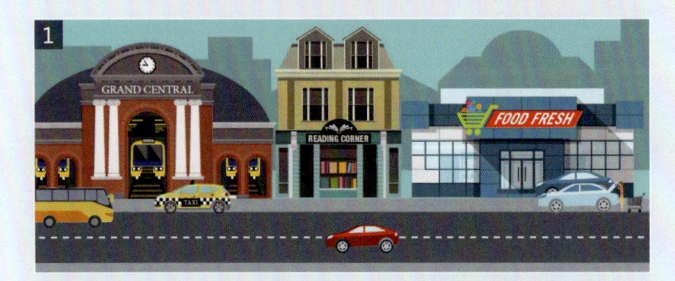

1 Read the text and choose the correct picture, 1–3.

> There is a train station and a bookshop, but there isn't a café. There isn't a hotel and there isn't a bank. There isn't a market, but there is a supermarket.

2 Read the Focus box and circle *and* and *but* in the text in Exercise 1.

Understanding *and* and *but* and

Use *and* to join words or parts of a sentence.
There's a cinema **and** (there's) a bank.
There's a market **and** (there's) a supermarket.
but
Use *but* to join two different/opposite ideas.
　+　　　　but　　　-
There's a market, **but** there isn't a supermarket.
　-　　　　but　　　+
There aren't any restaurants, **but** there is a café.

3 Choose the correct alternatives.
1 There isn't a bookshop, but there *is / isn't* a bank.
2 There is a bookshop, but there *is / isn't* a bank.
3 There isn't a café, but there *is / isn't* a bookshop.
4 There is a bookshop, but there *is / isn't* a café.
5 This is my book and this *is / isn't* my pen.
6 This is my desk, but this *is / isn't* my computer.

4 a Match pictures A–C with descriptions 1–3.

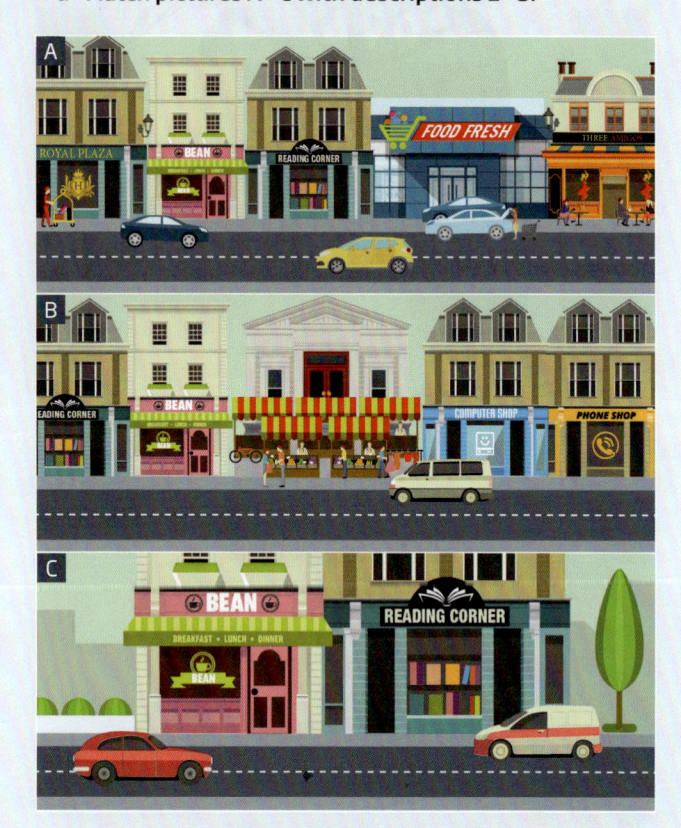

1 This is my town. There are no restaurants, but there's a great café. There is a bookshop, a phone shop and a computer shop. There isn't a supermarket, but there is a market.
2 I'm from a small town. There isn't a supermarket, but there is a café and a bookshop. There are no hotels, no cinemas and there isn't a train station.
3 This is a picture of my town. There is a café and a restaurant. There are no computer shops, but there is a bookshop. There is a hotel and a supermarket. It's a great town.

b Read 1–3 in Exercise 4a again and answer the questions.
1 Which place has a market, but no supermarkets?
2 Which places have a café, but no supermarkets?
3 Which place has a restaurant and a café?
4 Which place has a supermarket and a hotel?
5 Which place has a bookshop, but no computer shops?
6 Which places have a café and a bookshop?

c Work in pairs. Which place is good to live in?

3B Develop your listening

> **Goal:** understand a description of a house
> **Focus:** noticing intonation in lists

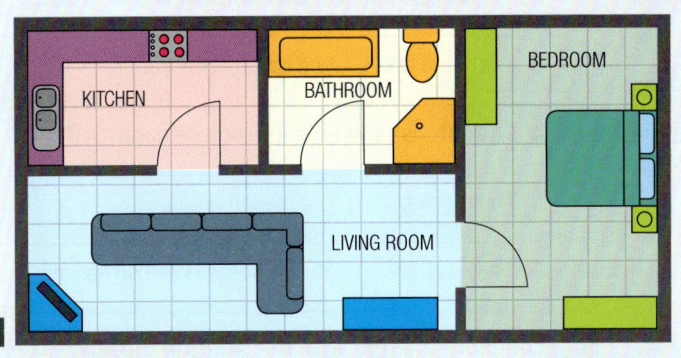

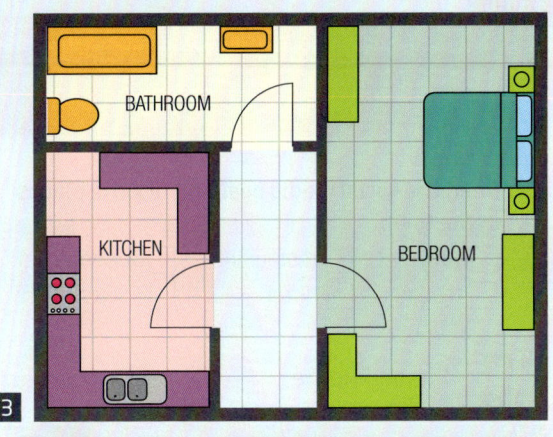

1 🔊 3.7 Listen and match pictures 1–4 with sentences a–d in the Focus box.

2 a 🔊 3.8 Read the Focus box and listen again. Complete 1–6 to show rising intonation (↗) or falling intonation (↘).

Noticing intonation in lists

a There's a kitchen ↗, a bathroom ↗, two bedrooms ↗ and a living room ↘.
b There's a kitchen ↗, a bathroom ↗ and a bedroom ↘.
c There's a bathroom ¹_____ and a bedroom ²_____.
d There's a kitchen ³_____, a bathroom ⁴_____, a bedroom ⁵_____ and a living room ⁶_____.

---

b Listen again and repeat.

3 a 🔊 3.9 Listen to questions and answers 1–4. Is the answer finished (F) or unfinished (U)?

1 **A:** What is there in the living room?
   B: A TV _____
2 **A:** What is there in the kitchen?
   B: A TV _____
3 **A:** How many rooms are there?
   B: Three bedrooms _____
4 **A:** What is there in the town?
   B: A café _____

b 🔊 3.10 Listen and check your answers.

c Listen again and complete the unfinished answers in Exercise 3a.

4 a 🔊 3.11 Listen to the descriptions of two flats. Write how many things the flat or town has got.

	Flat 1	Flat 2
Rooms	bedroom 2 living room 1 kitchen bathroom	bedroom living room kitchen bathroom
Furniture	table chair TV bed	table chair TV bed
Places in town	café(s) shop(s) park	café(s) shop(s) park

b Work in pairs. Which flat do you like?

3c Develop your writing

> **Goal:** write about your town
> **Focus:** using *and* and *but*

1
a Read the social media post and tick the places in the town.
- [ ] café
- [ ] restaurant
- [ ] supermarket
- [ ] market
- [ ] hotel
- [ ] train station

Simon Thorpe

In my town there is a café and a restaurant. The café is good, but the restaurant is expensive. There isn't a supermarket, but there is a market. It's big and cheap. There's a hotel, but there isn't a train station. The hotel is small and old.

b Read the post again. What adjectives does the writer use to describe each place?

2
Read the Focus box and circle *and* and *but* in the text in Exercise 1.

Using *and* and *but*

and
Use *and* to join words or parts of a sentence.
It's big. It's cheap. > *It's big **and** it's cheap.*
The hotel is small. The hotel is old. > *The hotel is small **and** old.*

but
Use *but* to join different/opposite ideas.
The café is good. The café is expensive. > *The café is good, **but** it's expensive.*
There's a market. There isn't a supermarket. > *There's a market, **but** there isn't a supermarket.*

3
Choose the correct alternatives.
1. There is a hotel *and / but* a bookshop in my town.
2. There is a bookshop, *and / but* there isn't a phone shop.
3. The hotel is bad *and / but* expensive.
4. There are no phone shops *and / but* no computer shops.
5. There are no Polish restaurants in my town *and / but* there is a Thai restaurant *and / but* a Mexican restaurant.

4
Join the sentences using *and* or *but*.
1. There is a bookshop. There is a supermarket.
2. There is a hotel. There is a cinema. There is a park.
3. There is a hotel. There isn't a restaurant.
4. The hotel is expensive. The hotel is good.
5. The market is big. The market is bad.
6. There is a park. There is a hotel. There isn't a café

5
Complete the text with the words in the box.

| and | but | is | isn't | it's | small |

Beth Davies

My town is a ¹_____ town in the UK. There ²_____ a café, a bookshop ³_____ a small supermarket, but there ⁴_____ a train station. The café is good, ⁵_____ the bookshop is old. The supermarket is small, but ⁶_____ good.

Prepare

6
Make notes in the table about your town or city.

Places	Y/N	Description (e.g. *good*, *bad*, etc.)
bank		
bookshop		
café		
cinema		
hotel		
park		
restaurant		
supermarket		
train station		

Write

7
a Write a description of your town or city. Use *and* and *but*. Use the text in Exercise 5 to help you.

b Work in pairs. Read and check your partner's description.

4A Develop your reading

> **Goal:** understand a short text
> **Focus:** understanding punctuation: apostrophes

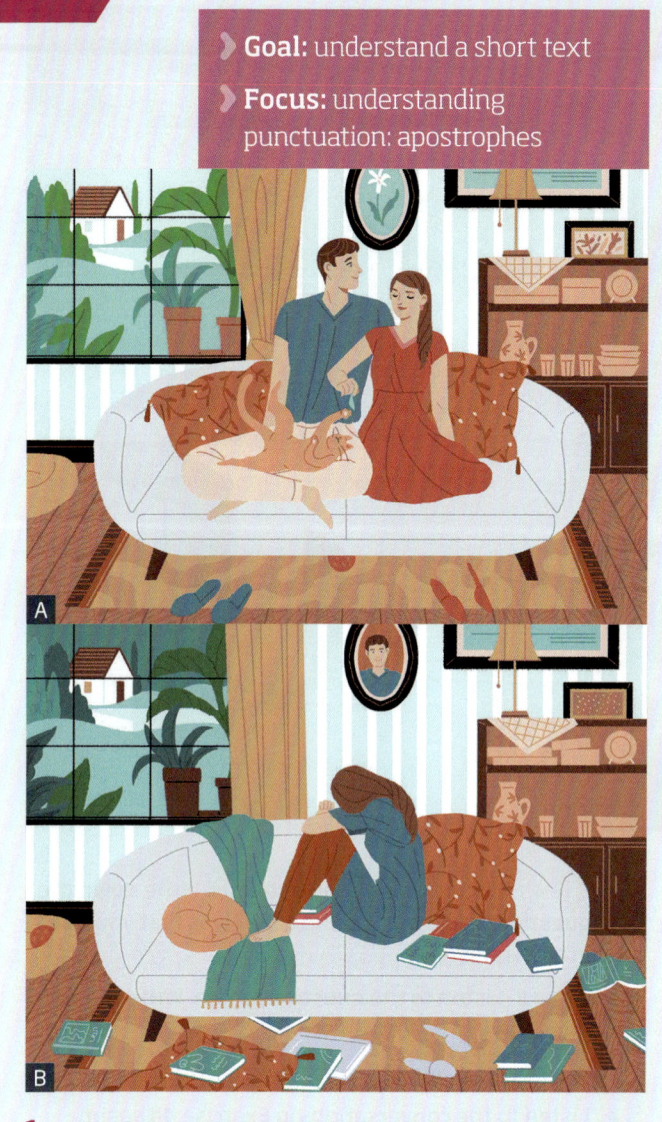

1 Read the text and choose the correct picture, A or B.

She lives in an old flat. She's got an old cat. His name's Peachy and he's quiet. Her husband's books are in the house. They are in the living room, the kitchen, the bathroom and the bedroom. There's a photo of her husband John. He's got brown hair and blue eyes. John's desk and chair are in the living room. John's keys are on the table. Her husband's not here.

2 Read the Focus box. Then circle the apostrophes in the text in Exercise 1. Are they for missing letters or possessive *s*?

Understanding punctuation: apostrophes

Use apostrophes (') for missing letters:
She's from Canada. = She **is** from Canada.
She isn't from Toronto. = She is n**o**t from Toronto.
She hasn't got blue eyes. = She has n**o**t got blue eyes.
Also use apostrophes for things people have got (called a possessive *s*):
This is my friend's book. (= one friend)
This is my friends' book. (= two or more friends)

3 Choose the correct meaning of *'s*.
1 This is Sarah's room. (*is / possessive s*)
2 Sarah's from a quiet town. (*is / possessive s*)
3 John's room is very small. (*is / possessive s*)
4 Lyra's not in her room. (*is / possessive s*)
5 Lola's a university student. (*is / possessive s*)
6 Where is her husband's office? (*is / possessive s*)
7 My friend's name is Tania. (*is / possessive s*)
8 Where are my pens? These are Tania's. (*is / possessive s*)

4 Look at the pictures and choose the correct option, a or b.

1 a This is my sister's room.
  b This is my sisters' room.

2 a This is my brother's flat.
  b This is my brothers' flat.

5 Read the text. Are the sentences true (T) or false (F)?

Hi, my name's Lola. Lola Lemon. I'm a taxi driver here in New York. It's a great city! It's busy and it's expensive, but I love it. I've got a small flat in Brooklyn. I live there with my sister, and our dog, Coco. He's black and white and has got big brown eyes. I'm very happy here!

1 Lola's surname is Apple.
2 She hasn't got a job.
3 Lola thinks New York is expensive.
4 Her flat is big.
5 Her sister's name is Coco.
6 Coco has got brown eyes.

4B Develop your listening

> **Goal:** understand a short, informal conversation
>
> **Focus:** understanding questions

1 Match photos A–D with the words in the box.

| hotel restaurant | hotel room | lift | swimming pool |

2 a 🔊 4.6 Listen to a conversation between two people. Where are they?

b Listen again. Tick the questions you hear.
1. Is there a restaurant in the hotel?
2. Is there a lift?
3. Is the hotel nice?
4. Is the restaurant in town good?
5. Where's my computer?
6. Where's my phone?
7. What's the wifi code?
8. Have you got the wifi code?
9. Have you got the room key?
10. Where's the room key?
11. Where's the lift?

3 Read the Focus box. Underline the question words, nouns and adjectives in Exercise 2b.

Understanding questions

Wh- questions
Listen for the question words and nouns:
Where's the lift?
What's the wifi code?

Yes/No questions
Listen for nouns and adjectives:
Is the restaurant in town good?
Have you got the room key?

---

4 a 🔊 4.7 Listen to five conversations. Write down the question words, nouns and adjectives that you hear in each question.

b 🔊 4.8 Listen to the questions again. Write the full questions.

c Work in pairs and compare your answers.

5 a Listen to the conversations in Exercise 4a again. Match conversations 1–5 with pictures A–E.

b What's the problem in each picture?

4c Develop your writing

> **Goal:** write a message to a friend
> **Focus:** using basic punctuation

1 Read the message from Ryan. Complete the table with the things that Ryan and Sam have got for the holiday.

> Hi Monika. We've got new things for our holiday. I've got sunglasses, cups and a bag. Sam's got books. Have you got a camera? Have you got your dad's credit card? Thanks!

Ryan	Sam

2 Read the Focus box. Then find examples of the punctuation in Ryan's message in Exercise 1.

Using basic punctuation

Use full stops (.) for sentences:
We've got new things for our holiday.
Use question marks (?) for questions:
Have you got a camera?
Use commas (,) in lists:
I've got sunglasses, cups and a bag.
Use apostrophes (') for missing letters:
Sam's got books. (= Sam has got books.)
Use apostrophes (') for possessives:
Have you got your dad's credit card?

3 Correct the sentences. Use the punctuation in the Focus box and capital letters.
  1. ive got a credit card
  2. have you got a camera
  3. weve got a camera a phone and food
  4. this is dannys coat and this is taylors coat
  5. is this your bag
  6. are these kayas sunglasses

4 Find and correct the five punctuation mistakes in the message from Samira.

> I've got my bag for the park I've got a bottle of water, food money and sunglasses. Bens got cups and we've got Jasmines chairs. Have you got a book. The park is on School Road.

Prepare

5 Make a list of five things to take to the park.

Write

6 a Write a message to Samira. Answer her question in the text in Exercise 4.

  b Work in pairs. Read and check your partner's message. Is the punctuation correct?

5A Develop your reading

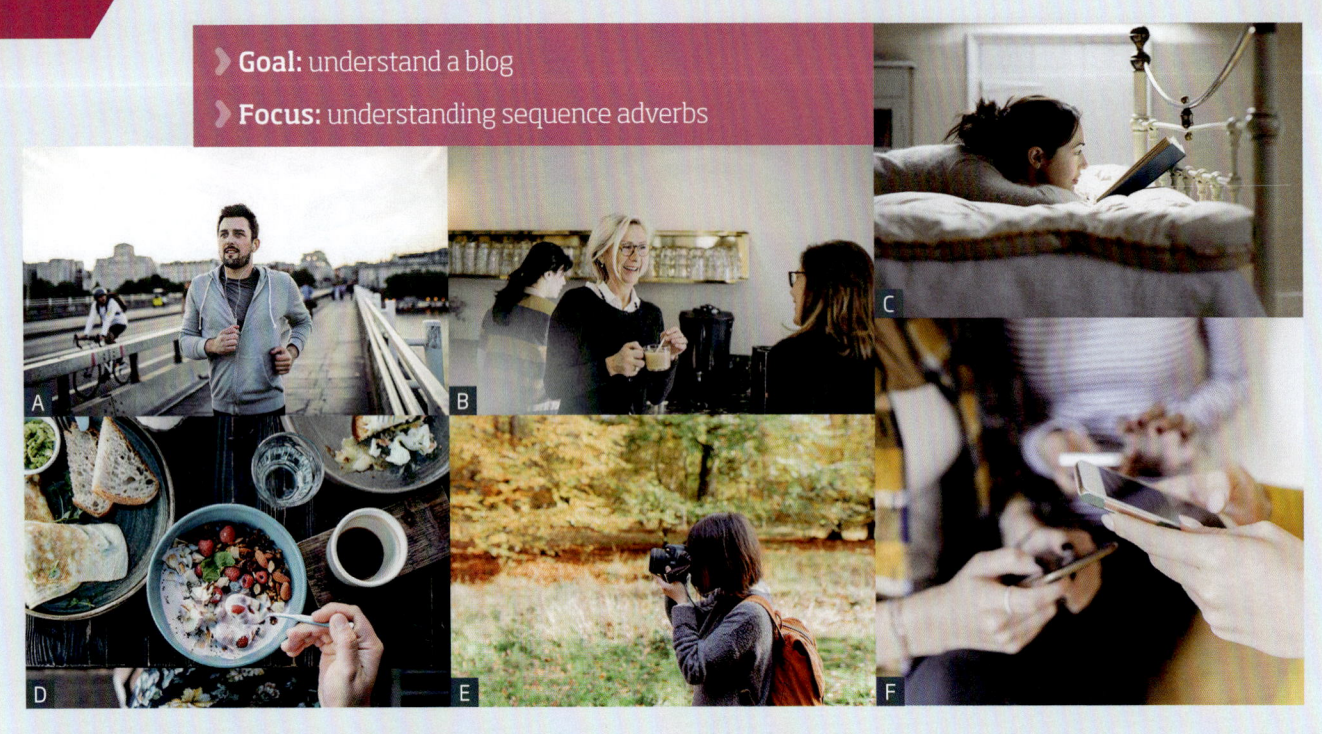

> **Goal:** understand a blog
> **Focus:** understanding sequence adverbs

1 Work in pairs. Look at the photos. Which things do you do every day?

2 Read the blog. Which photos in Exercise 1 does Mika describe?

How to have a good day – Mika

First, wake up at 6 a.m. Don't eat – run for 10 minutes, then have a good breakfast. Breakfast is important! After that, walk to work. Don't take the bus or the train.
Next, at the office, don't use your computer and phone all day. Drink tea with work friends or have lunch with them.
After work, go home and have a small dinner.
Finally, read a good book in the evening.

3 Read the Focus box. Underline the sequence adverbs in Exercise 2.

Understanding sequence adverbs

Sequence adverbs are words like *first, then, after that, next* and *finally*. They show the order of actions.

- **First**, I get up.
- **Then**, I have a shower.
- **Next**, I put on my clothes.
- **After that**, I have breakfast.
- **After** breakfast, I use my phone.
- **Finally**, I go to work.

4 Complete the text with the words in the box.

| After | Finally | First | Next |

¹_____, I have dinner. ²_____, I study and then I watch TV. ³_____ that, I use my computer. ⁴_____, I go to bed at 11 o'clock.

5 Read Karina's blog. Then complete her plan for the day.

How to have a good day – Karina

Well, I don't wake up early! I love sleeping.
In the morning, I drink coffee. Then, I watch TV.
Next, I go to the shops. I buy a cheap bag or sunglasses.
Then, I drink tea (and eat a sandwich maybe) in a quiet café. After that, I walk to the park.
I take photos of the people and the animals.
Then, I go home and watch TV. After dinner, I go to bed.
That's a good day.

12 a.m.–10 a.m. Sleep!
10 a.m. Drink coffee.
10.15 ¹_____
12.00 Go to the shops. Buy a bag/sunglasses.
1.00 ²_____
2.00 ³_____
3.30 Take photos of the people and the animals.
4.00 Go home.
4.15 Watch TV.
9.00 Have dinner.
10.00 ⁴_____

6 Which day do you like, Mika's day or Karina's day?

5B Develop your listening

> **Goal:** understand short, factual conversations
>
> **Focus:** using pictures to help you listen

2 a Read the Focus box. Look at picture B and answer the questions.

Using pictures to help you listen

Before you listen, look at the pictures. Think about questions like this:
- Where are the people?
- What can you see in the picture?
- What do they say?

This helps you get ready to listen.

b 🔊 5.8 Listen to the conversation and complete the sentences.
1 The woman says, 'Where is the _____?'
2 The man says, 'It's next to the _____.'

1 a Look at picture A and choose the correct option, a–c, to answer the questions.
1 Where are the people?
   a in a hotel
   b in a shop
   c in a train station
2 What does the woman say?
   a What time is the London train?
   b Is there a café here?
   c Where is the toilet?
3 What does the man say?
   a It's next to the bank.
   b It's at 3 o'clock.
   c It's over there.

b 🔊 5.7 Listen and check your answers.

c Listen again and choose the correct alternatives.
1 The woman wants the *London / Liverpool* train.
2 The train arrives in London at *5 / 9* o'clock.

3 a Look at picture C and answer the questions in the Focus box.

b 🔊 5.9 Listen and complete the sentences.
1 Their train is at _____.
2 The time is _____ now.

5c Develop your writing

> **Goal:** write an informal message
> **Focus:** using correct word order

1 Read the message. What does Jess ask for information about?
  a places in Paris
  b work in Paris
  c food in Paris

> Hey Pierre, I've got a work trip to Paris next week, and I've got one big question for you – what do French people eat?
> Jess xx

2 Read Pierre's answer and complete the table.

> Hi Jess,
> Paris? Great! We've got lots of good food here. 😊
> In the morning, we have a small breakfast at 8 a.m. We usually have tea or coffee and bread and jam. I sometimes have fruit.
> At 12 or 1 o'clock, we have lunch. We often have a big lunch. We have fish or meat. We usually have bread and salad. After lunch, I always have coffee.
> We usually have dinner at 7 or 8 o'clock. We don't have a big dinner. I often have soup, pasta or salad.
> See you soon!

	Morning	Afternoon	Evening
Time	8 a.m.	1	3
Food	tea/coffee, bread, fruit	2	4

3 Read the Focus box. Complete the table with another sentence from Exercise 2.

Using correct word order

Time	Subject	Verb	Object	Place/Time
At 7.30,	I	run		in the park.
At 1 o'clock,	I	go	home.	
	I	study	Japanese	from 3 o'clock to 5 o'clock.
After dinner,	I	watch	TV.	

Put adjectives after *be*, but before nouns.
*The food at the market **is good** and cheap.*
*I usually have a **big lunch**.*
Put frequency adverbs after *be*, but before other verbs.
*The park **is always** quiet at 7.30.*
*I **never eat** breakfast.*

4 Put the words in the correct order to make sentences. Use capital letters and full stops.
  1 eat / we / at 12 o'clock / lunch
     At 12 o'clock, we eat lunch./We eat lunch at 12 o'clock.
  2 often / I / drink / tea
  3 have got / parents / kitchen / my / big / a
  4 Sundays / lunch / café / at / I / sometimes / have / a / on
  5 we / eat / breakfast / usually / a / small
  6 always / on Saturdays / children / my / busy / are
  7 at 8 a.m. / breakfast / have / we / usually

5 a Correct the mistake in each sentence.
  a I have at 1 o'clock lunch.
  b I get up at 9 o'clock and have a breakfast big.
  c study Spanish after dinner and go to bed at 10.30.
  d I dinner at 6 o'clock.
  e I usually eat bread, fish and eggs, and tea I drink.
  f I get up early on Sundays never. 1
  g I have often meat and salad for dinner.
  h After breakfast, watch TV in the living room.
  i After lunch, I in the park walk.
  j I sometimes cheese sandwiches for lunch.

  b Put sentences a–j in the correct order to make a blog post.

Prepare

6 Make notes about food and drink in your country. What do you usually eat? When?

Write

7 a Read the message in Exercise 1 again. Answer Jess's message about your country.
  b Work in pairs. Read and check your partner's message to Jess. Is the word order correct?

6A Develop your writing

> **Goal:** write about a daily routine
> **Focus:** using time expressions

1 Read the blog post and look at photos A–D. Which person is Monica?

Daniel's blog

My grandmother Monica is 79, but she's not old. Every day she gets up at 6 o'clock. She goes to the swimming pool and swims for an hour. In the afternoon she meets her friends. They drink tea and play games. She cooks every day. She's a really good cook. She goes to bed at 9 o'clock. She says it's good to go to bed early.

2 Complete the table with Monica's routine.

Time	Action	
6 a.m.	She gets up.	
	1	for an hour.
In the afternoon	2	
	3	every day.
	4	at 9 o'clock.

3 Read the Focus box. Underline the time expressions and circle the commas (,).

Using time expressions

- At the start of a sentence:
At seven, I take the bus to the hospital.
At the weekend, I get up late.
On Sundays, I study.
- At the end of a sentence:
I get up **at 6 o'clock**.
I work **every day**.
I watch TV **in the evening**.

Many time expressions use *in*, *at* or *on*:
on Mondays   in the evening   at 4 o'clock

4 Complete the table with the words in the box. Use Exercise 1 to help you.

Tuesdays   9 o'clock   the weekend   the morning
the afternoon   six thirty   night

in	on	at

5 Make sentences using the prompts and *in*, *on* or *at*.
1 Tuesdays / she / works / at home
2 He / has / dinner / 8 o'clock
3 Her bus / arrive / at the office / 9 o'clock
4 She / study / Spanish / Wednesdays
5 He / drinks / three cups of coffee / the morning
6 They / go / to the cinema / the weekend

6 Look at the table. Write about Harry's routine.
Harry gets up at 1 o'clock in the afternoon. He …

Time	Action
13.00	get up
14.00	have breakfast
15.00	study French
17.00	eat lunch
18.00	start work at the restaurant
02.00	finish work, eat a sandwich
03.00	go to bed

Prepare

7 Make notes about the routine of a person you know.
grandfather / Luc / drive / two hours / every day

Write

8 a Write a blog post about the routine of the person in Exercise 7.

b Work in pairs. Check your partner's blog post. Are the time expressions and the commas correct?

101

6B Develop your listening

> **Goal:** understand short conversations
>
> **Focus:** linking between words

1 a Look at the photo. What's on the table?

b 🔊 6.8 Listen and complete the conversation.

Matt: Hi, Lukas. Would you like a ¹_____ tea?
Lukas: Yes, please.
Matt: Hmm. Where's the milk?
Lukas: ²_____ the table.
Matt: Ah! Thanks. Would you like ³_____ sandwich?
Lukas: No, thank you. So, er, how often do you clean the kitchen?
Matt: Hmm. We sometimes ⁴_____. Maybe once a week.
Lukas: Really?

2 a 🔊 6.9 Read the Focus box. Listen to the example sentences and underline the linking sounds in the fourth example.

Linking between words

Words that end in a consonant sound link with words that start with a vowel sound.

Would you like a cup of tea?
It's on the table.
Would you like an egg sandwich?
We sometimes clean it.

---

b Listen again and repeat the sentences.

3 a Underline the linking sounds.
1 Wash our cups.
2 It's on the chair.
3 An old car.
4 We often get up late.
5 A cup of coffee, please.
6 He's got a ticket.

b 🔊 6.10 Listen and check your answers. Then listen again and repeat.

4 a 🔊 6.11 Listen and write the words you hear.

b Listen again and repeat.

5 a Work in pairs. Say the phrases. Link the sounds.
1 this it
2 not a
3 cheese or
4 like a
5 it's a
6 milk and
7 like a cup of
8 is it on
9 they're on

b 🔊 6.12 Listen to two conversations. Do you hear the phrases in conversation 1 or 2?
1 this it ___1___
2 not a _____
3 like a _____
4 cheese or _____
5 it's a _____
6 like a cup of _____
7 milk and _____
8 is it on _____
9 they're on _____

c Listen again. Are the sentences true (T) or false (F)?
1 Anya's bag is red.
2 It's on a chair.
3 They have three types of sandwich.
4 The man wants a cup of tea.
5 The milk and sugar are on the table.

6c Develop your reading

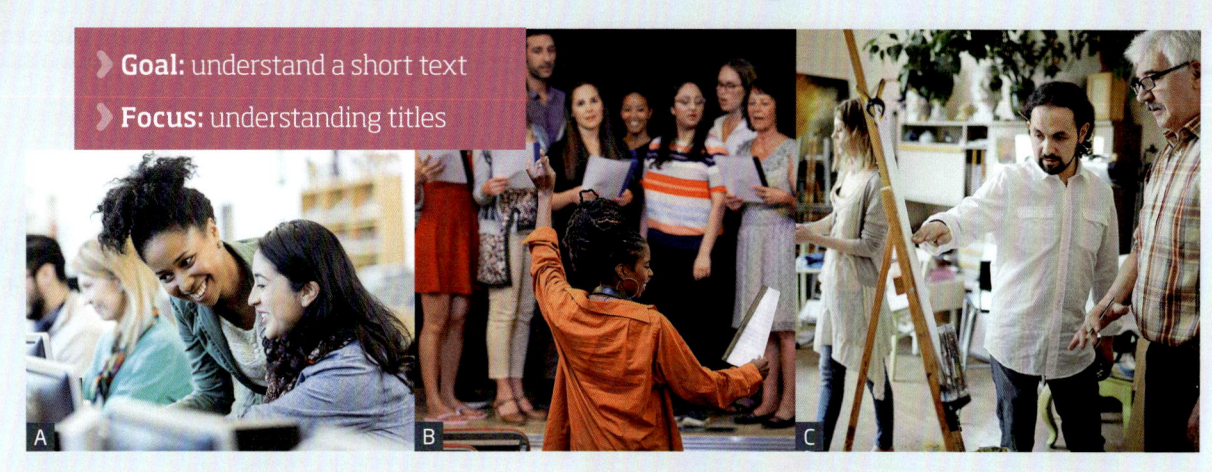

> **Goal:** understand a short text
> **Focus:** understanding titles

1 a Match photos A–C with texts 1–3.

1 **Singing Lessons**
Can't sing? We can teach you. Lessons on Wednesdays and Thursdays at 7 o'clock.

2 **Drawing Lessons**
Learn how to draw. Classes on Mondays at 3.30 at the university. We usually draw in the classroom, but we sometimes go to the park.

3 **Website Building Lessons**
Your teacher is Sandra James. She builds websites for companies. Tuesdays at 8 o'clock.

b Read the texts and answer the questions.
1 Who teaches about websites?
2 Where are the drawing lessons?
3 When are the singing lessons?

2 Read the Focus box. Underline the titles in Exercise 1a.

Understanding titles

A **title** tells us the topic of a text.
Make Italian Food — title
Greg Sumner can teach you to make great pasta and more! Lessons at the university on Wednesdays at 6 o'clock.
Use titles to help you to understand texts.

3 Match titles 1–6 with topics a–f.
1 Spain, Thailand and Turkey
2 New Oven for your Kitchen
3 Office Worker or Football Player?
4 Trains, Buses and Boats
5 Sandwiches, Pasta and Cakes
6 Parents and Children

a Countries d Family
b Travel   e Jobs
c Food   f Houses

4 Read the texts and complete them with the titles in the box.

Bike Club   Cinema Club
Make a Cake   Spanish Lessons

1 _____
Cook and then eat! Lessons on Sundays at 11 o'clock.

2 _____
Learn a second language. Your teacher is José from Madrid.

3 _____
Watch films with us every weekend. Meet on Saturdays at 7 o'clock.

4 _____
Meet us in the park on Sundays at 9 o'clock in the morning. Cycle with new friends.

5 Read the texts and answer the questions. Use the titles to help you find the correct text.

Help with the School Show
Can you make clothes? Can you take photos? Please help us! Call Dorota on 0344-555-3829.

The Office Shop
Buy desks, chairs, pens and things for work. Turn left at the bank.

Students Sport Club
Play football or tennis with us and be healthy! Saturday afternoons at the park.

Jobs at the Café
Can you make good coffee? Work with us on Saturdays and Sundays. Students OK.

1 When can students play sports?
2 Where can you buy a new desk?
3 When can you work at the café?
4 Who can you speak to about the school show?

7A Develop your writing

> **Goal:** write directions
> **Focus:** using sequence adverbs

1 How do you get to the sea? Look at the pictures and put sentences a–e in the correct order.

Directions to the sea

a After that, go past the field.
b Finally, turn right.
c Then, turn left.
d First, leave the hotel.
e Next, walk next to the river.

2 Read the Focus box. Circle the sequence adverbs in Exercise 1.

Using sequence adverbs

Use sequence adverbs to show the order you do something:

First, leave the hotel.
Then/Next/After that, turn left.
Then/Next/After that, walk next to the river.
Then/Next/After that, go past the field.
Finally, turn right.

3 Complete the directions to the park with sequence adverbs.
1 _____ , go out of the station.
2 _____ , turn right.
3 _____ , go straight on.
4 _____ , go past the hotel.
5 _____ , turn left at the bank. The park is on the left.

4 Put the words in the correct order to make directions.
1 take / to the station / a bus / First,
2 a train / take / Then, / to Liverpool
3 to Pier Head / After that, / take / a taxi
4 Next, / to Douglas / take / a boat
5 walk / Finally, / to the hotel

Prepare

5 Look at the map. Draw a route from the hotel to the train station.

Write

6 a Write directions for the route in Exercise 5. Use sequence adverbs.

How to get to the train station
1 _____
2 _____
3 _____
4 _____
5 _____

b Work in pairs. Check your partner's directions.

7B Develop your listening

> **Goal:** understand a short conversation about events
>
> **Focus:** understanding present and past

1 Match photos A–C with the words in the box.

| a meal   a meeting   a party |

2 🔊 7.9 Listen to speakers 1–4. What do they talk about? Choose the correct option, a–c.
1 a a party   b a meeting   c a meal
2 a a party   b a meeting   c a meal
3 a a party   b a meeting   c a meal
4 a a party   b a meeting   c a meal

3 Read the Focus box. Then listen again. Which of events 1–4 are in the past?

Understanding present and past

- Listen for the verb *be*:
He**'s** very happy.   He **was** very happy.
- Listen for time expressions:
Present
We **usually** have a party.
We **often** meet at a restaurant.
We go there **every day**.
Past
Last month, there was a nice party. The party was **yesterday/last week/last month/last year**.
The meeting was on **10th April**.

---

4 What type of word completes the sentences, the verb *be* (B) or a time expression (T)?
1 There _B_ a family lunch _T_ .
2 ___ , there ___ a big meeting in the office.
3 ___ there a party in the office ___ ?
4 There ___ a street party in my town ___ .
5 ___ there a meeting ___ ?
6 There ___ a birthday party for John ___ .
7 ___ , I ___ at a meeting with Tanya.
8 Sophie's birthday ___ in March. There's ___ a big party.

5 🔊 7.10 Listen and complete the sentences.
1 There _____ a family lunch _____ .
2 _____ , there _____ a big meeting in the office.
3 _____ there a party in the office _____ ?
4 There _____ a street party in my town _____ .
5 _____ there a meeting _____ ?
6 There _____ a birthday party for John _____ .
7 _____ , I _____ at a meeting with Tanya.
8 Sophie's birthday _____ in March. There's _____ a big party.

6 a 🔊 7.11 Listen to a conversation. What is the situation, a or b?
a mother and son talking at home
b work friends talking in a café

b Listen again and complete the table.

	usually happens	was in the past
1 work party		✓
2 bad weather		
3 birthday party in a restaurant		
4 birthday party at home		
5 office meeting		
6 Tony not at the meeting		

7C Develop your reading

› **Goal:** understand short texts
› **Focus:** finding dates, times and place names

1 Match photos A–C with texts 1–3.

1
Dance show
6th June
City High School
14.00 to 16.00

2
Cooking class
08/07/21 @ 3 p.m.
Red River Restaurant

3
Football game
Milltown sports park
Sun 9th June
1 o'clock

2 a Read the Focus box. How can you find a place name in a text?

> **Finding dates, times and place names**
> Look quickly to find dates, times and places in a text. Look for numbers and capital letters.
> • Dates
> *2/3/2021   5th August*
> • Times
> *7 o'clock*
> *4.30 p.m.* Use *p.m.* after 12 o'clock in the day.
> *6 a.m.* Use *a.m.* before 12 o'clock in the day.
> • Place names
> *The City Hotel   Paris*

b Read the texts in Exercise 1 again and complete the table.

Event	Date	Time	Place name
1 Dance show			
2 Cooking class			
3 Football game			

3 Read the information and tick the correct boxes.

	Date	Time	Place name
1 Chocolate Café			
2 6th August			
3 York			
4 3 o'clock			
5 Rome			
6 12.30			

4 a Read the messages. Underline the dates, circle the times and draw a box around the place names.

• **Mountain walk**
Come with us and walk up the mountain on Sun 9th October. Meet in the Mountain Café at 8 o'clock.

• **Horse riding**
Learn to ride a horse at River Park on 08/10/21. We are open from 11 a.m. to 4 p.m.

• **International food market**
Eat food from all over the world. South Park, Sat 1st Oct. 10.00–15.00.

• **Photo show**
See beautiful photos of rivers, lakes and hills in India by R Greenwood. City Hotel, 15/10/21 from 10 to 6.

b Read the messages again and answer the questions.
1 When does the horse riding start?
2 Where is the photo show?
3 What date is the international food market?
4 Where does the mountain walk start?

106

8A Develop your reading

› **Goal:** understand a short story
› **Focus:** understanding *a/an* and *the*

1 Read the first part of a story and look at photos 1 and 2. Which animal is the story about?

When I was young, I had a dog. His name was Snowy. The dog loved me and I loved my dog.

I lived in a small town. I didn't have any friends in the town. Well, I had one friend, Snowy. After school, I usually walked to a hill near my house and Snowy walked with me. I had a kite. It was red, yellow and blue. We watched the kite in the blue sky.

2 Read the story again. Put photos A–C in the order the writer talks about them.

3 Read the Focus box. Underline *a/an* and *the* in the text in Exercise 1.

Understanding *a/an* and *the*

Use *a/an* the first time you talk about something:
a + (consonant)
I watched **a** cat in my garden.
an + (vowel, *a e i o u*)
I watched **an** old cat in my garden.
Use *the* the second time you talk about something:
I watched **a** cat in the park. **The** cat was grey and white.

4 Put the next part of the story in the correct order.
  a The town's name was Holfur, and it had a great beach.
  b He played on the beach and I listened to the sea.
  c At the weekend, we often travelled to a town near the sea with my parents.
  d When we arrived in Holfur, Snowy was always so happy.

5 Read the final part of the story. Are the sentences true (T) or false (F)?

When I was 19, I travelled to a big city to study at university. Snowy stayed with my parents. When I came home for the holidays, Snowy was always happy to see me, and we walked to the hill with the kite.

Now, I sometimes go back to the small town. Snowy isn't there now, but I always walk to the hill with my son and the same red, yellow and blue kite.

  1 The writer studied at university in the small town.
  2 Snowy travelled to the big city with the writer.
  3 The writer saw Snowy when he went home.
  4 Snowy lives in the small town now.
  5 The writer has got a boy.

6 Do you likes dogs or other animals? Which ones?

8B Develop your writing

> **Goal:** write a description of your last birthday
>
> **Focus:** planning your writing

1 Look at the pictures and answer the questions.
1. What day is it?
2. Where are the people?
3. What do you usually do on this day?

2 Match the text with the correct picture, A–D, in Exercise 1.

What was your last birthday like?
Kerry Cantona

My birthday was last Saturday. In the morning, my friends took me to a small island by boat. It was really beautiful and I was very happy! We played games and then in the afternoon we cooked fish and ate it on the beach. Later, we all felt really bad – the fish wasn't good. We went back to our town. We went to the shops and we bought medicine. I felt really sad. It was a bad birthday!

3 Read the Focus box. Underline the time expressions in the text in Exercise 2.

Planning your writing
Before you write a description of an event in the past, think about your answers to these questions:
- **What** was the event?
- **When** was it?
- **Where** was it?
- **Who** was there?
- **What** happened?
- **Why** was the event good/bad?
- **How** did people feel after the event?

Use time expressions and sequence adverbs to help describe the story:
In the morning, we took a train to Morocco.
Then, we walked in the park.
After lunch, we sang songs.

4 Read the text in Exercise 2 again and answer the questions.
1. What was the event? *Kerry's birthday*
2. When was it?
3. Where was it?
4. Who was there?
5. What happened?
6. Why was the event good/bad?
7. How did Kerry feel after the event?

Prepare

5 a You're going to write a description of your last birthday. Answer the questions and make notes. The details can be real or imagined.
- When was it?
- Where was it?
- Who was there?
- What happened?
- Why was the event good/bad?
- How did people feel after the event?

b What happened at different times of the day? Complete the timeline. Use the past simple.

got up
|—————|—————|—————|
8.30
in the morning   in the afternoon   in the evening

Write

6 a Write your description of your last birthday.

b Check your description carefully.
- Have you answered all the questions in the Focus box?
- Are the past simple verbs correct?
- Are the time expressions correct?

8c Develop your listening

> **Goal:** understand directions
> **Focus:** listening for sequence adverbs

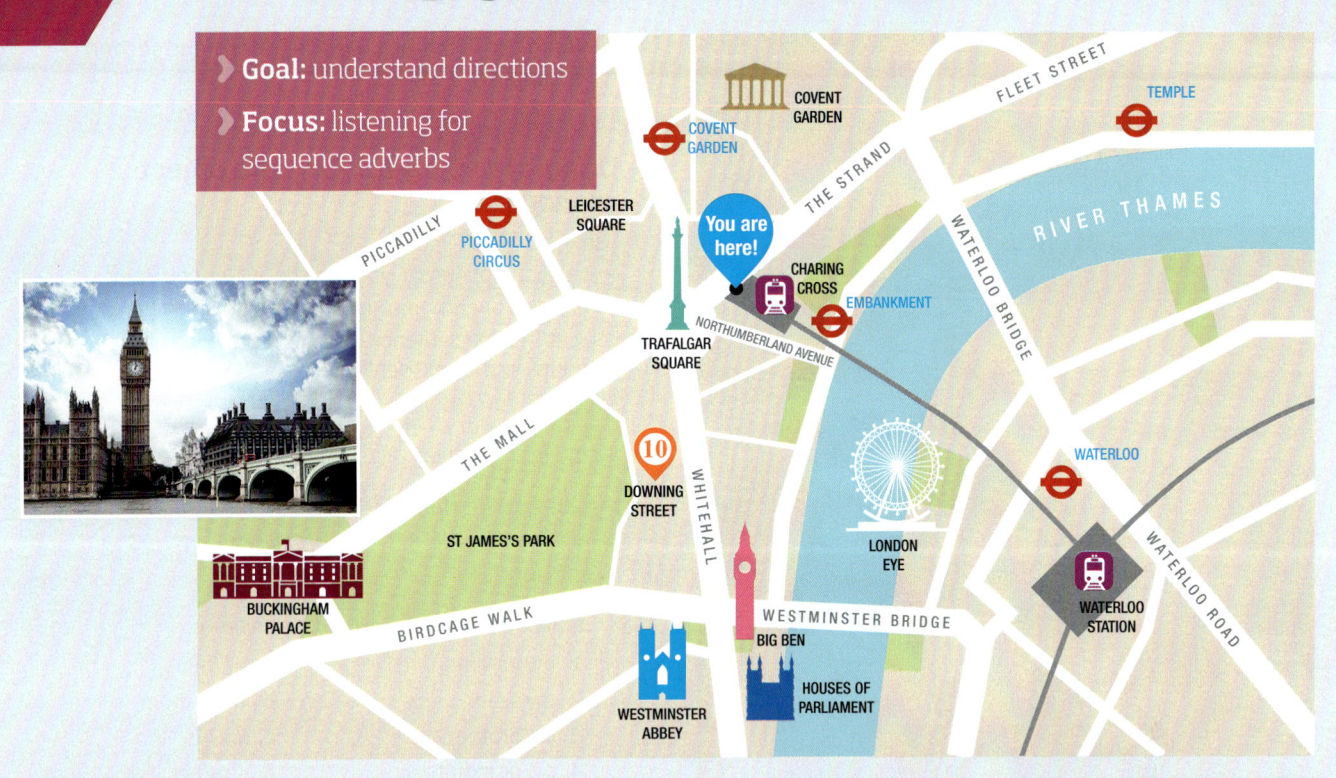

1 a Look at the map and the photo. What city is it? What can you see?

 b 8.11 Listen and put directions a–e in the correct order.
   a Finally, go straight on and you can see it.
   b After that, turn right at the river.
   c First, go out of Charing Cross Station.
   d Next, turn left onto The Strand.
   e Then, turn left again onto Northumberland Avenue.

 c Draw the route on the map in Exercise 1a. What is at the end of the route?

2 a Read the Focus box and underline the sequence adverbs.

Listening for sequence adverbs
Speakers use sequence adverbs to show the order of directions.
First, | *go out of Charing Cross Station.* | *Next,* | *turn left onto The Strand.* | *Then,* | *turn left again onto Northumberland Avenue.* | *After that,* | *turn right at the river.* | *Finally,* | *go straight on and you can see it.*

 b Listen again and repeat the directions.

3 a 8.12 Listen and complete the sentences with the correct sequence adverbs.
   1 _____ , go out of the station and turn right.
   2 _____ , walk down Summer Street.
   3 _____ , turn left at the hotel.
   4 _____ , walk past the bookshop.
   5 _____ , turn right at the supermarket.

 b Listen again and repeat.

4 8.13 Listen and put pictures A–E in the correct order.

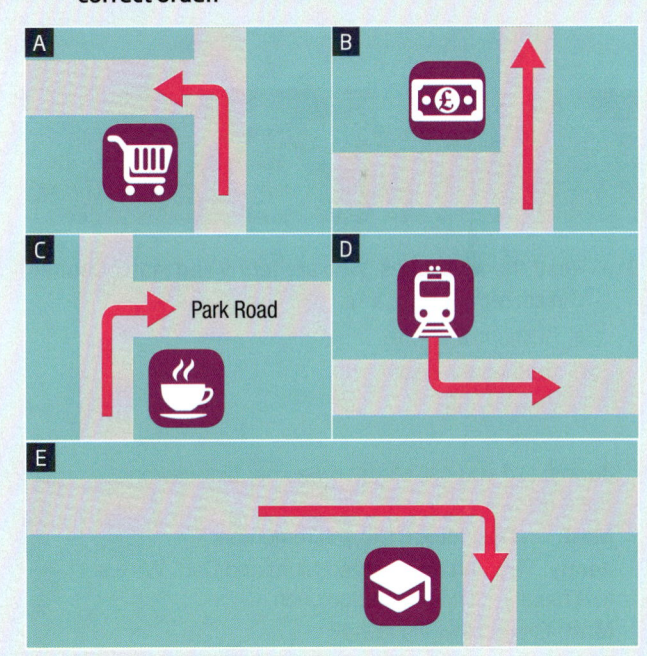

5 8.14 Listen and draw the route on the map.

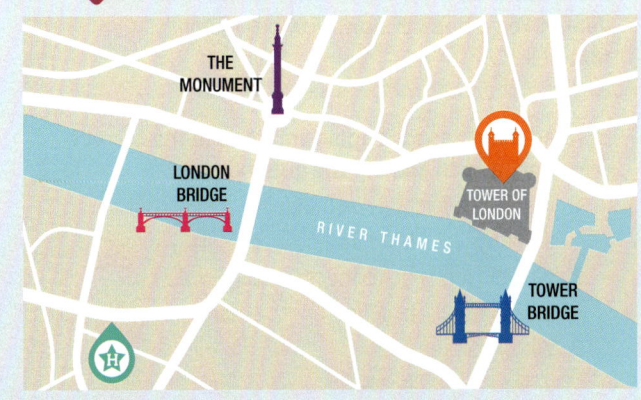

9A Develop your reading

> **Goal:** understand short messages
>
> **Focus:** understanding subject and object pronouns

1 a Read the messages. Who are Jenny and Matt? Choose the correct option, a–c.

   a husband and wife
   b brother and sister
   c mother and son

Jenny: Did you call Mum? It was her birthday on Sunday.
Matt: Oh no! I forgot! Did you remember?
Jenny: Yes, Jan and I visited Mum and Dad. We went to a restaurant with them for lunch.
Matt: Great! How was Dad?
Jenny: He was fine. He's busy at work, as always.
Matt: Yes. I saw him last month. He was really tired.
Jenny: Yeah, he's OK now. Now call Mum!
Matt: OK!

---

b Read the messages again and choose the correct option, a–c, to answer the questions.

1 Who had a birthday on Sunday?
   a Jenny   b Mum   c Matt
2 Who did Jenny go to the restaurant with?
   a Jan   b Mum   c Jan, Mum and Dad
3 Who was tired?
   a Dad   b Matt   c Jan

2 Read the Focus box. Who is *them* in the second example?

Understanding subject and object pronouns

Use
- subject pronouns: *I, you, he, she, it, we, you, they*
- object pronouns: *me, you, him, her, it, us, them*

Look at the first sentence to find the meaning of the pronouns in the next sentences.

Jenny: Did you call **Mum**? It was **her** birthday on Sunday.
Jenny: Yes, **Jan and I** visited Mum and Dad. **We** went to a restaurant with **them** for lunch.
Matt: How was **Dad**? … I saw **him** last month.

---

3 Match nouns 1–5 with pronouns a–e.

1 my parents   a he/him
2 my sister   b they/them
3 my brother and I   c we/us
4 my grandfather   d she/her
5 our house   e it

4 Read the sentences. Circle the meaning of the underlined object pronouns.

1 My parents live in Scotland. I call <u>them</u> every week.
2 I live with my grandmother. A nurse often visits <u>her</u>.
3 My husband and I bought a new flat. Please visit <u>us</u>.
4 I often talk to Tom. I had lunch with <u>him</u> last week.
5 This is a beautiful picture. Did you draw <u>it</u>?
6 Where's my bag? I know! <u>It</u>'s behind the chair.

5 Read the messages and answer the questions.

1 Who went to a restaurant?
2 What was OK?
3 Who bought the clothes?

Vanessa: Hey! Did you have a good weekend?
Fernando: Yeah. Martin and I went to the cinema. Then we met Jack and Mila and we went to a nice restaurant with them near the park. 🍔
Vanessa: Sounds great. What did you see at the cinema?
Fernando: *A Weekend in Tokyo*.
Vanessa: Was it good?
Fernando: It was OK.
Vanessa: And the restaurant?
Fernando: We had Thai food. It was really good. How was your weekend?
Vanessa: Great. I went shopping with my mum.
Fernando: Oh yeah?
Vanessa: Yeah, we went to Marco's and she bought me some clothes! 😄
Fernando: Great! What did you get?
Vanessa: A new coat and a bag.
Fernando: Wow!

9B Develop your listening

> **Goal:** understand people's feelings
>
> **Focus:** listening for how people feel

1 Match photos A–F with the activities in the box.

listen to music   play basketball   play video games
read a book   use the internet   watch a film

2 🔊 9.8 Listen to three conversations. Which activities in Exercise 1 do the speakers talk about?

3 Read the Focus box then listen to the conversations in Exercise 2 again. How do the people feel about each activity, interested or not interested?

Listening for how people feel

Speakers often use a rise-fall [⌒] intonation to show they're interested or excited.

A: I bought them for £10 on the internet!
B: Really? That's gʳᵉᵃᵗ!

A: My friend was in that film.
B: Oh, wᵒʷ!

---

4 a 🔊 9.9 Listen and choose the speakers that sound interested/excited, a or b.

1 That was great.   a / b
2 Oh, really?   a / b
3 Wow.   a / b
4 Oh, yeah.   a / b
5 That's amazing.   a / b
6 It's great.   a / b

b 🔊 9.10 Listen to the interested/excited answers again and repeat.

5 a 🔊 9.11 Listen and tick the conversations where the speakers sound interested/excited.

1 **A:** Hey! Do you want to do some exercise later?
   B: Yes, OK.
2 **A:** Oh, listen! This is my brother's song on the radio.
   B: Really? That's amazing.
3 **A:** I watched a film about Taylor Swift last night.
   B: Wow.
4 **A:** I saw Tom in a police car this morning.
   B: Oh, really?
5 **A:** Look – I cleaned the kitchen and the bathroom.
   B: Oh, yeah.

b Work in pairs. Roleplay the conversations. Practise using your voice to show how you feel.

9c Develop your writing

› **Goal:** write a short text
› **Focus:** using *because*

1 Read speech bubbles 1–4 and match them with photos A–D.

Why do you study English?

1 I study English because I like watching films. I love going to the cinema and I love watching American films.

2 I study English because I like listening to music. I like British music and I like singing the songs.

3 I study English because I have got a British friend. I met Tom in the UK and I often email him.

4 I study English because I use it for my job at the café. I sometimes speak English because people in the café can't always speak Spanish.

2 Read the Focus box and underline the reasons in the speech bubbles in Exercise 1.

Using *because*

Use *because* to give a reason for something.
A: Why do you study English?
B: I study English **because** <u>I like watching American films</u>.
　　　　　　　　　　　　　　　　　　　　　　　reason
A: Why did you buy a dictionary?
B: I bought a dictionary **because** <u>I like learning new words</u>.
　　　　　　　　　　　　　　　　　　　　　　　reason

3 Complete the sentences using *because* and the phrases in the box.

> I forgot　　I got up late　　it is quiet
> I use my computer　　it was difficult
> she speaks very fast

1 I do my homework in the library _____.
2 I failed the exam _____.
3 I didn't do my homework _____.
4 I don't have a notebook _____.
5 I didn't have breakfast _____.
6 I don't understand her _____.

4 Choose *like* or *don't like* and complete the sentences so that they are true for you.

1 I like / (don't like) travelling because *it is expensive* .
2 I like / don't like winter because _____.
3 I like / don't like taking the bus because _____.
4 I like / don't like dancing because _____.
5 I like / don't like eating cake because _____.
6 I like / don't like studying English because _____.

Prepare

5 Why do you study English? Think of some reasons and make notes.
　　I study English because I use it for work.

Write

6 a Write a short text about why you study English. Write about three different reasons.

b Work in pairs. Check your partner's text.

10A Develop your reading

> **Goal:** understand a short article
> **Focus:** understanding paragraphs

1 Read the text. Match the writer's goals (1–3) with photos A–C.

My goals for next year
1. I would love to change my job next year. I work in an office now and it's OK, but I would like to do something different. I'd like to work at a hotel.
2. I would like to learn how to dance. I love watching dancing on TV, but I can't dance. I would love to take lessons.
3. I would love to spend more time with my family, because I was really busy last year. I'd like to meet my parents every month and have dinner together.

2 Read the Focus box. Complete the third label with the correct topic.

Understanding paragraphs
Writers use a new paragraph for a new topic. The first sentence in a paragraph often tells you the topic.

My goals for next year
I would love to change my job next year. I work in an office now and it's OK, but I would like to do something different. I'd like to work at a hotel. Paragraph 1: jobs
I would like to learn how to dance. I love watching dancing on TV, but I can't dance. I would love to take lessons. Paragraph 2: dancing
I would love to spend more time with my family, because I was really busy last year. I'd like to meet my parents every month and have dinner together.
Paragraph 3: _____

3 Read the text. Match the writer's goals (1–3) with paragraph topics a–f. There are three extra topics you don't need.

My goals for next year
1. I'd like to study a language. I'd love to learn Turkish, because I often go to Turkey for work.
2. I'd love to cycle to work every day because I am not very healthy. I never do any exercise.
3. I'd like to go to the US. I'd love to go to New York and watch a play.

a cycling   d travel
b work   e plays
c food   f learning

4 a Read the text. Circle the words that tell you the topic of each paragraph.

My goals for next year
I would love to start a new sport next year. At school, I played football. I don't play now because there isn't a team near my home, but I'd like to be healthy. I'd like to start swimming.
I would like to move to a new house. I like my flat, but it is very small. I've got a lot of books and a lot of clothes. And I'd like to live near the station.
I would love to start an online business. I make bags and I sell them at the market, but I'd like to sell them on a website. I'd like to take photographs of my bags and make an online shop.

b Read the questions. Then find the correct paragraph in the text and answer the questions.
1. Would the writer like to live in a house or a flat?
2. Where would the writer like to sell bags?
3. What sport would the writer like to start?

10B Develop your listening

> **Goal:** understand a conversation about plans
>
> **Focus:** checking information and showing understanding

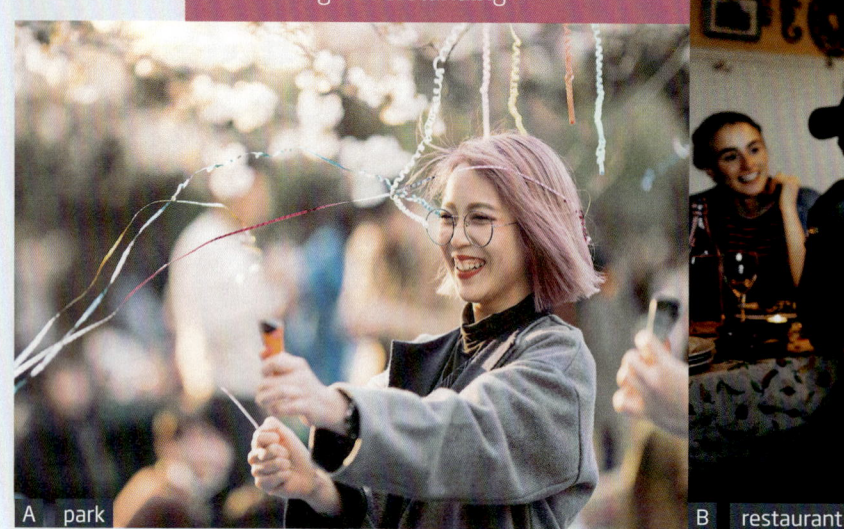

A park
B restaurant
C house

1 Work in pairs. Look at the photos. Which places are good for parties? Why?

Parks are a good place for parties because you can play games and sports.

2 a 🔊 10.10 Listen to a conversation between friends. Where is the party going to be?

b Listen again. Number the sentences in the order that you hear them.
   a Sorry, was that the 25th, Michael?
   b Great.
   c West Park? Not North Park?
   d OK, West Park, yes.
   e Sorry, did you say Gavin is going to bring snacks?

c Listen again. How do Ellie and Michael use the phrases in Exercise 2b? Write *1* or *2*.
   1 to show they understand
   2 to check information

3 Read and complete the Focus box with the phrases in the box.

   | Great.   The 25th?   Right. |

Checking information and showing understanding

Checking information
Sorry, was that the 25th?
Did you say the 25th or the 27th?
1 _____

Showing understanding
The 25th, OK.
Uh huh.
2 _____
3 _____

4 a 🔊 10.11 Listen to four conversations. Does the second speaker check the information or show understanding? Choose the correct alternatives.
   1 check / show understanding
   2 check / show understanding
   3 check / show understanding
   4 check / show understanding

b Listen again. Write the phrases the speaker uses to check information or show understanding.
   1 Right

5 🔊 10.12 Listen to a conversation and answer the questions.
   1 Where is the party?
   2 When is the party?
   3 Who is going to be there?

10c Develop your writing

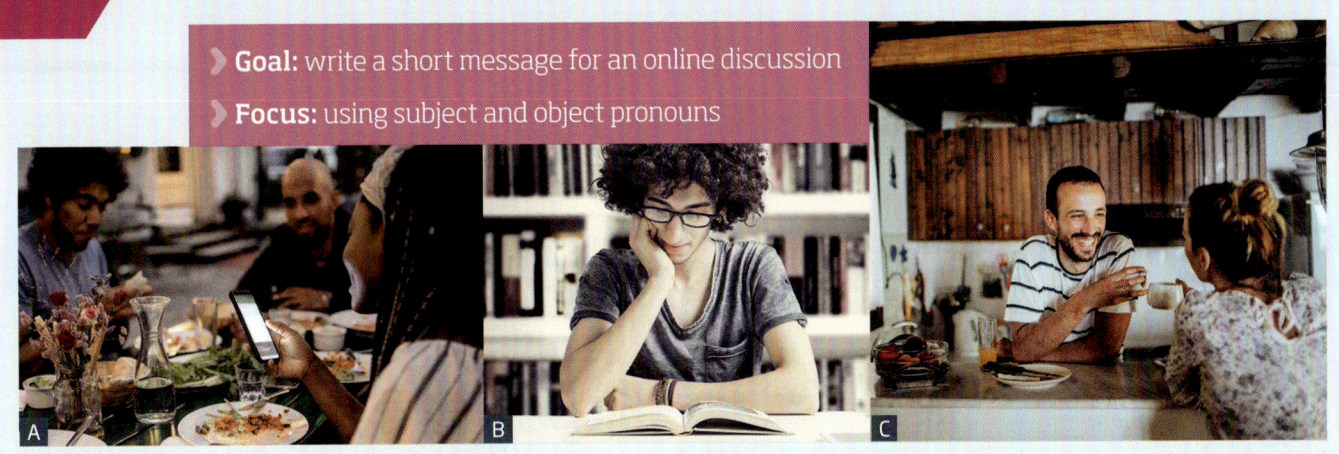

› **Goal:** write a short message for an online discussion
› **Focus:** using subject and object pronouns

A   B   C

1 Look at the photos. Where are the people?
2 Read the messages and answer the questions.
  1 Who is going to have a meal?
  2 Who is going to go to the library?
  3 Who is going to meet his sister?

Weekend plans?

Raquel
Hi, everyone.
What are your weekend plans?
I'm going to have dinner with Mike and Sam. They're old friends and I really like them.

Victor
I'm going to visit my sister. She lives in Wales with her husband. They bought a new house and I'm going to see it for the first time.

Josh
I'm going to study in the library, because I've got an exam on Monday. ☹

---

3 Read the Focus box. Complete 1–3 with the correct pronouns.

Using subject and object pronouns

Don't write the same names a lot. Use
- subject pronouns: *I, you, he, she, it, we, you, they.*
- object pronouns: *me, you, him, her, it, us, them.*

I'm going to have dinner with Mike and Sam. ~~Mike and Sam~~ **They**'re old friends and I really like ~~Mike and Sam~~ **them**.
I'm going to visit my sister. ~~My sister~~ ¹_____ lives in Wales with her husband. ~~My sister and her husband~~ ²_____ bought a new house and I'm going to see ~~the new house~~ ³_____ for the first time.

4 Choose the correct alternatives.
  1 My friend and I went to the cinema. *We / I / He* saw a good film.
  2 I don't often see my parents. *We / I / They* live in Canada, but I live in the UK.
  3 My friend Rosa doesn't like Japanese food, but *she loves / it loves / we love* Thai food.
  4 I took the train to my grandfather's house last week. *He lives / It lives / We live* in Liverpool.

5 Complete the sentences with the correct object pronouns.
  1 I met my brother in the morning and took _____ to the countryside.
  2 My sister and I love going to see my grandma. We often go to the beach with _____ .
  3 I'm going to go shopping with my friends. I'm going to meet _____ at the train station.
  4 My brother plays games with _____ online. We love video games.

6 Complete the text with the correct pronouns.

My family and I are going to go shopping on Saturday morning. ¹_____ are going to buy food for the evening. Our friends are going to have dinner with ²_____ . My mother is going to make Spanish food. ³_____ is very good at cooking. Our friends are going to arrive at 7 o'clock. ⁴_____ live in Italy and we don't see ⁵_____ very often.

Prepare

7 Complete the table with notes about your weekend plans.

Saturday	Sunday

Write

8 a Write a message for an online discussion about your weekend plans.
  b Work in pairs. Check your partner's text.

115

Grammar bank

GRAMMAR

1A be: *I* and *you*

+	I'm Juan. I'm a university teacher. You're on time.		
?	Am I late?	+	Yes, you are.
		-	No, you aren't.
?	Are you a teacher? Are you from Spain?	+	Yes, I am.
		-	No, I'm not.

with *Where*

Where are you from?	I'm from Mexico.

Short forms

I'm = I am	you're = you are	aren't = are not

Word order

+   I'm on time.   subject (*I/you*) + *be*

?   Am I on time?   *be* + subject (*I/you*)

Use

- subject (*I/you*) + *be*: *I'm from Rome.* NOT *Am from Rome.*
- *be* with names: *I'm Mikel.*
- *be* for where a person is from: *Where are you from? I'm from Segovia, in Spain.*
- short answers with *yes/no* questions: *Are you Angela Hamilton? Yes, I am.*
- short forms in conversation: *Hi, Sally. Sorry I'm late.*

Don't use

- short forms in positive short answers: *Are you in Class 5? Yes, I am.* NOT *Yes, I'm.*

1B be: *he/she/it*

+	-
He's a nurse.	He isn't from the UK.
She's a doctor.	She isn't from Canada.
It's a small hospital.	It isn't a big hospital.

?	+	-
Is he from the UK?	Yes, he is.	No, he isn't.
Is she a doctor?	Yes, she is.	No, she isn't.
Is it in London?	Yes, it is.	No, it isn't.

with *Where*

Where's she from?	She's from Spain.

Short forms

he's = he is	it's = it is
she's = she is	isn't = is not

Word order

+   She's a doctor.   subject (*he/she/it*) + *be*

?   Is she a doctor?   *be* + subject (*he/she/it*)

Use

- subject (*he/she/it*) + *be*: *She's nice.* NOT *Is nice.*
- *he* for ♂, *she* for ♀ and *it* for things.
- *be* + *a/an* for jobs: *He's an office worker.*
- short answers with *yes/no* questions: *Are you a teacher? Yes, I am.*
- *be* to describe people and things: *She's a doctor. The school is small.*
- short forms in conversation: *Mark isn't from New York.*

Don't use

- short forms in positive short answers: *Is he a student? Yes, he is.* NOT *Yes, he's.*

1C be: *you/we/they*

+	-
You're British.	You aren't American.
We're office workers.	We aren't football players.
They're nurses.	They aren't doctors.

?	+	-
Are you British?	Yes, we are.	No, we aren't.
Are we a good team?	Yes, you are.	No, you aren't.
Are they in the UK?	Yes, they are.	No, they aren't.

with *Who*

Who are they?	They're my friends.

Short forms

we're = we are	they're = they are

Word order

+   They're friends.   subject (*you/we/they*) + *be*

?   Are they friends?   *be* + subject (*you/we/they*)

Use

- *we* and *you* for ♂ and ♀.
- *you* for 1 and 2+ people.
- *they* for ♂, ♀ and things.
- short answers with *yes/no* questions: *Are you friends? Yes, we are.*
- short forms in conversation: *They aren't from New York.*

Don't use

- short forms in positive short answers: *Are they American? Yes, they are.* NOT *Yes, they're.*

PRACTICE

1A

1 Choose the correct alternatives.
1. *I / I'm* Mike Collins.
2. *Am / I'm* from Izmir, in Turkey.
3. I *not / 'm not* from London.
4. *You / You're* in Class 7.
5. You *aren't / 'm not* late.
6. *You are / Are you* from Japan?
7. Yes, *I'm / I am*.
8. Where *you are / are you* from?

2 Complete the conversation with the words in the box.

Are you	I'm	I'm from	I'm not	Where are you

A: Hello, ¹ _I'm_ Max. Nice to meet you.
B: Nice to meet you, too. I'm Paola.
A: ² _____ from Spain?
B: No, ³ _____ . I'm from Italy.
A: Oh, where in Italy?
B: ⁴ _____ Turin. ⁵ _____ from?
A: Adelaide, in Australia.

1B

1 Complete the conversation. Use short forms where possible.

Maria: ¹ _Is_ Joe from the UK?
Alina: Yes. He ² _____ from Edinburgh.
Maria: Is ³ _____ a student?
Alina: No, he ⁴ _____ . He's a nurse at the hospital.
Maria: Oh, is ⁵ _____ a small hospital?
Alina: No, ⁶ _____ really big.
Maria: And, Joe, ⁷ _____ he nice?
Alina: Yes, ⁸ _____ very nice!

2 Look at the pictures and make sentences using the prompts.
1. nurse / teacher
   He's a nurse. He isn't a teacher.
2. taxi driver / doctor
3. teacher / farmer
4. football player / nurse
5. office worker / pilot

1C

1 Match 1–6 with a–f.
1. Are you and your friend from Spain?
2. Who are Harry and Rachel?
3. Are you and Vicky students?
4. Where are Adam and Lidia from?
5. Are your friends British?
6. Where are your friends?

a. Yes, we are. We're at university in London.
b. They're in class.
c. No, we aren't. We're Argentinian.
d. They're my friends.
e. Lublin, in Poland.
f. No, Mehmet and Meral are Turkish.

2 Make the sentences negative.
1. My friends are American.
   My friends aren't American.
2. We're in Class 6 today.
3. They're from Thailand.
4. Karel and Suki are Polish.
5. Annie and Nick are from the UK.
6. We're in the same class for English.
7. They're from New York.
8. Beth and Simon are at work today.

Want more practice? Go to your Workbook or app.

GRAMMAR

2A Possessive 's, I/my, you/your, etc.

Possessive 's
name + 's *Rafael is Cristina's husband.*
word + 's *My friend's name is Lily.* (= one friend)
word + s' *My friends' class is 3A.* (= more than one friend)

Use
- to show possession: *That's Lyn's dog. Where's Joe's photo?*

I/my, you/your, etc.

I, you, etc.	possessive adjectives
I	my
you	your
he	his
she	her
it	its
we	our
they	their

Use
- *my, your*, etc. + noun: *My office is in Stuttgart.*
- *my, your*, etc. for singular and plural nouns: *our friend, our friends* NOT *ours friends*
- *his* for a ♂: *Tom and his sister*
- *her* for a ♀: *Sue and her dad*
- *its* for things and animals. *That's their dog. Its name's Bella.*
- *its* for possession: *its photo* = the dog's photo, but *it's* for *it is*: *It's from Spain.*

Notice: *'s* can be
- possessive: *Helen's father is a pilot.*
- the short form of *is*: *Helen's a teacher.* (= Helen is a teacher.)

2B *this, that, these* and *those*, plural nouns

this, that, these and those

this key   **that** key 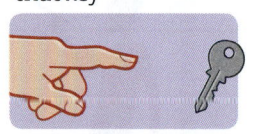
these keys    **those** keys

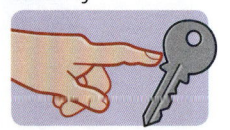

- *this/that* + *is* + singular noun: *This is my computer. That computer is good.*
- *these/those* + *are* + plural noun: *These are my books. Those books are great!*
- *this/that/these/those* + noun: *This photo is nice.*
- *this/that/these/those* - noun: *This is a photo of my family.*
- *this is* with people: *This is my friend, Julia.*

Plural nouns

		singular (1)	plural (2+)
most nouns	+ -s	pen, phone, photo	pens, phones, photos
after -x, -s, -ss	+ -es	address	addresses
nouns ending consonant + -y	-y + -ies	family	families

Use
- *a* with singular nouns: *It's a clock.* NOT *It's clock.*
- *an* before *a, e, i, o, u*: *an office worker*
- *a* before other sounds (*b, c, d, f*, etc.): *a book, a cup*

Don't use
- *a/an* with plural nouns: *They're books.* NOT *They're a books.*

2C Question words with *be*

Question words (e.g. *Who, How, What, Where, When,* etc.) come before the verb *be*.
The verb *be* comes before the subject (e.g. *she, they, their names,* etc.).

Who are you?	I'm your new teacher.
How old is he?	He's 99 years old!
What is her name?	Her name is Anna Chubb.
Where are they from?	They're from Canada.
When is your class?	At 9.30 a.m.

Use
- question words to ask about something: *What's your name? Where are you from?*
- question word + *be* + subject: *How old is she? Who are Jack and Eddie?*

PRACTICE

2A

1 Change the underlined words. Use the words in brackets.
1 Samia is his wife. (Nick) *Samia is Nick's wife.*
2 Ana is her sister. (Raquel)
3 His office is near here. (Peter)
4 That's her school. (my friend)
5 They're his students. (Mike)
6 Eddie is their son. (Fran and Steve)
7 His children are at university. (my brother)
8 Rover is their dog. (my parents)

2 Complete the sentences with the words in the box.

| her | his | its | my | our | their | your (x2) |

1 Hi, I'm Katya. What's _your_ name?
2 We're from Florida. _____ names are Josie and Leo.
3 This is my sister. _____ name's Lin.
4 My dad is a doctor. _____ name's William.
5 These are my friends from Spain. _____ names are Francisco and Julio.
6 I'm Chris and this is _____ brother, Mark.
7 Is this your dog? What's _____ name?
8 Is this a photo of _____ family? They're nice.

2B

1 Correct the underlined words.
1 Is these a photo of your brother? *this*
2 What's in these box?
3 These is my friends from university.
4 That are my books on the table.
5 How do you say this words in English?
6 This are my friend, Jack.
7 Where are those student from?
8 Those aren't my keys. Those are my keys on this table.

2 Look at the pictures and make sentences.
1 _They're cups._
2 _____
3 _____
4 _____
5 _____
6 _____

2C

1 Complete the questions with a question word.
1 _Where_ is your family from?
2 _____ are those people in the meeting room?
3 _____ is your phone number?
4 _____ old are the students in your class?
5 _____ are your mum and dad's names?
6 _____ is my computer? It isn't in my room.
7 _____ old is your sister?
8 _____ is your English class? Is it at 11 a.m.?

2 Match the questions in Exercise 1 with answers a–h.
1 c
a Diana and Tony
b She's 25.
c a small city in Poland
d It's 07700 900614.
e They're my friends from university.
f It's on the table.
g They're 19.
h No, it's at 10 a.m.

Want more practice? Go to your Workbook or app.

GRAMMAR

3A *There is / There are*

	Singular	Plural
+	There's a park. There is a park.	There are three cafés.
-	There isn't a bank.	There aren't any supermarkets. There are no supermarkets.

Use

- *there is/there are* to talk about something for the first time, or say where something is: *There's a train station in my town.* NOT *Is a train station in my town.* *There are three cinemas in the town.* NOT *Are three cinemas in the town.*
- *there's a* + singular noun: *There's a new student in my class. There's a bank in town.*
- *there aren't any* + plural noun: *There aren't any hotels.* (not any = 0)
- *there are no*: *There are no cafés in my town.* (no = 0)
- *there's* with a list: *There's a supermarket, a bookshop, a phone shop and a computer shop.*

3B *Is there a/an …? / Are there any …?*

	Singular	Plural
?	Is there a shower?	Are there any flats?
+	Yes, there is.	Yes, there are.
-	No, there isn't. No, there is not.	No, there aren't. No, there are not.

BUT **Is there** wifi?

with *How many*

How many bedrooms are there?	There is one. There are two.

Word order

+ There's a park. → Is there a park?
+ There are two banks. → Are there any banks?

Use

- *Is there a* + singular noun in questions: *Is there a supermarket?*
- *Are there any* + plural noun in questions: *Are there any shops?*
- *How many* + plural noun in questions about a number: *How many flats are there?*
- only the number in short answers: *How many bedrooms are there? There are two./Two.*

Don't use

- short forms in positive short answers: *Is there wifi? Yes, there is.* NOT *Yes, there's.*

3C Position of adjectives

be + adjective
It's **big**.
It **isn't expensive**.
This town **is busy**.

adjective + noun
This is **a quiet town**.
There's **an old cinema**.
There are **cheap shops and restaurants**.

Use

- adjectives to talk about people and things: *She's quiet. That's a cheap computer.*
- adjectives after the verb *be*: *My flat is small.*
- adjectives before nouns, after *a/an* or *the*: *It's a small flat.*
- *an* + vowel (*a, e, i, o, u*): *an old oven, an expensive TV*

Don't

- add *-s* to adjectives: *It's a big town. They're big towns.* NOT *They're bigs towns.*
- change adjectives after *he/she*: *He's a new student. She's a new student.*
- put the adjective after the noun: *It's a small flat.* NOT *It's a flat small.*

PRACTICE

3A

1 Choose the correct alternatives.
¹ *There's / Is* a supermarket in the town. There ² *isn't / aren't* a market. ³ *There / There's* a train station, and there ⁴ *is / are* two cafés. There are ⁵ *any / no* restaurants. There ⁶ *is / are* a big park and a bank. There is a cinema and there ⁷ *is / are* two bookshops. There ⁸ *are / aren't* any hotels.

2 Complete the sentences with *a*, *any* or *no*.
1 There aren't __any__ chairs in the room.
2 There isn't _____ park in my town.
3 There aren't _____ shops.
4 There's _____ bank and _____ office.
5 There aren't _____ hotels.
6 There's _____ train station.
7 There are _____ cinemas in my town.
8 There isn't _____ market and there isn't _____ supermarket.

3B

1 Choose the correct alternatives.
1 *Is / Are* there any supermarkets?
2 How many *room / rooms* are there in your flat?
3 *Is / Is there* wifi in the hotel?
4 Are there *a / any* Spanish students in your class?
5 *There's / Is there* a TV in the bedroom?
6 How *many / any* people are there in your office?

2 Match questions 1–6 in Exercise 1 with answers a–f.
a Three - it's a small flat.
b No, there isn't. It's in the living room.
c No, there aren't. But there's a market.
d Yes, there is - in the café and in the rooms.
e There are about 20, from all over the world.
f Yes, there are. Pablo and Ana are from Madrid.

3 Write questions for these answers.
1 _____*Is there a shower in the flat?*_____
Yes, there is. There's a shower in the bathroom.
2 _____
No, there isn't. There's wifi in the café.
3 _____
There are two, a big bedroom and a small bedroom.
4 _____
Yes, there is. It's a small lift, but it's OK.
5 _____
There are two - there's a big table in the kitchen and a small table in the living room.

3C

1 Correct the mistake in each sentence.
1 It's a old house.
2 Look at those news shops.
3 It's a restaurant small.
4 The Grand is a hotel expensive.
5 That's good a restaurant.
6 These phones are cheaps.
7 Those flats new are.
8 It's not a house big - it's small.

2 Put the words in the correct order to make sentences.
1 good / They're / students
   They're good students.
2 town / busy / a / It's
3 are / Houses in this town / expensive
4 isn't / big / Our hotel
5 our / is / teacher / Paul Bryan / new
6 is / car / Anna's / expensive
7 in this town / Is / a big / there / cinema ?
8 restaurants / There / no / here / are / good

Want more practice? Go to your Workbook or app.

GRAMMAR

4A have/has got

+	I/You/We/They	've got/have got brown hair.
	He/She/It	's got/has got green eyes.
-	I/You/We/They	have not/haven't got blue eyes.
	He/She/It	has not/hasn't got red hair.

Use has/have got to talk about
- possessions: **I've got** a new phone. She**'s got** a new car.
- family and friends: **Sara's got** a brother and a sister. **She hasn't got** any friends here.

Don't use
- have got to talk about age, use be: I'm 35 (years old). NOT I've got 35 years.

4B have/has got: questions

Question	Short answer	
Have I/we/you/they **got** a ticket?	+	Yes, I/we/you/they **have**.
	-	No, I/we/you/they **have not/haven't**.
Has he/she/it **got** a phone?	+	Yes, he/she/it **has**.
	-	No, he/she/it **has not/hasn't**.

with How many

How many bottles of water have you got?	(I've got) three.

Don't use
- short forms in positive short answers: *Have the rooms got a TV? Yes, they have.* NOT *Yes, they've.*
- got in short answers: *Has he got a room in this hotel? Yes, he has.* NOT *Yes, he has got.*

4C Imperatives

+	–
Visit Greenwich.	**Don't** visit Greenwich.
Take photos.	**Don't** take photos.
See a show.	**Don't** see a show.
Go to Buckingham Palace.	**Don't** go to Leicester Square.
Speak English to your partner.	**Don't** speak Spanish in class.
Sit down here.	**Don't** sit down there.
Do your homework.	**Don't** do Exercise 5a.

Use *please* to be polite.
Please sit down./Sit down, **please**.
Please walk./Walk, **please**.
Please don't run./Don't run, **please**.

Use imperatives in
- instructions: *Put your bag here, please.*
- advice: *Talk to your mother or your friend.*
- orders: *Sit down!*

Don't
- use *you* with imperatives: *Sit down.* NOT *You sit down.*
- change the form of the verb: *Talk to me, please.* NOT *Talks to me, please.*

PRACTICE

4A

1 Choose the correct option, a or b.

1. We _b_ a new computer.
   a got   b 've got
2. My brother _____ a dog.
   a is got   b has got
3. I _____ a sister and a brother.
   a 've got   b 's got
4. You _____ grey hair!
   a have got   b has got
5. I've got green eyes. I _____ blue eyes.
   a not got   b haven't got
6. We _____ red hair.
   a hasn't got   b haven't got
7. Darius _____ any good friends.
   a hasn't got   b isn't got
8. Emily _____ brown hair.
   a 's got   b is got

2 Make the sentences negative.

1. Dmitri's got a sister.
   Dmitri hasn't got a sister.
2. We've got a big bathroom.
3. Sam and Emma have got a dog.
4. Rob's got a beard.
5. I've got a class today.
6. You've got a lot of time.
7. My father's got a credit card.
8. They've got children.

4B

1 Put the words in the correct order to make questions.

1. got / family / a / you / big / Have ?
   Have you got a big family?
2. blue / got / she / coat / Has / a ?
3. got / Has / new / he / a / passport ?
4. phone / Has / a / got / camera / your ?
5. children / Ali and Sara / How many / got / have ?
6. we / water / got / have / of / How many / bottles ?

2 Match the questions in Exercise 1 with answers a–f.

1 c

a Yes, he has.
b They've got two.
c Yes, I have.
d You've got four.
e Yes, it has.
f No, she hasn't.

3 Write questions for these answers.

1. _____ *Have you got a credit card?* _____
   No, I haven't got a credit card.
2. _____
   Yes, the shop has got a lift.
3. _____
   Yes, we've got a camera.
4. _____
   The house has got two bathrooms.
5. _____
   I've got one brother and two sisters.
6. _____
   She's got three computers.

4C

1 Correct the mistake in each sentence.

1. Drink please this water.
2. Takes a photo of this food.
3. You put that book on the table.
4. No run here, please.
5. Use please the camera, not the phone.
6. Eat not and drink in school.

2 Complete the sentences with the positive or negative imperative of the verbs in the box.

| buy | ~~read~~ | run | sit down | take | use | walk |

1. *Don't read* this book. It's really bad!
2. Please _____ photos in the museum.
3. Here's a chair. Please _____ .
4. The tickets are expensive. _____ them.
5. We're at the cinema. _____ your phone here.
6. _____ to the park. _____ !

> Want more practice? Go to your Workbook or app.

GRAMMAR

5A Present simple: *I/you/we/they*

Use the present simple to talk about routines.

+	I/You/We/They	**go**	to work.
-	I/You/We/They	**don't work.**	

Use **at** + times: *I go to work **at 8 o'clock.***
Use **on** + days: ***On Saturdays,** I get up at 10 o'clock.*
Use **from** day/time **to** day/time: ***From Monday to Friday,** I get up at 7 o'clock. On Wednesdays, I work **from 2 o'clock to 10 o'clock.***

Use

- the same form of the verb for *I/you/we/they*: *I get up late. They get up late.*
- *don't* (= do not) + verb in negative sentences: *We don't have lunch at the office.*
- *7.30/seven thirty/half past seven*

Put *on* (+ day) and *at* (+ time) at the beginning or end of a sentence: *On Sundays, we walk in the park./We walk in the park on Sundays.*

5B Present simple questions: *I/you/we/they*

Question	Short answer	
Do I/you/we/they **drive** to work?	+	Yes, I/you/we/they **do.**
	-	No, I/you/we/they **don't.**

with question words

How	**do** you travel to work?	I cycle.
What time	**do** you leave home?	At 6.00.
What time	**do** you arrive at work?	At 8.00.

Word order

+ They have dinner at 8.00.

? Do they have dinner at 8.00?

Use

- *do* + *I/you/we/they* + verb in present simple questions: *Do you work in an office?* NOT *Work in an office? Work you in an office?*
- *do* or *don't* in short answers: *Do you work at the weekend? Yes, I do./No, I don't.* NOT *Yes, I work./No, I don't work.*

5C Present simple with frequency adverbs

Use frequency adverbs to say how often you do things.
*I **always** drink tea in the morning.*
*I **usually** eat chocolate at work.*
*I **often** eat cakes.*
*I **sometimes** eat fish or salad.*
*I **never** drink coffee.*
Frequency adverbs go after the verb *be*:
*I'm **always** late for work.*
Frequency adverbs go before other verbs (e.g. *eat, have, drink*).
Ask questions about frequency with *How often*:
***How often** do you eat meat?*
***How often** are you late for work?*

0% ←————————————————→ 100%
↓   ↓   ↓   ↓   ↓
never sometimes often usually always

Use

- *always, usually, often* after *don't*: *I don't always eat breakfast.*
- *always, usually, often, sometimes* in questions: *Do you usually have eggs for breakfast?*
- a positive verb with *never*: *I never work on Sundays.* NOT *I don't never work on Sundays.*

Don't use

- *sometimes* in negative sentences: *I don't often cycle to university.* NOT *I don't sometimes cycle to university.*

PRACTICE

5A

1 Correct the mistake in each sentence.
1. I am get up late on Sundays.
2. You no study on Saturdays and Sundays.
3. We are have breakfast in a café on Fridays.
4. My friends don't go to classes at Mondays.
5. I don't not go out from Monday to Friday.
6. My brothers and sisters not go to bed late.

2 Make positive (+) or negative (-) sentences using the prompts.
1. I / get up / 6.30 (+)
   I get up at 6.30.
2. She / have breakfast / the kitchen (-)
   She doesn't have breakfast in the kitchen.
3. He / go / work / 8.00 (+)
4. We / study English / home (+)
5. They / have lunch / 12.00 (-)
6. I / go / bed late / Sundays (+)
7. They / watch TV / Saturdays (+)
8. He / work / an office (-)

5B

1 Make questions using the prompts.
1. you / walk / school? *Do you walk to school?*
2. your friends / go / work / bike?
3. What time / you / leave / home?
4. your mum and dad / travel / boat?
5. you / take / bus / the office?
6. How / your friends / travel / university?

2 Match the questions in Exercise 1 with answers a–f.
1 e

a At about 8.00, but 7.00 on Fridays.
b No, I don't. I walk.
c No, they don't. They don't like boats.
d They travel by car.
e Yes, we do. There isn't a bus.
f Yes, they do. They've all got bikes.

3 Write questions for these answers.
1. *What time do you take the train on Fridays?*
   We take the train at 8.00 on Fridays.
2. _____
   My friends go to the park by bike.
3. _____
   No, I don't. Taxis are expensive. I go to work by bus.
4. _____
   My brother and I drive to the cinema.
5. _____
   I arrive home at about 6.00.

5C

1 Put the frequency adverbs in brackets in the correct place.

always
1. My parents ∧ eat chicken on Sundays. (always)
2. I eat Turkish food with my friends. (sometimes)
3. How do you eat chocolate? (often)
4. He is late for work. (usually)
5. They drink coffee. (never)
6. I don't have sugar in tea or coffee. (usually)
7. We are busy at work. (always)
8. I eat eggs for breakfast. (never)

2 Look at the table. Then complete the sentences with the frequency adverbs in the box.

| always | never | often | sometimes | usually |

	Mon	Tues	Weds	Thurs	Fri	Sat	Sun
have a sandwich for lunch	✓	✓	✓	✓			
have dinner at home	✓	✓	✓	✓	✓	✓	✓
eat unhealthy food	✓	✓					
drink water with dinner	✓	✓	✓	✓	✓		
drink coffee with breakfast							

1. I *often* have a sandwich for lunch.
2. I _____ have dinner at home.
3. I _____ eat unhealthy food.
4. I _____ drink water with dinner.
5. I _____ drink coffee with breakfast.

Want more practice? Go to your Workbook or app.

GRAMMAR

6A Present simple: *he/she/it*

+	He	**gets up**	early.
	She	**works**	at home.
	It	**starts**	at nine.
-	He	**doesn't have**	dinner at home.
	She	**doesn't work**	every day.
	It	**doesn't leave**	at 6 o'clock.

For most verbs, + -s:
He arrive**s** home late.
For verbs ending in consonant + -y, ~~y~~ and + -ies:
She stud**ies** Spanish.
For verbs ending in -ch, -o, -s, -sh, -ss, -x, + -es:
She watch**es** TV.

Use

- the present simple for things people do every day/week: *Manuela calls her mother every day.*
- *doesn't* (= does not) + verb in negative sentences: *My brother doesn't drive to work.*
- *has* for the *he/she/it* form of *have*: *She has breakfast in a café.* NOT ~~She haves breakfast in a café.~~
- time expressions (e.g. *at the weekend, in the morning*) at the beginning or end of a sentence: *He studies Spanish on Sundays./On Sundays, he studies Spanish.*

Don't use

- verb + -s in negative sentences: *Hiroshi doesn't live here.* NOT ~~Hiroshi doesn't lives here.~~
- *don't* with *he/she/it* in negative sentences: *Fatima doesn't work at the weekend.* NOT ~~Fatima don't work at the weekend.~~

6B Present simple questions: *he/she/it*

Yes/No questions

?	**Does** she **clean** the bathroom?
+	Yes, she **does**.
-	No, she **doesn't**.

Wh- questions

What	jobs **does** he **do** around the house?
How often	**does** he **clean** the kitchen?
Where	**does** he **walk** the dog?
When	**does** it **open**?
Who	**does** Bonnie **live** with?

Word order

+ Szymon cooks dinner at the weekend.

? Does Szymon cook dinner at the weekend?

Use

- present simple questions to ask about what people do: *Does Andrea clean the kitchen?*
- *does* + *he/she/it* + verb in present simple questions: *Does she play video games?* NOT ~~Do she play video games?/Plays she video games?~~
- *does* or *doesn't* in short answers: *Does he live here? Yes, he does./No, he doesn't.* NOT ~~Yes, he lives.~~

Don't use

- -s/-es/-ies with the verb in present simple questions: *Does he make his bed?* NOT ~~Does he makes his bed?~~

6C *can/can't* for ability

+	I/You/He/She/It/We/They	**can**	sing.
-	I/You/He/She/It/We/They	**can't**	drive.

Yes/No questions

Question		Short answer
Can you **use** a computer?	+	Yes, I **can**.
	-	No, I **can't**.
Can he **play** football?	+	Yes, he **can**.
	-	No, he **can't**.

with question words

What	**can** you **cook**?	I **can cook** fish.
How many	languages **can** you **speak**?	Two. English and Spanish.

Word order

+ She can swim.

? Can she swim?

Use

- *can* + verb to talk about skills: *I can dance.*
- *can't* + verb in negative sentences: *She can't dance.*
- *can* + subject in questions: *Can you sing?*
- *can* or *can't* in short answers: *Can you cook? Yes, I can./No, I can't.*
- the same verb form for *I/you/he/she/it/we/they* + *can/can't*: *He can drive.* NOT ~~He cans drive.~~

Don't use

- *to* after *can*: *Can Marek ride a horse?* NOT ~~Can Marek to ride a horse?~~

PRACTICE

6A

1 Correct the mistake in each sentence.
1 My dad no have meat every day.
2 My brother is walks to work.
3 The shop manager finishs at 8 o'clock.
4 Jack don't go to work on Saturdays.
5 My sister cycle from our house to the station.
6 My friend doesn't goes to the gym.
7 Helen not play sports in the morning.
8 My friend studys Spanish and English.

2 Choose the correct alternatives.
1 The class *start* / *starts* at 8.30.
2 Rob and Ellie *live* / *lives* in Paris.
3 My son *have* / *has* lunch at school.
4 I *don't* / *doesn't* have breakfast every day.
5 Jakub *don't* / *doesn't* work at the weekend.
6 Gina *studies* / *studys* languages at university.
7 Kim doesn't *eat* / *eats* meat.
8 My parents *don't* / *doesn't* work now.

6B

1 Complete the conversation with the correct form of the verbs in brackets or *does/doesn't* in short answers.

Tadashi: Who ¹*do you live* with, Gosia? (you / live)
Gosia: My friend Elena. We live in a flat near the station.
Tadashi: ²_____ the flat? (you / clean)
Gosia: Well, I clean the living room and my bedroom.
Tadashi: ³_____ the kitchen? (Elena / clean)
Gosia: Yes, she does. She cleans the kitchen and the bathroom.
Tadashi: ⁴_____ dinner for you? (she / cook)
Gosia: No, she ⁵_____ , but she makes great cakes!
Tadashi: ⁶_____ the washing? (you / do)
Gosia: Yes, I do, but Elena ⁷_____ the dishes. (wash)
Tadashi: ⁸_____ her bed? (she / make)
Gosia: Yes, she does that too.
Tadashi: She's a good friend!

2 Look at the pictures and make questions and answers.

1 *What time does Keira cook dinner?*
   She cooks dinner at 6 o'clock.
2 _____?
   _____
3 _____?
   _____
4 When _____?
   _____
5 _____?
   _____
6 _____?
   _____

6C

1 Complete the conversations with the correct form of *can* and the verbs in the box.

| cook | ~~drive~~ | play | ride a horse | speak | swim |

1 **A:** *Can* you *drive*?
   B: Yes, *I can*, but I haven't got a car.
2 **A:** How many languages _____ you _____ ?
   B: Two. I _____ Polish and English.
3 **A:** _____ your dad _____ ?
   B: Yes, _____ . He makes great cakes.
4 **A:** _____ your mum _____ ?
   B: Yes, _____ . She rides it at the weekend.
5 **A:** _____ your sister _____ ?
   B: No, _____ . She doesn't go in the water.
6 **A:** What sports _____ they _____ ?
   B: They _____ football and tennis.

2 Make sentences using *can*, *can't* and the prompts.
1 We / speak / English / not Spanish
   We can speak English, but we can't speak Spanish.
2 My dad / sing / not dance
3 Jack / ride a horse / not ride a bike
4 They / read Japanese / not write it
5 I / draw / not paint
6 My sister / ride a bike / not drive

Want more practice? Go to your Workbook or app.

GRAMMAR

7A Wh- questions

Wh- question word	Example
Use *what* for things.	**What**'s the name of the place?
Use *how* for the way you do something.	**How** do you spell that?
Use *when* for days, months and times.	**When** do you usually go there?
Use *who* for people.	**Who** do you go with?
Use *where* for places.	**Where** is it?
Use *how much* for prices.	**How much** is a ticket?
Use *how many* for the number of things.	**How many** lakes are there?
Use *how old* for ages.	**How old** is the hotel?
Use *what time* for times.	**What time** does the boat leave?

Use
- question words to ask for information: *What time is it? How much is this cake?*
- the question word before the verb (*be, do/does, have/has, can*, etc.): *Where do you work? What have you got in your bag?*

Don't use
- a subject (*you, he*, etc.) after a question word: *When do you cook dinner?* NOT *When you cook dinner?*
- a noun after *Who, When* or *Where*: **Where do** you play tennis? NOT *Where place do you play tennis?*

You can use adjectives after *How*: *How old are you? How big is the lake?*

7B was/were, there was/were

was/were

+	I/He/She/It	**was**	thirty-one this year.
−		**wasn't** (was not)	quiet.
+	You/We/They	**were**	great.
−		**weren't** (were not)	there.

there was/were

+	There	**was**	a party.
−	There	**wasn't** (was not)	a lift.
+	There	**were**	trees and fields.
−	There	**weren't** (were not)	any buses or cars.

Use
- *was/were* to talk about the past: *I was on holiday last week.*
- *wasn't/weren't* in negative sentences: *I wasn't at work yesterday.*
- *was/were* with *yesterday, last night, last week*, etc: *They weren't here last night.*
- *there was/were* to talk about something in the past for the first time: *There was a bank in the town then.*

Don't use
- subject + *'s* or *'re* in the past: *He was busy. They were quiet.* (He's = He is; They're = They are)
- *was/were* without a subject or *there*: *There were a lot of people.* NOT *Were a lot of people.*

7C was/were (questions)

Yes/No questions

Question			Short answer	
Was	he/she/it	OK?	+	Yes, he/she/it **was**.
			−	No, he/she/it **wasn't**.
Were	you	cold?	+	Yes, I **was**.
			−	No, I **wasn't**.
Were	we/they	with you?	+	Yes, we/they **were**.
			−	No, we/they **weren't**.

Wh- questions

Where	**were**	they?
What	**was**	it about?
How much	**was**	it?

there was/were (questions)

Yes/No questions

Question			Short answer	
Was	there	a meeting?	+	Yes, **there was**.
			−	No, **there wasn't**.
Were	there	a lot of people?	+	Yes, **there were**.
			−	No, **there weren't**.

Wh- questions

What food	**was there**	at the party?

Use
- *was/were* to ask questions about the past: **Were** *Simon and Beth with you? Where* **was** *your friend last night?*

Don't use
- *was/were* without a subject or *there*: *Were there a lot of people?* NOT *Were a lot of people?*

PRACTICE

7A

1 Choose the correct alternatives.
1 *What's / Who's* the time?
2 *How / How many* bedrooms are there?
3 *Who / What time* cooks dinner in your family?
4 *How much / How many* is a sandwich and a tea?
5 *How much / How often* do you ride your horse?
6 *Where / When* are the mountains in your country?
7 *Who / How* do you spell your name?
8 *When's / What's* the meeting?
9 *How much / How old* is your brother?

2 Match the questions in Exercise 1 with answers a–h.
1e
a Every weekend.
b They're in the north.
c It's £5.25.
d B - O - U - R - K - E.
e It's half past seven.
f It's on Tuesday.
g He's eighteen – it's his birthday today!
h Three.
i My husband. He cooks great dinners.

7B

1 Correct the mistake in each sentence.
1 I'm at the cinema last night.
2 You aren't at home last Sunday.
3 My parents was on holiday last week.
4 You was late for work yesterday.
5 Yesterday weren't a good day.
6 Penpak isn't at work last month.
7 There wasn't any taxis.
8 Was good food at the restaurant.
9 Last week, I am on holiday in Italy.
10 There wasn't any films on TV last night.
11 The food were really expensive!
12 Yesterday, there is a big party in my office.

2 Write the sentences in the past. Use *was, were, wasn't* or *weren't* and the words in brackets.
1 I'm at work this week. (last week) *I was at work last week.*
2 You're late today. (yesterday)
3 My birthday's on Sunday this year. (Saturday / last year)
4 They aren't at home this evening. (last night)
5 Harry and Louise are in Thailand in April. (March)
6 Marek's party is in May this year. (March / last year)
7 There are no cakes in the café today. (yesterday)
8 There isn't a train every day in December. (January)
9 We are on holiday today. (in July)
10 Sara and I are at a party this evening. (last night)
11 There isn't a birthday in our family this month. (last month)
12 There are no good films at the cinema this year. (last year)

7C

1 Put the words in the correct order to make questions.
1 class / the / difficult / Was ? *Was the class difficult?*
2 you / How old / on your last birthday / were ?
3 train tickets / were / the / How much ?
4 last / in the kitchen / Were / night / you ?
5 last / were / you / weekend / Where ?
6 were / students / at your school / How many / there ?
7 party / Saturday / last / a / Was / there ?
8 yesterday / What time / your English class / was ?
9 was / in your living room / the TV / How much ?
10 you / yesterday / Who / with / were ?

2 Make questions and short answers using the prompts and *was/were*.
1 your brother / happy? (✓)
   Was your brother happy? Yes, he was.
2 your train / OK / last night? (✗)
3 your friends / at your birthday party? (✓)
4 your sister / a good student? (✗)
5 there / a restaurant / at the hotel? (✓)
6 there / many people / at the meeting? (✗)
7 your teacher / at school yesterday? (✓)
8 there / a good market / in your town? (✗)

Want more practice? Go to your Workbook or app.

GRAMMAR

8A Past simple (regular verbs)

+	I/You/He/She/It/We/They	**lived** in a village.
-		**didn't live** in a city.

Spelling

	Rule	Example
most verbs	+ -ed	walk → walk**ed**
verbs ending in -e	+ -d	like → like**d**
verbs ending in consonant + -y	~~y~~ + -ied	study → stud**ied**
verbs ending in vowel + -y	+ -ed	play → play**ed**
many verbs ending in consonant + vowel + consonant	double the final consonant + -ed	stop → stop**ped** travel → travel**led** BUT visit → visit**ed**

Use

- the same verb form for *I/You/He/She/It/We/They* in the past simple: *I **played** video games and **the** children **played** football.*
- *didn't* (*did not*) + verb in the negative: *I didn't like the hot summer in Thailand.* NOT ~~I didn't liked~~ ...
- the past simple to talk about:
– an action at a time in the past: *The lesson started at 11.30.*

```
            the lesson started
past ─────────|────────────── now
           11.30
```

– a situation in the past: *I lived in Poland for six years.*

```
         lived in Poland
past ────|────────|──────── now
       1998-2004
```

– repeated actions in the past: *I walked to school every day.*

```
        walked to school
past ──|────|────|────|────|──── now
      Mon  Tues  Wed  Thurs  Fri
```

- time expressions with past simple verbs, e.g. *last week, yesterday, on Saturday*

8B Past simple (irregular verbs)

Some verbs don't add *-d/-ed/-ied* in the past simple positive, but they have different forms. We call them **irregular** verbs: *Last Sunday I got up late.* NOT ~~I getted up~~.
Irregular verbs and regular verbs are the same in the negative: *Last Sunday I didn't get up late.*
Regular past simple verbs usually end in *-ed*. *I watched TV. I walked to the office.*
Irregular past simple verbs have different forms: *feel* → *felt, go* → *went, lose* → *lost*
→ Irregular verbs list page 160
The negative of irregular past simple verbs is *didn't* + verb: + *I went to work.* - *I **didn't go** to work.*

Use

- irregular past simple verbs to talk about the past: *I bought a new coat last week.*
- *didn't* + verb for the past simple negative with both regular and irregular verbs: *I didn't like the food.* NOT ~~I didn't liked the food~~. *We didn't go by train.* NOT ~~We didn't went by train~~.

Notice: some irregular past simple verbs are the same as the present simple, e.g. *put*: *I usually put my phone on the desk. Yesterday I put my phone on the chair.*

8C Past simple (questions)

Yes/No questions

Question		Short answer
Did you **have** a good weekend?	+	Yes, I **did**.
	-	No, I **didn't**.
Did they **have** fun?	+	Yes, they **did**.
	-	No, they **didn't**.

Wh- questions

Where	**did**	Emily	**go**?
When	**did**	she	**visit** Tokyo?
How	**did**	you	**get** there?
What	**did**	you	**do**?

Use

- *did* + subject + verb for past simple questions with both regular and irregular verbs: *Did you like the hotel?* NOT ~~Did you liked the hotel?~~ *Did you take a good camera?* NOT ~~Did you took a good camera?~~
- a question word before *did* in *wh*-questions: *How did you travel?*
- *did* or *didn't* in short answers: *Did you have a good weekend? Yes, I did./No, I didn't.* NOT ~~Yes, I had./No, I didn't have.~~

PRACTICE

8A

1 Complete the text with the past simple form of the verbs in the box.

change   clean   not cook   ~~not like~~
start   not stay   stop   wash   work

Enzo ¹*didn't like* his office job. So in spring he ²_____ a new job – he ³_____ at the café in the park. He ⁴_____ the food, but he ⁵_____ the dishes and ⁶_____ the tables. It was good in the summer, but the autumn was cold and Enzo ⁷_____ at the café. He ⁸_____ his job at the café and ⁹_____ his job again – to a job in an office!

2 Write the sentences in the past simple. Use *yesterday*.
1. He plays football. *He played football yesterday.*
2. I don't walk to work.
3. We visit Paris by train.
4. She tries different food.
5. Dad cooks dinner.
6. You don't listen to music.
7. She doesn't stay in an expensive hotel.
8. I work in the hospital.

8B

1 Correct the mistake in each sentence.
1. Last week I losed my house keys.
2. I didn't forgot my coat – I didn't wear it.
3. We were make dinner yesterday.
4. I buyed a new phone last week.
5. We didn't haved a good holiday.
6. He puts the book on the table this morning. Where is it?
7. She didn't went home from work late.
8. I did eat chicken for dinner last night.

2 Correct the sentences. Use the information in brackets.
1. She lost her ticket. (her phone)
   She didn't lose her ticket. She lost her phone.
2. I forgot her name. (phone number)
3. Your camera broke. (your bag)
4. My dad took a bus. (a taxi)
5. She spoke to Alan on Monday. (Dave)
6. My friend bought new sunglasses. (a coat)
7. The train left at 11.30. (12.30)
8. You made Thai food. (Japanese food)

8C

1 Complete the conversations with the past simple form of the verbs in brackets.
1. A: Where _did_ you _go_ on holiday last year? (go)
   B: We _went_ to Santander, in the north of Spain.
2. A: _____ your mum _____ a good birthday? (have)
   B: Yes, she _____ thanks. She _____ a party on Saturday evening.
3. A: What restaurant _____ you and your friends _____ to last weekend? (go)
   B: We _____ to the new Turkish restaurant in the town.
4. A: _____ the plane _____ on time? (leave)
   B: No, it _____ . It _____ an hour late.
5. A: What _____ the children _____ at school today? (learn)
   B: They _____ Spanish verbs.
6. A: _____ you _____ the food for dinner this evening? (forget)
   B: No, we _____ . The shop was closed.

2 Make questions using the prompts in brackets.
1. *Where did you go at the weekend?*
   (Where / you / go / at the weekend)
2. _____ ?
   (How / you / travel to the lake)
3. _____ ?
   (you / go / in Enrico's car)
4. _____ ?
   (What / you / do there)
5. _____ ?
   (you / have / a good time)
6. _____ ?
   (What time / you / leave)

3 Complete the answers to the questions in Exercise 2 with the verb in brackets. Then match 1–6 with a–f.
a. We _____ by car. (go)
b. Yes, we did. We _____ a great time! (have)
c. We _____ at about 7 o'clock. (leave)
d. No, we didn't. Elena _____ . (drive)
e. We *went* to the lake in the mountains. (go) *1*
f. We _____ lunch by the lake and walked in the mountains. (eat)

Want more practice? Go to your Workbook or app.

GRAMMAR

9A Object pronouns (*me, him, her*, etc.)

- Use subject pronouns before the verb: *I live in London.*
- Use object pronouns after the verb: *My parents sometimes visit **me** at the weekend.*

subject pronouns	object pronouns
I	me
you	you
he	him
she	her
it	it
we	us
they	them

Use

- the pronouns *I/me, you/you, he/him, she/her, we/us* and *they/them* for people (and animals): *This is Sarah. I like her.*
- the pronouns *it/it* and *they/them* for animals and things: *English is easy. I like it.*
- an object pronoun after a preposition (e.g. *of, with, to*, etc.): *I've got a great photo of you.*
- an object pronoun after the verb *be*: *Who's that in the photo? – It's me!*

Don't

- repeat a noun. Use an object pronoun: *She doesn't watch football. She doesn't like it.*
- leave out an object pronoun: *Your sister is nice. I like her.* NOT *I like.*

9B *like/enjoy/love/hate* + *-ing*

Statements

+	I/You/We/They	like/enjoy/love/hate	**walking** the dog.
–		don't like	**watching** TV.
+	He/She/It	likes/enjoys/loves/hates	**reading** books. **running** in the park.
–		doesn't like	

Yes/No questions

Do	I/you/we/they **like**	**reading** books?
Does	he/she/it **like**	**doing** exercise?

Wh- questions

What	**do** you **like**	**doing** at the weekend?
	does she **like**	

Spelling rules: *-ing* forms

most verbs	+ *-ing*	go → go**ing** do → do**ing** tidy → tidy**ing** read → read**ing**
verbs ending in *-e*	*e* + *-ing*	take → tak**ing** make → mak**ing** have → hav**ing**
many verbs ending in consonant + vowel + consonant	double the final consonant + *-ing*	get → get**ting** stop → stop**ping** BUT visit → visit**ing**

Use

- *like/enjoy/love/hate* +verb + *-ing* to talk about activities you (don't) like: *I enjoy reading books.*
- *do* and *don't* in short answers: *Do you like doing homework? Yes, I do./No, I don't.* NOT *Yes, I like./No, I don't like.*

You can use these verbs with a noun or a verb: *He loves **music**. He loves **listening to** music.*

9C *why* and *because*

Ask for reasons with *why*

Question	Example
Why + *be*	**Why is** English difficult for you?
Why + *do* + subject + verb	**Why do you study** English? **Why didn't you study** English at school? **Why do you study** here?
Why + *have* + subject + *got*	**Why have you got** four lessons this week?

Give reasons with *because*

Statement + *because* + reason

*Bianca studies English **because** she uses it for her work.*
*English is difficult for Bianca **because** she can't remember all the new words.*

Use

- *why* to ask for a reason: *Why does Mario like taking English exams?*
- *because* to give a reason: *Because his English is good.*
- *because* to join two sentences: *Mario likes taking English exams. His English is good.* → *Mario likes taking English exams because his English is good.*

PRACTICE

9A

1 Choose the correct option, a, b or c.

1 My brother never calls _____.
   a I   b he   c me
2 _____ loves Italian food.
   a She   b Her   c I
3 This coffee is really bad. Don't drink _____.
   a it   b them   c coffee
4 _____ work for a computer company.
   a Him   b They   c Them
5 _____ don't like sport very much.
   a We   b Us   c Me
6 Can I visit _____ this weekend?
   a me   b your   c you
7 A: Is Jack here this evening?
   B: Yes, that's _____ with Sandro.
   a he   b him   c them
8 His sister's name's Kiera. Do you know _____?
   a her   b him   c she

2 Replace the underlined words with an object pronoun.

1 I like chicken. I eat <u>chicken</u> every week. *it*
2 Joe and Lisa were at school with us. Come and talk to <u>Joe and Lisa</u>.
3 Their daughter is very nice. Everyone likes <u>their daughter</u>.
4 Where's my phone? I can't find <u>my phone</u>.
5 I hate eggs. I never eat <u>eggs</u>.
6 My brother lives in the US. I see <u>my brother</u> every summer.
7 My son lives near my husband and me. He visits <u>my husband and me</u> every week.
8 I studied English at school. I didn't study <u>English</u> in the UK.

9B

1 Write the *-ing* form of the verbs.

1 do — *doing*
2 swim — _____
3 use — _____
4 listen — _____
5 walk — _____
6 have — _____
7 stop — _____
8 play — _____
9 go — _____
10 write — _____

2 Make statements or questions using the prompts.

1 I / enjoy / take photos *I enjoy taking photos.*
2 He / not like / lose things
3 My son / hate / get up early
4 My children / enjoy / play cards
5 Ellen / love / do sport
6 your dad / like / read books?
7 you / enjoy / swim?
8 your friends / enjoy / watch football?
9 you / like / listen to the radio?

9C

1 Match sentences 1–6 with reasons a–f.

1 I went to the library. *e*
2 I failed the exam.
3 I passed the exam.
4 I watched this film.
5 I read a book every month.
6 I took an English course.

a I love reading.
b I studied every day.
c I like the people in it.
d My English isn't very good.
e It has a lot of good books.
f I didn't study every day.

2 Write complete sentences. Use 1–6 and a–f from Exercise 1 and *because*.

1 *I went to the library because it has a lot of good books.*
2 _____
3 _____
4 _____
5 _____
6 _____

3 Make questions and answers using the prompts and *because*.

1 Why / you / not be / at the office yesterday? I / go / to a meeting in town
   Why weren't you at the office yesterday? Because I went to a meeting in town.
2 Why / Hamid / not at school today? he / got a job interview
3 Why / Serena / have not got / a computer? she / not like / computers
4 Why / you / leave work early yesterday? I / go to / the cinema with my friends
5 Why / your parents / can speak / good Spanish? they / live / in Mexico for four years

Want more practice? Go to your Workbook or app.

GRAMMAR

10A would like/love to

+	I'd/would like to	start	a business.
	I'd/would love to	change	jobs.
-	I wouldn't like to	go	to a cold place.

Yes/No questions

?	Would you like to	have	more money?
+	Yes, I would.		
-	No, I wouldn't.		

Wh- questions

What	would you like to	do?
When	would you like to	start your business?

Use

- *would like/love to* + verb to say what you want to do now: *I'd like to ask a question. We'd love to stay for dinner.*
- *would like/love to* + verb to talk about dreams for the future: *I'd like to be a dancer one day. He'd love to travel round the world.*
- *would like/love* + noun to say what you want now: *I'd love a cup of coffee.*
- *like/love* + *-ing* to talk about what you like doing: *We love listening to music. They like visiting other cities.* NOT ~~They'd like visiting other cities.~~ or ~~They like visiting another city in the future.~~

10B be going to

+	I'm/am	going to	talk to Teri.
-	I'm/am not	going to	buy small snacks.
+	You/We/They're/are	going to	watch a film.
-	You/We/They aren't/are not	going to	meet my friends.
+	He/She/It's/is	going to	be at the restaurant.
-	He/She/It isn't/is not	going to	be at my house.

Use

- *be* + *going to* + verb to talk about future plans and intentions: *We're going to try tennis at the weekend. The government isn't going to spend a lot of money on houses.*

10C be going to: questions

Yes/No questions

Question				Short answer	
Am	I	going to	drive?	+	Yes, you **are**.
				-	No, you **aren't**.
Are	you	going to	go on holiday?	+	Yes, I **am**.
				-	No, **I'm not**.
Is	he/she	going to	cycle?	+	Yes, he/she **is**.
				-	No, he/she **isn't**.
Is	it	going to	be at the café?	+	Yes, it **is**.
				-	No, it **isn't**.
Are	we/they	going to	visit?	+	Yes, we/they **are**.
				-	No, we/they **aren't**.

Wh- questions

When	are you	going to	go?
What	are you	going to	do there?
Where	are you	going to	take them?

Use

- *be going to* + verb to ask about future plans and intentions: *Are they going to start a new business?*
- *be* + subject + *going to* + verb in *yes/no* questions: *Are you going to have a party next weekend?*
- *be* in short answers: *Is he going to study at university? Yes, he is./No, he isn't.* NOT ~~Yes, he's going./No, he isn't going.~~

134

PRACTICE

10A

1 Correct the mistake in each sentence.
1 I'd like being a doctor one day.
2 We'd loving to see you at the weekend.
3 I not would like to live in another country.
4 Do you like travelling round the world one day?
5 I like my job so I don't like to change it.
6 My sister would liking to be a dancer.
7 John would like work for a travel company.
8 Anne and Maxine do like to travel after university.

2 Complete the questions with the correct form of *would like to* and the verbs in the box.

| do | go out | ~~listen to~~ | spend | visit | watch |

1 A: What music *would* you *like to listen to*?
  B: You can choose. I love all music.
2 A: _____ you _____ this evening?
  B: No, thanks. Can we stay at home?
3 A: What job _____ you _____ after university?
  B: I'd love to be a singer.
4 A: What countries _____ you _____ one day?
  B: Mexico and Argentina, I think.
5 A: _____ you _____ the football game on TV?
  B: No, thanks. I don't really like sport.
6 A: _____ you _____ some time with me and the children tomorrow?
  B: Yes, that's a great idea.

10B

1 Choose the correct alternatives.
1 *I / I'm* going to visit my family next weekend.
2 We *aren't / don't* going to go on holiday in the summer.
3 *Your / You're* going to buy the fruit.
4 My friends *going / are going* to be at my party.
5 The party *doesn't / isn't* going to be at our house.
6 My mum's going *move / to move* to a new house.
7 *I'm not / I don't* going to go to the post office at the weekend.
8 Amy and Max *not / aren't* going to come to the cinema with us.

2 Make sentences using the prompts and the correct form of *be going to*.
1 I / cycle to work tomorrow *I'm going to cycle to work tomorrow*.
2 Mum / not buy a new car
3 We / go to the beach next weekend
4 My friends / start a business next year
5 We / not go to the film club
6 I / not look for a new job
7 Mike / make a dessert
8 You / not be at home on Saturday

10C

1 Complete the conversation with one word in each space.

A: Are you going ¹*to* stay at home on Friday evening?
B: No, I'm ² _____ . I'm going to go to a meeting of a new book club.
A: Oh, is this your first meeting?
B: No, it ³ _____ . The club started last month. We're ⁴ _____ to talk about a new book on Friday.
A: Where ⁵ _____ you going ⁶ _____ meet? In a café?
B: No, at my house. We ⁷ _____ going to meet at a different house each month.
A: That's great. Have a good time!

2 Complete the questions with the correct form of *be going to* and the words in brackets.
1 What *are you going to do* after work tonight? (you / do)
2 _____ you next weekend? (your friends / visit)
3 Where _____ on his holiday? (your son / stay)
4 _____ at this shop next year? (your manager / be)
5 When _____ jobs? (Marek / change)
6 _____ English next year? (you / study)
7 _____ at Sam's house next weekend? (the party / be)
8 _____ to drive? (your sister / learn)

3 Match the questions in Exercise 2 with answers a–h.
a No, she isn't. She likes taking the train.
b In July. He's going to start his new job then.
c No, it isn't. It's going to be at Joe's house.
d Yes, I am. I'm going to use it in my new job.
e No, they aren't. They're busy with work and studies.
f Yes, he is. I'm going to stay here too.
g I'm going to meet my friends for a coffee. *1*
h He's got a room in a small hotel in the mountains.

Want more practice? Go to your Workbook or app.

Vocabulary bank

1B Jobs

1 Look at the photos and complete 1–12 with the words in the box.

| artist | bus driver | manager | police officer | receptionist | shop assistant |
| soldier | ~~student~~ | tennis player | tour guide | waiter/waitress | writer |

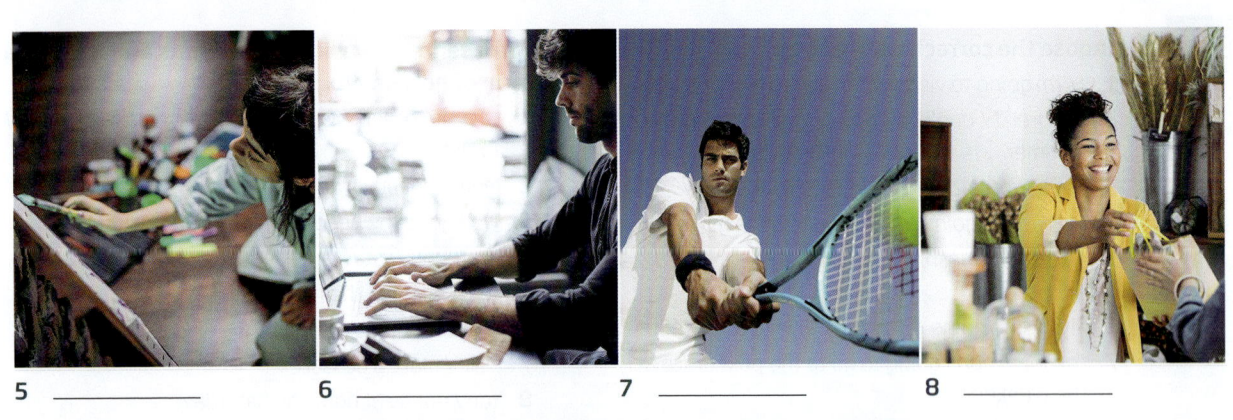

1 _student_
2 _____
3 _____
4 _____
5 _____
6 _____
7 _____
8 _____
9 _____
10 _____
11 _____
12 _____

2 Work in pairs. Do you know anyone who does the jobs in Exercise 1?
   My mum is a bus driver.

2A Family

1 Look at the photos and complete the sentences with the words in the box.

aunt   boyfriend   cousins   girlfriend   grandad   grandma   nephew
niece   ~~parents~~   uncle

Beth: They are my mum and dad. They are my ¹*parents*.

Yuri: They are my father's parents. He's my ²_____ and she's my ³_____ .

Rick: They are my dad's brother and his wife. He's my ⁴_____ and she's my ⁵_____ .

Marcus: They are my aunt and uncle's children. They are my ⁶_____ .

Eve: They are my brother's children. He is my ⁷_____ and she is my ⁸_____ .

Elsa: He's not in my family. He's my ⁹_____ and I'm his ¹⁰_____ .

2 Work in pairs. Tell your partner the names of people in your family.

My uncle's name is Vladimir.

2B Everyday objects

1 Look at the picture and complete 1–12 with the words in the box.

backpack   credit card   glasses   handbag
keyboard   laptop   money   ~~newspaper~~
passport   screen   umbrella   wallet

1 *newspaper*
2 _____
3 _____
4 _____
5 _____
6 _____
7 _____
8 _____
9 _____
10 _____
11 _____
12 _____

2 Work in pairs. What objects are in your bag?

my credit card, my glasses, …

137

3B At home

1 Look at the photos and complete 1–12 with the words in the box.

basement   bath   cupboard   curtains   door   floor   fridge   hall
mirror   roof   washing machine   window

1 *basement*
2 _____
3 _____
4 _____
5 _____
6 _____
7 _____
8 _____
9 _____
10 _____
11 _____
12 _____

3C Adjectives (1)

1 Look at the photos and choose the correct alternatives.
1 The kitchen is *clean* / *dirty*.
2 Wow! That's *a cheap* / *an expensive* phone!
3 My new car is *big* / *small*.
4 There's *an old* / *a new* lift in the train station.
5 The shop is *open* / *closed*.
6 It's a *dark* / *light* blue cup.

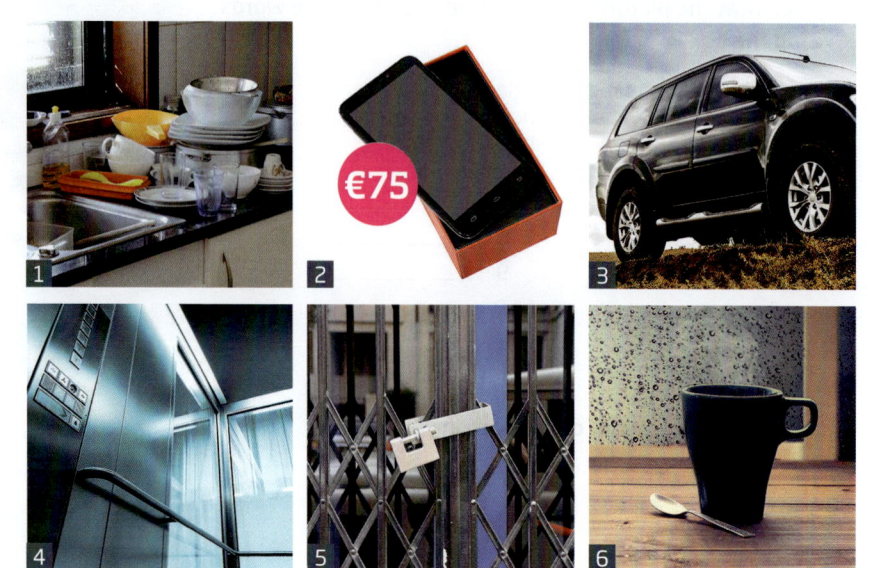

2 Work in pairs. Describe things to your partner. Use the adjectives in Exercise 1.
  My phone is old.

4A Parts of the body

1 Look at the photo and complete 1–17 with the words in the box.

| arm | chest | ear | elbow | eye | face | finger | hair | hand | head |
| knee | leg | mouth | neck | nose | shoulder | stomach | | | |

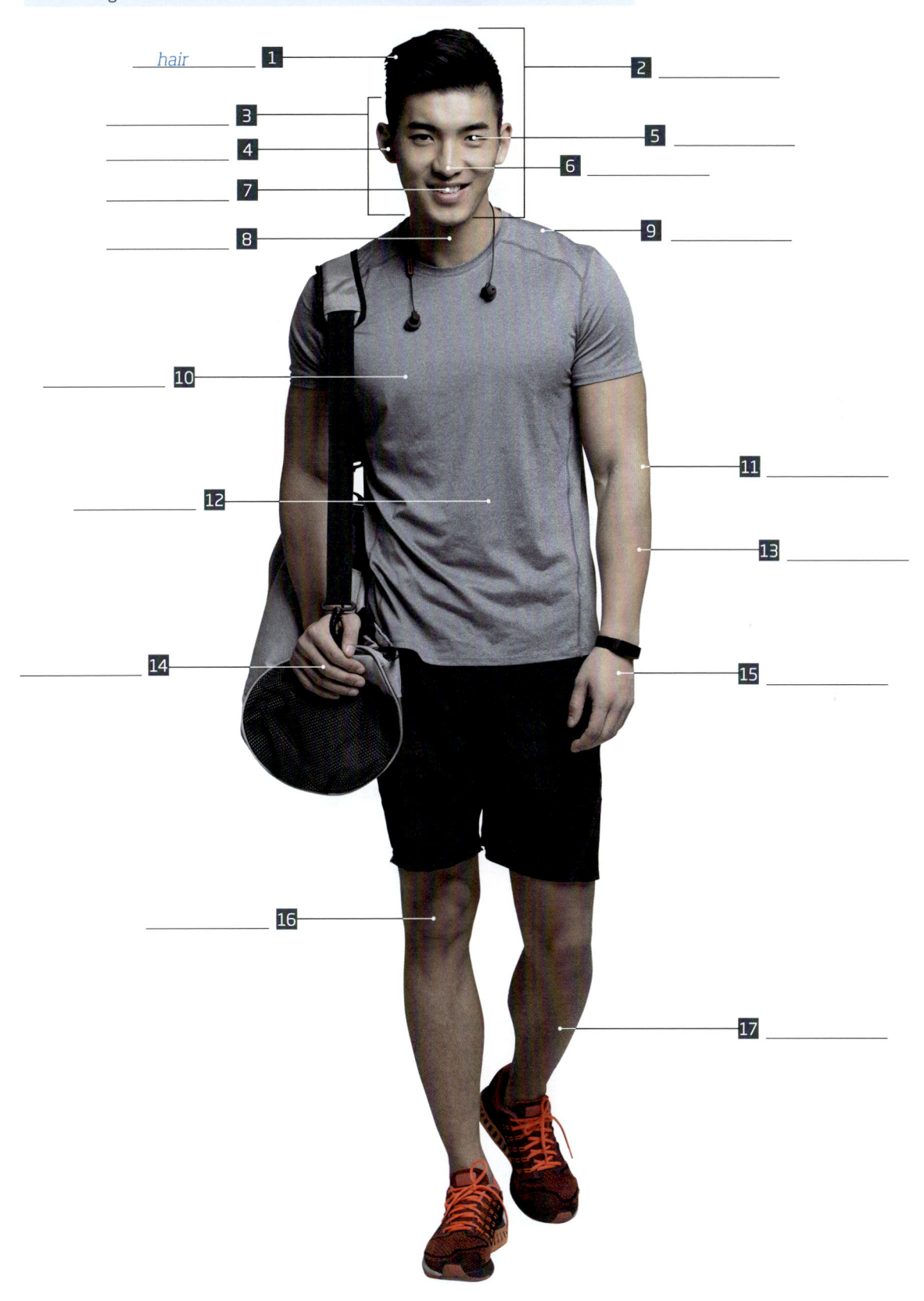

hair 1 _____ 2 _____
3 _____
4 _____ 5 _____
       6 _____
7 _____
8 _____ 9 _____
10 _____
11 _____
12 _____
13 _____
14 _____ 15 _____
16 _____
17 _____

2 Work in pairs. What other parts of the body do you know in English?

5A Everyday activities

1 Look at the photos and complete 1–10 with the words and phrases in the box.

finish work go shopping have a coffee have a shower meet friends
play a game read a book relax run start work

1 _run_   2 _____   3 _____   4 _____   5 _____
6 _____   7 _____   8 _____   9 _____   10 _____

2 Which activities in Exercise 1 do you do every day?

5C Food and drink

1 Look at the photos and complete 1–12 with the words in the box.

apple banana burger carrot chips orange potato rice
soup strawberry tomato water

1 _apple_   2 _____   3 _____   4 _____   5 _____   6 _____
7 _____   8 _____   9 _____   10 _____   11 _____   12 _____

2 Which things from Exercise 1 do you:
- have every day?
- eat/drink in the morning?
- have in a restaurant?

6C Skills

1 Look at the photos. What can the people do? Complete the phrases with *ride, make, play* or *speak*.

1 *ride* a motorbike
2 _____ a short film
3 _____ a horse
4 _____ the guitar
5 _____ Japanese food
6 _____ a bicycle
7 _____ four languages
8 _____ bread
9 _____ the violin
10 _____ chess
11 _____ Spanish
12 _____ golf

2 Work in pairs. Which of the skills in Exercise 1 can you do?
   I can play chess and I can speak two languages.

7C Adjectives (2)

1 Look at the photos and complete the sentences with the adjectives in the box.

bored   clever   difficult   famous   fast   favourite   interesting
nice   old   sad   slow   ~~tired~~

1 I'm _tired_. Where's my coffee?
2 That's a _____ bag. I like it. 
3 This film is _____. 
4 This man is very _____ in my country. 
5 I'm _____. What's on TV? 
6 My brother is very _____. 
7 This is my _____ coat. I wear it every day. 
8 This book is really _____. It's about Japan. 
9 This isn't my new phone. It's my _____ one. 
10 This taxi is so _____. I'm late! 
11 Wow, your dog is _____! 
12 Today's crossword is really _____.

8B Irregular verbs

1 Match past simple verbs 1–12 with present simple verbs a–l.

Past simple		Present simple	
1	taught	a	send
2	spent	b	leave
3	sat	c	find
4	sent	d	write
5	saw	e	teach
6	left	f	make
7	gave	g	win
8	found	h	sit
9	drove	i	drive
10	made	j	spend
11	won	k	give
12	wrote	l	see

2 Look at the pictures and complete the sentences with the correct past simple verbs from Exercise 1.

1 He _sent_ me some beautiful flowers.
2 I _____ work at 9.30 p.m. 
3 I _____ a film with my sister. 
4 I _____ to my girlfriend from Rome. 
5 She _____ me her telephone number. 
6 We _____ in the park and listened to the birds. 
7 I _____ a wallet in the street. 
8 I _____ to the sea. 
9 We _____ a lot of money in the shops. 
10 I _____ dinner for my parents. 
11 I _____ our tennis game. 
12 The teacher _____ us the names of animals in English. 

143

9B Hobbies

1 Look at the photos and complete 1–12 with the hobbies in the box.

baking   camping   cooking   cycling   fishing   gardening   painting
running   sightseeing   skateboarding   ~~snowboarding~~   travelling

1 *snowboarding*
2 _____
3 _____
4 _____
5 _____
6 _____
7 _____
8 _____
9 _____
10 _____
11 _____
12 _____

2 Work in pairs. Which of the hobbies in Exercise 1 do you like?

I like running and cooking.

10A Collocations

1 Complete the word map with the nouns and phrases in the box.

a club   to a big city   with my kids   a band   a house   jobs
to a small town   to another country   cars   with my friends
a computer   bread   with my grandparents   clothes

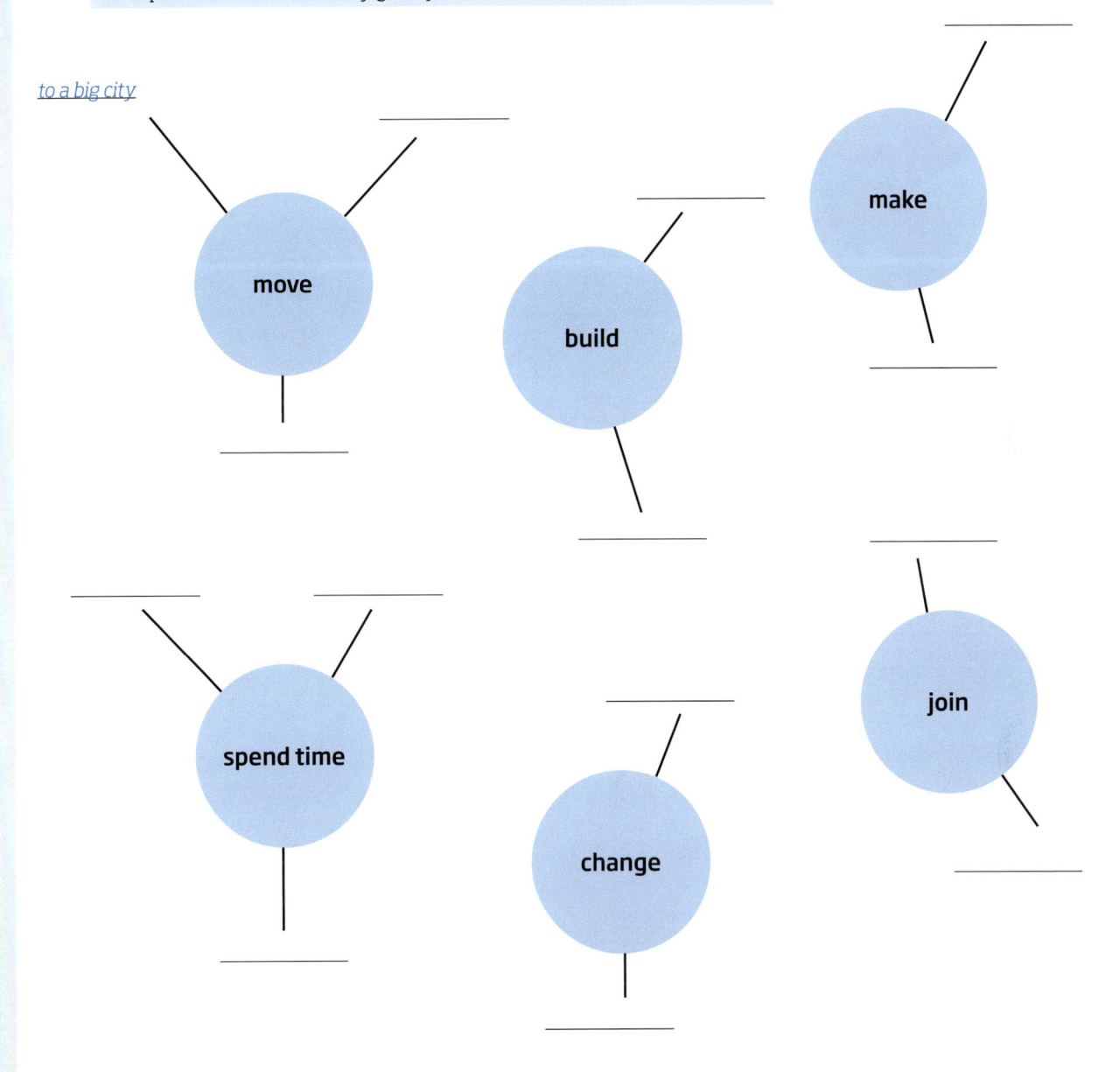

to a big city

- move: to a big city, to a small town, to another country
- build: a house, a computer
- make: bread, clothes
- spend time: with my kids, with my friends, with my grandparents
- change: cars, jobs
- join: a club, a band

2 Work in pairs. Which of the sentences are true for you?

1 I want to join a band.
   That's not true. I don't want to join a band.
2 I want to change cars.
3 I want to move to a big city.
4 I want to spend more time with my friends.
5 I want to learn to make bread.
6 I want to make clothes.
7 I want to build my own house.
8 I want to change jobs.
9 I want to spend more time with my kids.
10 I want to move to a small town.

Communication review

Reach the end (Units 1-2 review)

Work in groups. Roll the dice and move your counter to the correct square. Read and answer the question on the square. If you cannot answer it, go back to your previous square. The first person to reach *Finish* wins.

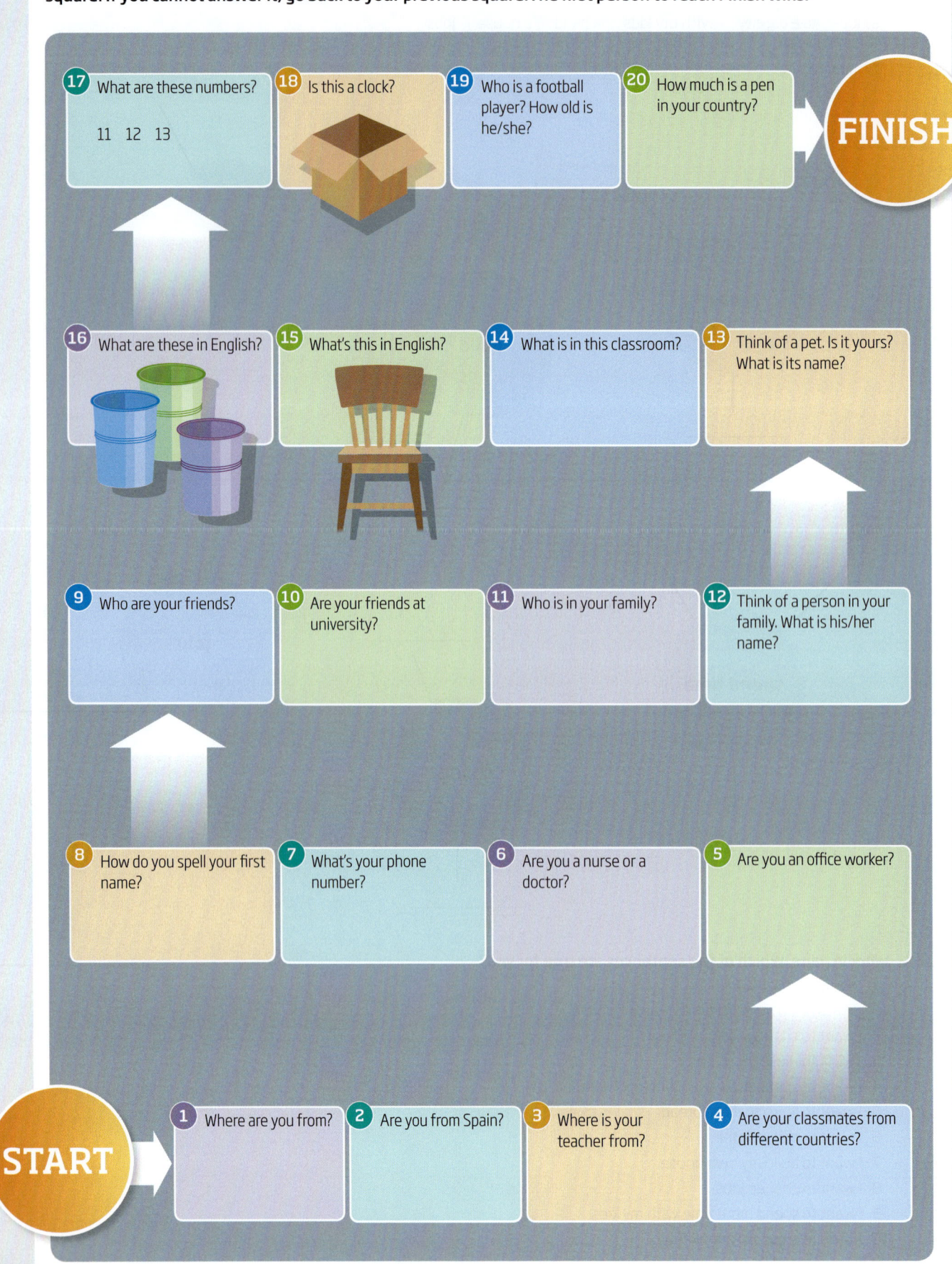

START

1. Where are you from?
2. Are you from Spain?
3. Where is your teacher from?
4. Are your classmates from different countries?
5. Are you an office worker?
6. Are you a nurse or a doctor?
7. What's your phone number?
8. How do you spell your first name?
9. Who are your friends?
10. Are your friends at university?
11. Who is in your family?
12. Think of a person in your family. What is his/her name?
13. Think of a pet. Is it yours? What is its name?
14. What is in this classroom?
15. What's this in English?
16. What are these in English?
17. What are these numbers? 11 12 13
18. Is this a clock?
19. Who is a football player? How old is he/she?
20. How much is a pen in your country?

FINISH

Cross the board (Units 3-4 review)

Work in pairs or two teams. Choose a number. Complete the sentence correctly and win the hexagon. Make a line of hexagons from left to right and you win!

1. In my town, there are …
2. In this room, there aren't any …
3. _____ there a cinema in your town?
4. _____ there any restaurants near your house or flat?
5. In my kitchen, there is …
6. In my living room, there are …
7. Is _____ wifi in this classroom?
8. In my town, the shops aren't busy, they're _____ .
9. That café isn't cheap, it's very _____ .
10. There _____ a big supermarket near my house.
11. My town _____ small.
12. Excuse me, is _____ a bank near here?
13. Turn left, then _____ straight ahead. It's on the right.
14. My teacher has got _____ hair and _____ eyes.
15. My friend is in her _____ .
16. I have got …
17. My friend has got …
18. I haven't got a _____ in my bag.
19. _____ many books have you got in your bag?
20. _____ you got green eyes?
21. _____ the hotel got a lift?
22. Please don't _____ photos here.
23. _____ this Italian food. It's very good.
24. The class is _____ eight forty-five.
25. _____ time is it now?

Three in a line (Units 5-6 review)

Games 1 and 2: work in pairs or two teams. Game 3: work in two teams. Choose a square and start the game. If you get the answer correct, you win the square. Try to get a line in a row.

Game 1: Say.

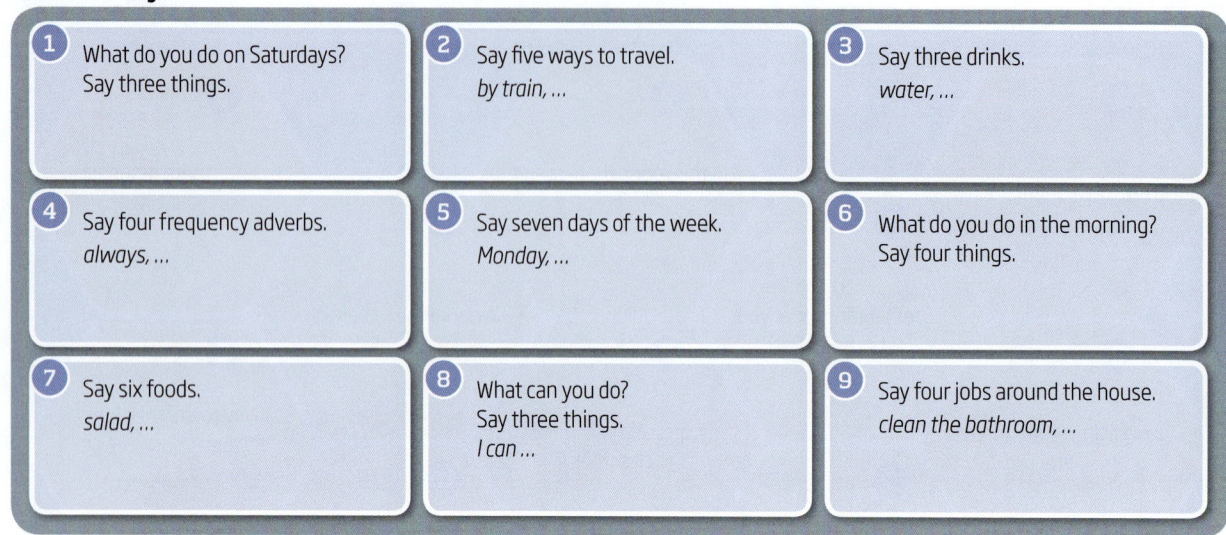

1 What do you do on Saturdays? Say three things.	**2** Say five ways to travel. *by train, ...*	**3** Say three drinks. *water, ...*
4 Say four frequency adverbs. *always, ...*	**5** Say seven days of the week. *Monday, ...*	**6** What do you do in the morning? Say four things.
7 Say six foods. *salad, ...*	**8** What can you do? Say three things. *I can ...*	**9** Say four jobs around the house. *clean the bathroom, ...*

Game 2: Complete the sentences.

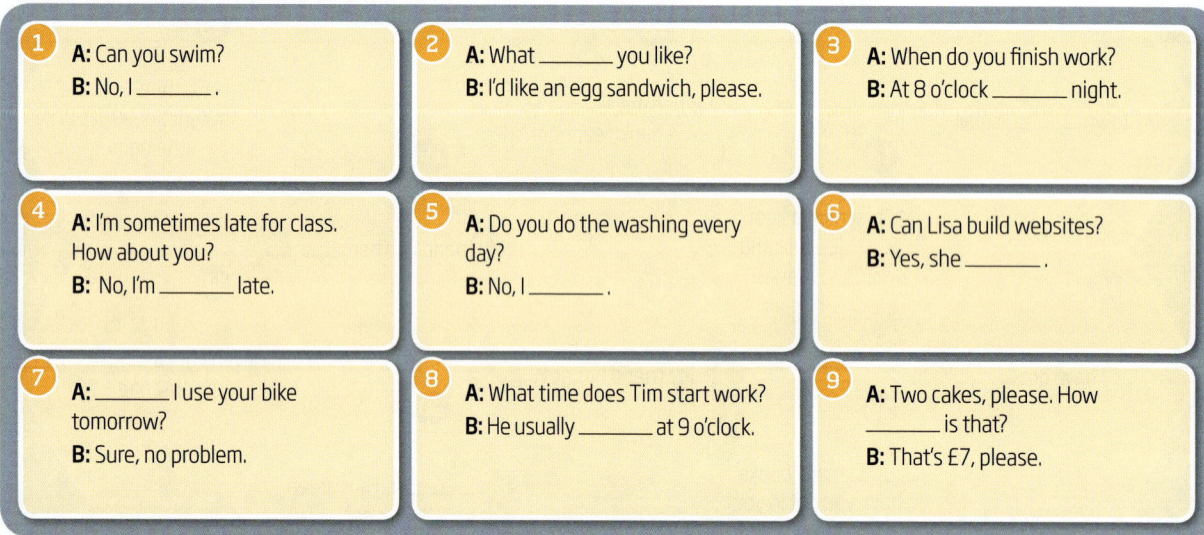

1 A: Can you swim? B: No, I _____ .	**2** A: What _____ you like? B: I'd like an egg sandwich, please.	**3** A: When do you finish work? B: At 8 o'clock _____ night.
4 A: I'm sometimes late for class. How about you? B: No, I'm _____ late.	**5** A: Do you do the washing every day? B: No, I _____ .	**6** A: Can Lisa build websites? B: Yes, she _____ .
7 A: _____ I use your bike tomorrow? B: Sure, no problem.	**8** A: What time does Tim start work? B: He usually _____ at 9 o'clock.	**9** A: Two cakes, please. How _____ is that? B: That's £7, please.

Game 3: Complete the questions then ask and answer in your team.

1 _____ time do you leave home on Wednesdays?	**2** Can you _____ three languages?	**3** How _____ you travel to class?
4 How often _____ you go to bed late?	**5** Do you _____ the bus every day?	**6** _____ often do you drink coffee?
7 _____ do you live with?	**8** Think of a family member. _____ he/she go to the gym every week?	**9** _____ jobs around the house do you do?

Snakes and ladders (Units 7–8 review)

Work in pairs or groups. Throw the dice, move your counter forward the correct number of squares and answer the question. If correct, stay on the square. If incorrect, move back to the square you were on before. If you land on a square with a ladder, answer the question, then move up the ladder. If you land on a square with a snake, go down it. The first person to reach *Finish* wins.

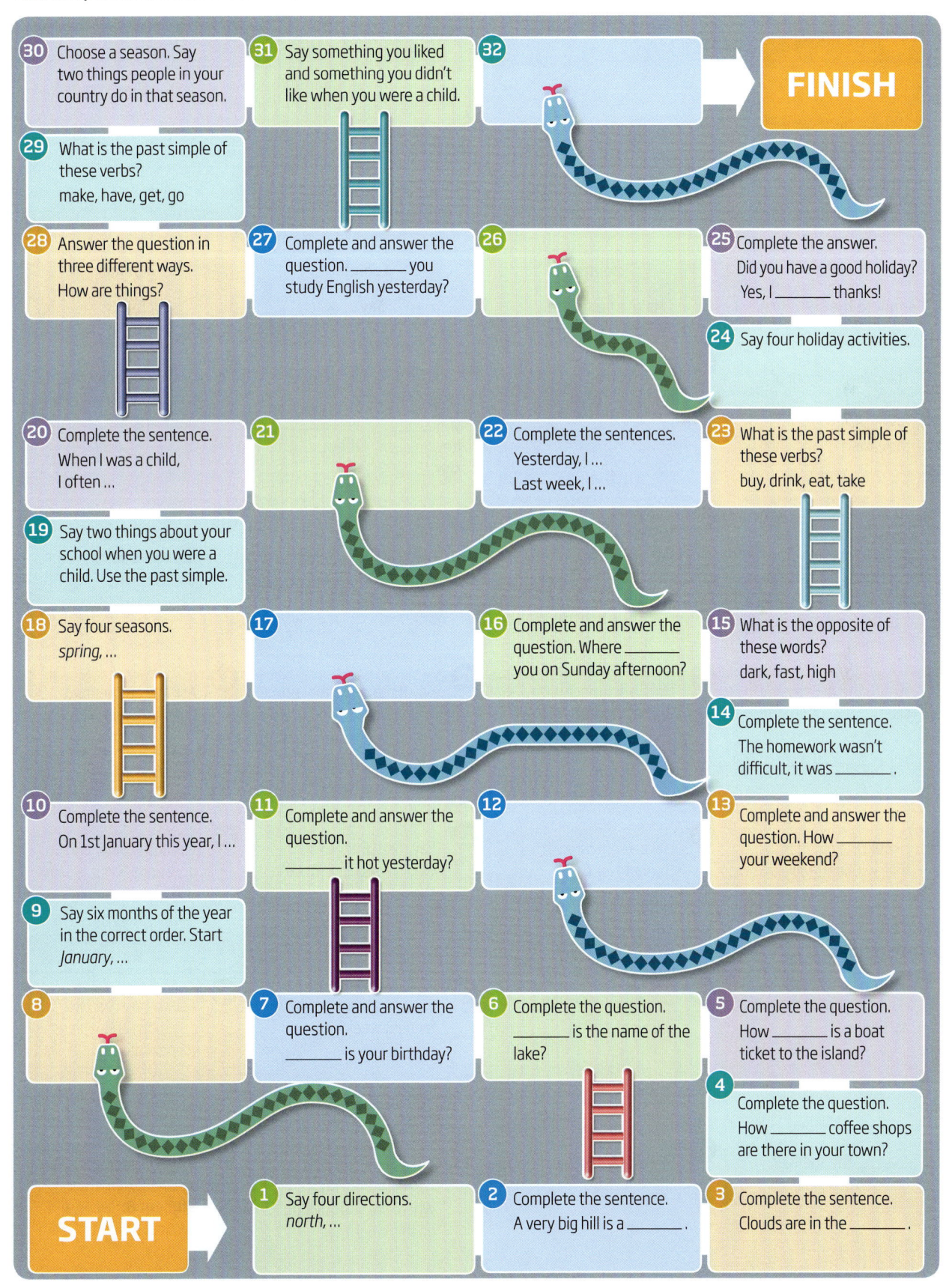

30 Choose a season. Say two things people in your country do in that season.

31 Say something you liked and something you didn't like when you were a child.

32

FINISH

29 What is the past simple of these verbs?
make, have, get, go

28 Answer the question in three different ways. How are things?

27 Complete and answer the question. _____ you study English yesterday?

26

25 Complete the answer. Did you have a good holiday? Yes, I _____ thanks!

24 Say four holiday activities.

20 Complete the sentence. When I was a child, I often …

21

22 Complete the sentences. Yesterday, I … Last week, I …

23 What is the past simple of these verbs?
buy, drink, eat, take

19 Say two things about your school when you were a child. Use the past simple.

18 Say four seasons. *spring*, …

17

16 Complete and answer the question. Where _____ you on Sunday afternoon?

15 What is the opposite of these words?
dark, fast, high

14 Complete the sentence. The homework wasn't difficult, it was _____ .

10 Complete the sentence. On 1st January this year, I …

11 Complete and answer the question. _____ it hot yesterday?

12

13 Complete and answer the question. How _____ your weekend?

9 Say six months of the year in the correct order. Start *January*, …

8

7 Complete and answer the question. _____ is your birthday?

6 Complete the question. _____ is the name of the lake?

5 Complete the question. How _____ is a boat ticket to the island?

4 Complete the question. How _____ coffee shops are there in your town?

START

1 Say four directions. *north*, …

2 Complete the sentence. A very big hill is a _____ .

3 Complete the sentence. Clouds are in the _____ .

149

Points race (Units 9–10 review)

Work in two teams, A and B. Choose a square to complete. Count your points. If a team can't complete a square correctly, then the other team can try.
When all squares are complete, the team with the most points wins!

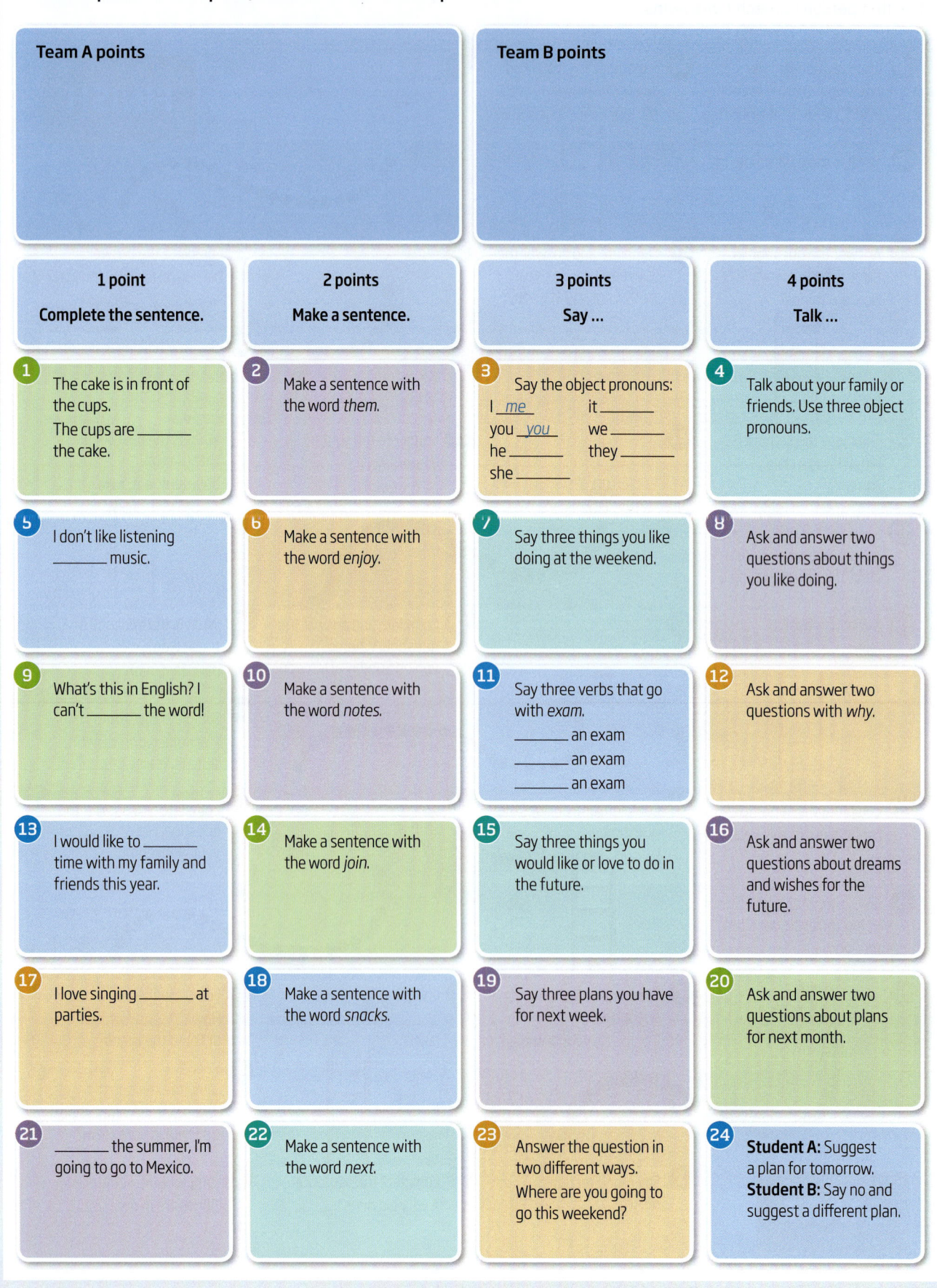

Team A points

Team B points

1 point Complete the sentence.	2 points Make a sentence.	3 points Say …	4 points Talk …
1 The cake is in front of the cups. The cups are _____ the cake.	**2** Make a sentence with the word *them*.	**3** Say the object pronouns: I _me_ it _____ you _you_ we _____ he _____ they _____ she _____	**4** Talk about your family or friends. Use three object pronouns.
5 I don't like listening _____ music.	**6** Make a sentence with the word *enjoy*.	**7** Say three things you like doing at the weekend.	**8** Ask and answer two questions about things you like doing.
9 What's this in English? I can't _____ the word!	**10** Make a sentence with the word *notes*.	**11** Say three verbs that go with *exam*. _____ an exam _____ an exam _____ an exam	**12** Ask and answer two questions with *why*.
13 I would like to _____ time with my family and friends this year.	**14** Make a sentence with the word *join*.	**15** Say three things you would like or love to do in the future.	**16** Ask and answer two questions about dreams and wishes for the future.
17 I love singing _____ at parties.	**18** Make a sentence with the word *snacks*.	**19** Say three plans you have for next week.	**20** Ask and answer two questions about plans for next month.
21 _____ the summer, I'm going to go to Mexico.	**22** Make a sentence with the word *next*.	**23** Answer the question in two different ways. Where are you going to go this weekend?	**24** **Student A:** Suggest a plan for tomorrow. **Student B:** Say no and suggest a different plan.

Communication bank

Lesson 1B

8 Student A

Read the profiles of Julia Smith and Pavel Kowalski and think of questions to complete the information. Then turn back to page 9, Exercise 9.

Is Julia a doctor?

Name: Julia Smith
Job: _____
City: _____
Country: _____

Name: Pavel Kowalski
Job: _____
City: _____
Country: _____

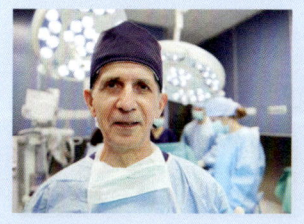

Name: Javier Martinez
Job: pilot
City: Los Angeles
Country: the US

Name: Yuki Mori
Job: farmer
City: São Paulo
Country: Brazil

Lesson 2C

9 Student A

Read the profiles and think of questions to complete the information. Then turn back to page 19, Exercise 10.

Where's Lena from?

Name: Lena Baros
Country: _____
Age: 93
Job: _____

Name: Niran Meeboon
Country: Thailand
Age: _____
Job: _____

Name: Silvia Lopez
Country: Mexico
Age: _____
Job: doctor

Name: Thiago Moreno
Country: _____
Age: 81
Job: office worker

Lesson 1B

8 Student B

Read the profiles of Javier Martinez and Yuki Mori and think of questions to complete the information. Then turn back to page 9, Exercise 9.

Is Javier a football player?

Name: Javier Martinez
Job: _____
City: _____
Country: _____

Name: Yuki Mori
Job: _____
City: _____
Country: _____

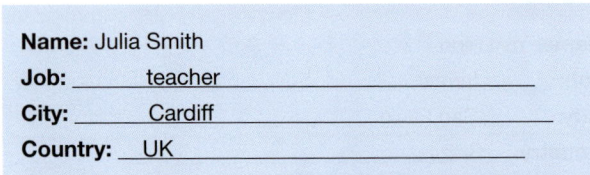

Name: Julia Smith
Job: _____teacher_____
City: _____Cardiff_____
Country: ____UK_____

Name: Pavel Kowalski
Job: _____doctor_____
City: _____Kraków_____
Country: ____Poland_____

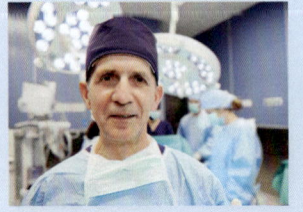

Lesson 2C

9 Student B

Read the profiles and think of questions to complete the information. Then turn back to page 19, Exercise 10.

How old is Lena?

Name: Lena Baros
Country: _Poland_____
Age: _____
Job: ____farmer_____

Name: Niran Meeboon
Country: _____
Age: ____58_____
Job: ____taxi driver_____

Name: Silvia Lopez
Country: _____
Age: ____87_____
Job: _____

Name: Thiago Moreno
Country: ___Argentina_____
Age: _____
Job: _____

Lesson 3A

10 Student A

Look at the picture. Write sentences about places in the town. Then turn back to page 23, Exercise 11.

There are two cafés.

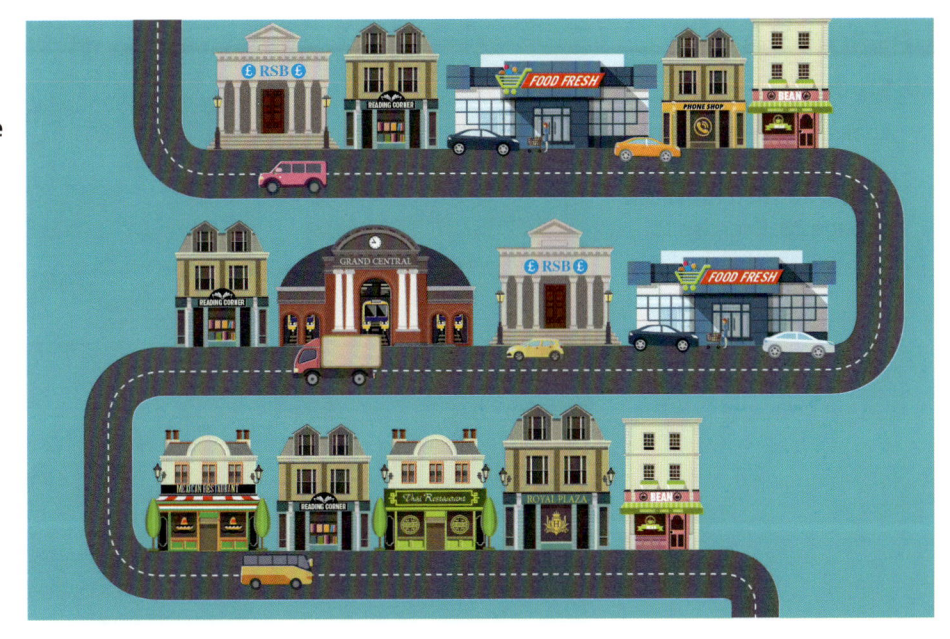

Lesson 3B

11a Student A

Read the information and complete the table for flat 1 on page 25, Exercise 10.

Flat 1   CITY FLAT, TOKYO ★★★★

£150 per night

10 minutes to the station
- living room
- kitchen
- bedroom
- bathroom

In this flat:

Lesson 9C

3 Student A

a Ask Student B the exam questions and check their answers. Give them one point for a correct answer. Tell Student B their score. Did they pass or fail the exam?

You passed/failed the exam.

English exam

1 Who works in a hospital? Answer: doctors or nurses
2 Where do people buy food? Answer: supermarkets or markets
3 What word means 'not busy'? Answer: quiet
4 What can travel on a lake? Answer: a boat
5 What is the past simple of the verb *buy*? Answer: bought

3–5 points: pass

0–2 points: fail

b Answer Student B's questions.

I don't know! I can't remember!

Lesson 3A

10 Student B

Look at the picture. Write sentences about places in the town. Then turn back to page 23, Exercise 11.

There are three cafés.

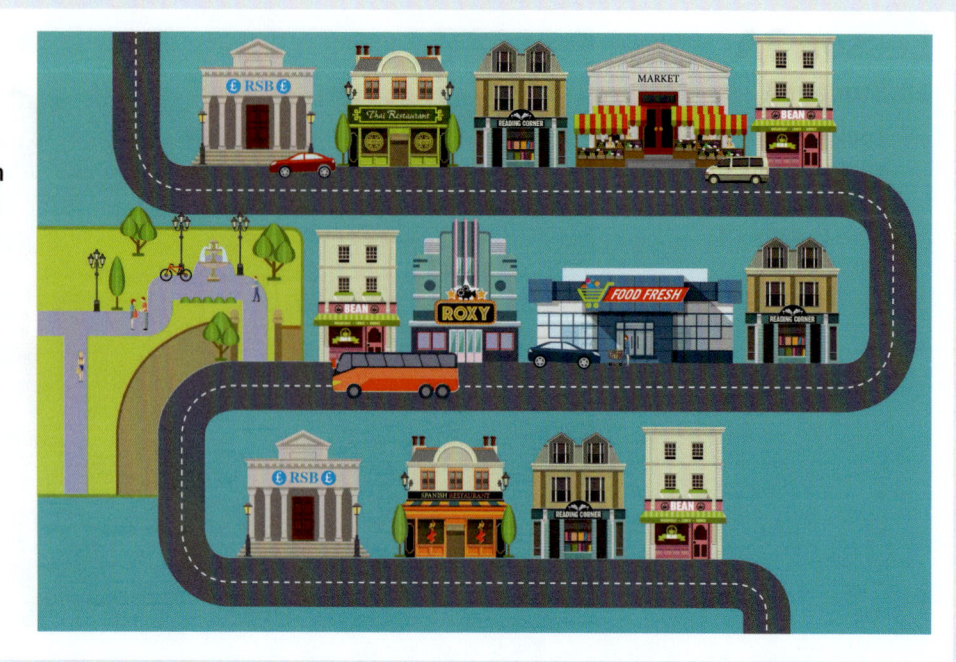

Lesson 3B

11a Student B

Read the information and complete the table for flat 2 on page 25, Exercise 10.

Flat 2 — CITY FLAT, TOKYO ★★★★

£80 per night
2 minutes to the station
- bedroom
- bathroom

In this flat:

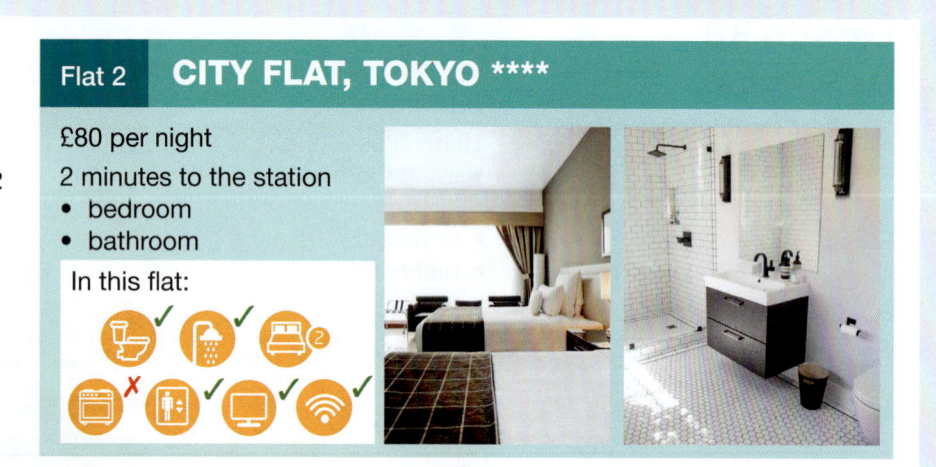

Lesson 5C

10a Look at 1–7 in the table. Write questions with *How often …?* Use Exercise 9a to help you. Then write two more questions.

b Turn back to page 43, Exercise 11.

Are you healthy?

Question	never	sometimes	often	usually	always
1 walk or cycle to work *How often do you walk or cycle to work?*					
2 drink tea or coffee					
3 have lunch					
4 work after 6 o'clock					
5 have salad for dinner					
6 go to bed at 10 o'clock					
7 play sports on Saturdays or Sundays					
8					
9					

Lesson 4B

9 Student A

a Think of ten things to put in a bag for Canada. Choose from the list.

- ☐ bottle of water
- ☐ books
- ☐ camera
- ☐ clock
- ☐ coat
- ☐ computer
- ☐ credit card
- ☐ cup
- ☐ keys
- ☐ money
- ☐ passport
- ☐ pen
- ☐ my phone
- ☐ photo of my family
- ☐ sunglasses
- ☐ ticket

b Prepare to ask your partner about these things. Have they got them in their bag for the office?

Have you got a bottle of water?

- ☐ bottle of water
- ☐ money
- ☐ computer
- ☐ pen
- ☐ keys

Turn back to page 33, Exercise 10.

Lesson 4D

6 Student B

a Look at the train information. Prepare to say the times.

Train to	Time
London	10.45
Rome	11.05
Brussels	16.00
Amsterdam	20.20
Barcelona	21.30

b Answer your partner's questions. Use the information in Exercise 6a.

It's at …

c Ask your partner about the times of the trains and complete the table.

What time is the train to Chicago?

Train to	Time
Chicago	
Boston	
Washington DC	
Philadelphia	
Kansas	

Lesson 4B

9 Student B

a Think of ten things to put in a bag for the office. Choose from the list.

- ☐ bottle of water
- ☐ books
- ☐ camera
- ☐ clock
- ☐ coat
- ☐ computer
- ☐ credit card
- ☐ cup
- ☐ keys
- ☐ money
- ☐ passport
- ☐ pen
- ☐ my phone
- ☐ photo of my family
- ☐ sunglasses
- ☐ ticket

b Prepare to ask your partner about these things. Have they got them in their bag for Canada?

Have you got your passport?

- ☐ passport
- ☐ ticket
- ☐ coat
- ☐ books
- ☐ camera

Turn back to page 33, Exercise 10.

Lesson 4D

6 Student A

a Look at the train information. Prepare to say the times.

Train to	Time
Chicago	8.25
Boston	10.40
Washington DC	13.15
Philadelphia	15.35
Kansas	23.00

b Ask your partner about the times of the trains and complete the table.

What time is the train to London?

Train to	Time
London	
Rome	
Brussels	
Amsterdam	
Barcelona	

c Answer your partner's questions. Use the information in Exercise 6a.

It's at …

Lesson 6B

9 a Look at the table. Complete 7–10 with more jobs around the house. Then make questions for 1–10 in note form.

Who cooks dinner? How often do you/does he/she …?
When do you/does he/she …?

	Who?	How often?	When?
1 cooks dinner			
2 washes the dishes			
3 goes to the supermarket			
4 cleans the kitchen			
5 cleans the bathroom			
6 does the washing			
7			
8			
9			
10			

b Turn back to page 49, Exercise 10a.

Lesson 7D

5 Student A

a You are a customer at a train station in Paris. You want to buy a return train ticket to one of the places in the photos. Student B is the assistant. Ask questions and roleplay the conversation.

A: Excuse me. What time is the next train to … , please?

Madrid   Barcelona   Valencia

b You are an assistant at a train station in Paris. Student B is a customer. Answer Student B's questions using the information in the table and roleplay the conversation.

Train to	Brussels	Geneva	Zurich	Geneva	Brussels	Zurich
Platform	8	3	9	12	4	2
Leaves	10.35	10.40	10.45	11.00	11.05	11.15
Arrives	12.55	14.20	17.30	14.02	12.27	15.15
Single	€55	€34	€42	€45	€63	€52
Return	€90	€57	€70	€74	€112	€98

Lesson 9C

3 **Student B**

a Answer Student A's questions.
I don't know! I can't remember!

b Ask Student A the exam questions and check their answers. Give them one point for a correct answer. Tell Student A their score. Did they pass or fail the exam?
You passed/failed the exam.

> **English exam**
> 1 Who is your father's father? Answer: your grandfather
> 2 What do people sit on? Answer: chairs or sofas
> 3 What word means 'not cheap'? Answer: expensive
> 4 What month is after June? Answer: July
> 5 How many eyes do people have? Answer: two
> 3–5 points: pass
> 0–2 points: fail

Lesson 7D

5 **Student B**

a You are an assistant at a train station in Paris. Student A is a customer. Answer Student A's questions using the information in the table and roleplay the conversation.

Train to	Barcelona	Madrid	Valencia	Madrid	Valencia	Barcelona
Platform	11	7	6	10	5	1
Leaves	13.10	13.20	13.25	13.30	13.40	13.45
Arrives	20.30	09.30	13.05	23.00	11.25	19.15
Single	€64	€98	€65	€130	€75	€72
Return	€117	€175	€115	€245	€142	€135

b You are a customer at a train station in Paris. You want to buy a single train ticket to one of the places in the photos. Student A is the assistant. Ask questions and roleplay the conversation.
B: Excuse me. What time is the next train to …, please?

Brussels   Geneva   Zurich

Lesson 10C

12 a Ask your partner about his/her plans and complete the table. Ask questions like:
- What are you going to do?
- When are you going to do it?
- How long are you going to do it for?

Turn back to Exercise, 12b page 83.

Calendar

January	February	March

April	May	June

July	August	September

October	November	December

Irregular verbs

Verb	Past simple	Past participle
be	was	been
become	became	become
begin	began	begun
bite	bit	bitten
blow	blew	blown
break	broke	broken
bring	brought	brought
build	built	built
buy	bought	bought
catch	caught	caught
choose	chose	chosen
come	came	come
cost	cost	cost
cut	cut	cut
do	did	done
draw	drew	drawn
drink	drank	drunk
drive	drove	driven
eat	ate	eaten
fall	fell	fallen
feel	felt	felt
find	found	found
fly	flew	flown
forget	forgot	forgotten
freeze	froze	frozen
get	got	got
give	gave	given
go	went	gone
grow	grew	grown
have	had	had
hear	heard	heard
hide	hid	hidden
hit	hit	hit
hold	held	held
hurt	hurt	hurt
keep	kept	kept
know	knew	known
learn	learned/learnt	learned/learnt
leave	left	left
lend	lent	lent
let	let	let
lie	lay	lain
lose	lost	lost
make	made	made
mean	meant	meant
meet	met	met
pay	paid	paid
put	put	put
read	read	read
ride	rode	ridden
ring	rang	rung
run	ran	run
say	said	said
see	saw	seen
sell	sold	sold
send	sent	sent
shine	shone	shone
show	showed	shown
shut	shut	shut
sing	sang	sung
sit	sat	sat
sleep	slept	slept
smell	smelled/smelt	smelled/smelt
speak	spoke	spoken
spend	spent	spent
spill	spilled/spilt	spilled/spilt
stand	stood	stood
swim	swam	swum
take	took	taken
teach	taught	taught
tell	told	told
think	thought	thought
throw	threw	thrown
understand	understood	understood
wake	woke	woken
wear	wore	worn
win	won	won
write	wrote	written